Women's Reproductive Rights

Women's Rights in Europe Series

Series Editors: **Christien L. van den Anker, Audrey Guichon, Sirkku K. Hellsten and Heather Widdows**

Titles include:

Sikku K. Hellsten, Anne Maria Holli and Krassimira Das kalova (*editors*)
WOMEN'S CITIZENSHIP AND POLITICAL RIGHTS

Heather Widdows, Itziar Alkorta Idiakez and Aitziber Emaldi Cirión (*editors*)
WOMEN'S REPRODUCTIVE RIGHTS

Forthcoming titles:

Christien van de Anker and Jeroen Doormernik (*editors*)
TRAFFICKING AND WOMEN'S RIGHTS

Audrey Guichon, Christien van den Anker and Irina Novikova (*editors*)
WOMEN'S SOCIAL RIGHTS AND ENTITLEMENTS

Women's Rights in Europe Series
Series Standing Order ISBN 1–4039–4988–3

You can receive future title in this series as they are published by placing a standing order. Please contact your bookseller or, in case of difficulty, write to us at the address below with your name and address, the title of the series and the ISBN quoted above.

Customer Services Department, Macmillan Distribution Ltd, Houndmills, Basingstoke, Hampshire RG21 6XS, England

Women's Reproductive Rights

Heather Widdows
Centre for Global Ethics
University of Birmingham, UK

Itziar Alkorta Idiakez
University of the Basque Country, Spain

and

Aitziber Emaldi Cirión
University of Deusto, Spain

First published in 2006 by
PALGRAVE MACMILLAN
Houndmills, Basingstoke, Hampshire RG21 6XS and
175 Fifth Avenue, New York, N.Y. 10010
Companies and representatives throughout the world.

PALGRAVE MACMILLAN is the global academic imprint of the Palgrave Macmillan division of St. Martin's Press, LLC and of Palgrave Macmillan Ltd. Macmillan® is a registered trademark in the United States, United Kingdom and other countries. Palgrave is a registered trademark in the European Union and other countries.

ISBN-13: 978-1-4039-4993-6 hardback
ISBN-10: 1-4039-4993-X hardback

This book is printed on paper suitable for recycling and made from fully managed and sustained forest sources.

A catalogue record for this book is available from the British Library.

Library of Congress Cataloging-in-Publication Data

Women's reproductive rights / edited by Heather Widdows, Itziar Alkorta Idiakez, and Aitziber Emaldi Cirión.
    p. cm.—(Women's rights in Europe)
    Includes bibliographical references and index.
    ISBN 1-4039-4993-X
    1. Women's rights – Europe. 2. Human reproduction – Political aspects – Europe. I. Widdows, Heather, 1972– II. Alkorta Idiakez, Itziar. III. Emaldi Cirión, Aitziber, 1970– IV. Series.

HQ1236.5.E85W645 2005
363.9′6′094—dc22   2005050048

10 9 8 7 6 5 4 3 2 1
15 14 13 12 11 10 09 08 07 06

Transferred to digital printing in 2007.

Contents

List of Figures   vii

List of Tables   viii

Acknowledgements   ix

Foreword   xi

Notes on Contributors   xiii

Introduction   1
Heather Widdows

Part I   Tensions in Europe: Critical Issues in Reproductive Rights

1   Abortion – A Reproductive Right   17
    Catherine Kenny

2   Adoption: Practices and Regulations   33
    Fiona MacCallum

3   Birth Rate and Women's Rights in Europe   50
    Paloma de Villota

4   Teenage Pregnancy   71
    Olga Tóth

5   Minority Groups and Reproductive Rights   88
    Nidhi Trehan and Isabel Crowhurst

Part II   The Impact of Technology: Scientific Advances and Reproductive Rights

6   Women's Rights in European Fertility Medicine Regulation   111
    Itziar Alkorta

7   How is Technology Changing the Meaning of Motherhood
    for Western Women   124
    Lori B. Andrews

v

8   Preimplantation Diagnosis: Problems and
     Future Perspectives   140
     Aitziber Emaldi Cirión

9   The Impact of New Reproductive Technologies
     on Concepts of Genetic Relatedness and
     Non-relatedness   151
     Heather Widdows

**Part III   Into the Future: Projections for
              Reproductive Rights**

10 Reproductive Rights in the Twenty-First Century   167
     Hille Haker

11 Ownership, Property and Women's Bodies   188
     Donna Dickenson

12 Beyond Europe: Rhetoric of Reproductive Rights in
     Global Population Policies   199
     Sirkku K. Hellsten

Bibliography   214

Index   236

List of Figures

3.1   Women's employment rates by presence of children,
      2000 (aged 25–54)   52
3.2   Women's activity rate by civil status and number
      of children – Luxembourg   52
3.3   Results of the survey   54
3.4   Women's activity rate and vital cycle (2001)   55
3.5   Activity rate and vital cycle men and women, 2001   57
3.6   Relationship between fertility and female labour
      force participation (1964)   58
3.7   Relationship between fertility and female labour
      force participation (1994)   59
3.8   Family/children benefits as % of total benefits (2000)   65
3.9   Family/children benefits as % of GDP (2000)   65
3.10 Transfers for the care of one, two or three children in the
      European Union   69
4.1   Abortion rate among teenagers per year   78

List of Tables

3.1   Social benefits provided for the family and
children   63

3.2   Provision of publicly funded childcare services   66

4.1   The main features of 'European marriage type'
and 'non-European marriage type'   73

4.2   Rates of teenage birth per year (per 1000 women
aged 15–19), in the European countries
and the United States, for 1980, 1995–6 and 2000   76

4.3   Change in the level of teenage birth rate in
European countries and in the United States,
1980–2000   77

4.4   Proportion of births and abortions in women
under 20   79

4.5   Change in the proportion of teenage births in
European countries and in the United States,
1980–2000   80

4.6   Level of government concern and existence of policies
towards teenage pregnancy in European
countries and in the United States for 1995 and 2000   83

4.7   Special government programmes to curtail the
number of teenage pregnancies   84

Acknowledgements

This series is the result of the involvement of a large number of people in the work of the Network for European Women's Rights (NEWR). We would like to thank them all for their input, although we cannot name them all here.

We want to thank especially those who spent time and energy discussing the four themes of NEWR during a series of intensive and engaging workshops across Europe and in the final conference in Birmingham.

We would also like to thank Donna Dickenson for initiating the project and leading it for two years and Christien van den Anker for taking over this leadership for the final year of the project, as well as the project partners Francesca Bettio, Krassimira Daskalova, Jeroen Doomernik, Anne Maria Holli, Maria Katsiyianni-Papakonstantinou, Lukas H. Meyer and Irina Novikova for their contributions.

We could not have done the project without the commitment and persistence of Audrey Guichon and the consistent support of Jose Vicente. We thank Rebecca Shah for taking over from Audrey in the final months of the NEWR project and for her thorough editing work in this series.

We thank the European Commission for funding the NEWR project under its 5th Framework Programme.

We hope that this series of books will contribute positively to the debate on women's rights and to improving the lives of all women in Europe.

With regard to this book, *Women's Reproductive Rights*, we would like to thank those who participated in the workshops on this topic. Unfortunately the participants are too numerous to name but it is they who made this project possible. Without their input the project and this volume would have been very different. In particular, we are grateful to the many activists and NGO representatives who gave up their valuable time to enlighten academics about the burning issues in reproductive rights across Europe. These 'on the ground' perspectives were invaluable in determining the content and issues which this book addresses, and it was they that ensured that the focus of the workshops and the book remained on issues which are fundamental to women in Europe today.

We would also like to thank the institutions that hosted the workshops, the University of Birmingham, the University of Bremen and University of the Basque Country and Universidad de Deusto.

Heather Widdows
Itziar Alkorta Idiakez
Aitziber Emaldi Cirión

Foreword

This series is a timely initiative to counter the mounting opposition and challenge to the progress made thus far in transforming mainstream human rights discourse from a feminist perspective. Expansion of the concept of human rights to address violations experienced by women due specifically to their sex has considerably altered international and domestic law and demystified the public/private distinction that justified women's subordination.

The Convention on the Elimination of All Forms of Discrimination against Women, adopted in 1979 by the United Nations General Assembly was an important step in the recognition of the universality of human rights, a view that became officially endorsed at the Vienna World Conference on Human Rights in 1993. Also referred to as the 'International Bill of Rights of Women' the Convention enjoys a ratification of 180 member states today. Yet, after over quarter of a century since the adoption of the Convention and the numerous human rights instruments that followed, what remains universal is the gross violation of women's rights worldwide.

Notwithstanding the notable progress achieved in the advancement of women in the past decades, women in all parts of the world still face obstacles in accessing rights, such as the rights to education, health, political participation, property, and to decide over matters related to their sexuality, reproduction, marriage, divorce and child custody, among others. Women's bodies are the zones of war and the sites of politics and policies as revealed in the armed conflicts around the world, transgressions over their reproductive and sexual rights, trafficking, dress codes as well as immigration and refugee policies, etc. Even in countries where traditional patriarchy is transformed, as in the European experience, gender-based discrimination and violence against women continues to persist in modified, subtle and discrete forms.

In many of the countries, in the European region, where human rights standards and institutions are in place, women's formal political participation is still extremely low, reproductive rights are an area of continuous contestation and struggle, social entitlements are at risk and single mothers and minority and immigrant women are at the highest risk of poverty. We need to learn more and understand how gender hierarchies are reproduced under diverse conditions and in different places. The books in this series promise to do that. They illustrate the need for increased attention from researchers, NGOs and policymakers throughout Europe for these instances of violations of women's rights.

This series comes at a time when the European process of enlargement has shown that respect for women's rights within different regions in Europe is diverse. It is fascinating to see that specific rights for women are protected better in some countries than others while it may also be the case that in the same region other rights for women are less observed. By illustrating these trends and inconsistencies, this series allows for comparison across the region as well as for reflection on the policy gaps across Europe.

The four books cover the areas of trafficking, political participation, social entitlements and reproductive rights in detail, from a multidisciplinary perspective and with contributions from activists, professionals, academics and policymakers. State of the art debates are reflected upon and burning issues in women's rights are brought together in one series for the first time. The depth of the arguments, coverage of recent developments and clear focus on their implications for gender equality are the most commendable aspects of the series. The books push forward the agenda for all of us and remind us that women's rights are not protected equally and intrinsically. In fact, the contributions confirm that we still have a long way to go to achieve women's equality in contemporary Europe.

This unique and compelling collection is a must for everyone striving for rights, equality and justice!

Yakın Ertürk

Notes on Contributors

Itziar Alkorta Idiakez is Associated Professor for Private Law in the University of the Basque Country (Spain). She is the author of a monography on comparative European ART regulation (*Medicina reproductiva: Derecho español y comparado*, Pamplona: Aranzadi, 2003) and she has published many articles on Genetic's and Reproductive Technologies' Regulation. She is a researcher in the European Comission's Fifth and Sixth Research Framework Programmes and at the Hastings Center (New York). She has been an advisor on biomedical law to Carlos III National Institute of Health (Spain), the Basque Government, and various governmental agencies.

Lori Andrews is a Distinguished Professor of Law at Chicago-Kent College of Law and Director of the Institute for Science, Law and Technology. She received her BA *summa cum laude* from Yale College and her JD from Yale Law School. Andrews has been an advisor on biomedical law to the US Congress, foreign governments and various federal agencies. She chaired the US Working Group on the Ethical, Legal, and Social Implications of the Human Genome Project. She has written ten books, including *Genetics: Ethics, Law and Policy* (West Publishing, 2002) (with Mark Rothstein and Maxwell Mehlman).

Isabel Crowhurst is currently a doctoral student in the Department of Sociology, and a researcher at the Centre for Civil Society, London School of Economics and Political Science. Her research interests include gender violence and women's international migrations, in particular, issues revolving around female migrants in Western European countries. Most recently she was Marie Curie Fellow at the University of Poitiers' MIGRINTER, where she researched the social response to female migrants operating in the Italian sex industry.

Paloma de Villota is a full time Professor Doctor of Applied Economy at Universidad Complutense de Madrid. Her research interests include, the labour market, fiscal and social policies and budgets from a gender perspective. She has worked on many studies, for example, with the European Commission, the Instituto de Estudios Fiscales as well as Universities, and published many books on the subject, including

Reflexiones sobe el Impuesto sobre la Renta de las Personas Fsicas desde la perspectiva de gnero (Instituto de Estudios Fiscales, 2005).

Donna Dickenson holds a joint chair in Law and Philosophy at Birkbeck College, University of London, where she is also Executive Director of the Advanced Study Centre in the Humanities. She has been a member of clinical ethics committees in London and Oxford and is co-author with Prof. K. W. M. Fulford of *In Two Minds: Case Studies in Psychiatric Ethics* (Oxford University Press, 2000). She has written and edited a number of books including, *Property, Women and Politics: Subjects or Objects?* (Polity Press, 1997a).

Aitziber Emaldi Cirión is a Professor of Law at the University of Deusto in Bilbao, Spain where she teaches courses in 'Biotechnology, bioethics and law'. She received her doctorate in Law *Summa cum laude* from University of Deusto. She also holds the Chair of Law and the Human Genome and thus is responsible for publications of monographs and periodicals, specialising in the areas of genetics, bioethics and law, and for organising seminars and congresses about these matters. Her publications and research interests include, genetic counselling, the protection of genetic data, ways to protect biotechnological innovations, genetic manipulation, biobanks, cloning and transgenic organisms.

Hille Haker holds the Chair for Religious Ethics at Frankfurt University having previously been at Harvard and prior to that at Tuebingen, where she co-directed the project 'Gender studies/feminist ethics' in the sciences. Her main research interests are theories of ethics, ethics and literature and bioethics; particularly reproductive medicine and human genetics. Her books include *Moral Identity: Literary Life Stories as a Medium of Ethical Reflection* (Francke, 1999, published in German), *Ethics of Genetic Diagnosis at the Beginning of Life* (Mentis 2002, published in German) and a co-edited collection taken from the proceedings of the international conference 'Ethics Gender Sciences' (Mentis, 2005).

Sirkku Hellsten is Reader in Development Ethics at the Centre for the Study of Global Ethics having spent four years as Coordinator for the Philosophy Programme for the Philosophy Unit/Department of Political Science at the University of Dar es Salaam, whilst also conducting research as Senior Research Fellow in an international development ethics project funded by the Academy of Finland. She also holds the title of Docent of Social and Moral Philosophy at the University of Helsinki, Finland.

Catherine Kenny is currently completing her Ph.D. at the Irish Centre for Human Rights. Her main research interests are women's human rights, asylum and immigration law and European Union law. She is a member of the Advisory Committee of the Women's Human Rights Alliance. She has taught Human Rights Law at the Irish School of Economics and was previously a Legal Officer in the Irish Refugee Council.

Fiona MacCallum is a Lecturer in Psychology at the University of Warwick. She recently completed her Ph.D. thesis at City University, London, investigating families with children conceived through embryo donation. Her research interests are in the area of parent–child relationships and children's social and emotional development, in particular, studying parenting and child development in non-traditional family forms.

Olga Tóth is a senior researcher at the Institute of Sociology, Hungarian Academy of Sciences. She conducted a series of empirical studies on family and gender. Her main research topics are: family formations and violence in the family. She has published in Hungarian and in English.

Nidhi Trehan, Ph.D. candidate at the London School of Economics, is currently a Marie Curie Fellow at the University of Padova's Centre for Human Rights, where she is researching the Romani civil rights movement. She has long been concerned with human rights: from 1996 to 1997 she worked with the European Roma Rights Centre; in 2002 she was research consultant for the UNHCR in Skopje, Macedonia; most recently, she was researcher for the 'Migration, Economics & Citizenship' project (Royal Society of Arts, UK). She has published in the areas of human rights, identity politics, NGOs and migration.

Heather Widdows is a Senior Lecturer and the Acting Director of the Centre for the Study of Global Ethics at the University of Birmingham. She is a moral philosopher whose research interests include the nature and status of moral value, communication across value frameworks and belief-systems and practical ethical issues in the global context, particularly the bioethical areas of genetic, research and reproductive ethics. She has published on all these issues including a recent book *The Moral Vision of Iris Murdoch* (Ashgate Publishing, 2005).

Introduction

Heather Widdows

This volume on 'Women's Reproductive Rights' is the outcome of a European funded project on Women's Rights as Human Rights (NEWR: Network of European Women's Rights). The project ran for three years (from 2002 to 2005) and considered four themes of particular importance to contemporary women's rights; namely, trafficking of women, reproductive rights, political participation and social entitlements. This volume is a direct outcome of the second theme of the project, that of reproductive rights, considered from the perspective of women's rights as human rights. However, although this book is part of the series resulting from the NEWR project it is also intended to stand alone as a useful and informative collection of essays for those interested in reproductive rights from across disciplinary perspectives (from lawyers to philosophers) and for those at all levels (from school pupils wishing to find out information about practices across Europe to university students and research academics addressing the more complex aspects of women's rights). In addition, the volume, like the project itself, is not meant to speak only to academics, but to be relevant and useful to activists and policy-makers (who were involved at all stages of the project). Consequently, this volume is concerned with the practical and theoretical questions of women's reproductive rights and their importance to all women (particularly in Europe, but also in the global context). Therefore the volume addresses the most fundamental issues of women's reproductive rights in the contemporary context, it provides information about the current state of women's reproductive rights, critical analysis of the various positions in the debate and it offers visions of what reproductive rights could and should be in the future and their place within the bundle of women's rights. To this end the book discusses the nature of reproductive rights as they are currently

1

conceived at the beginning of the twenty-first century by combining discussions of the status of such rights in law and practice with conceptual exploration about how such rights are defined and perceived in social and political contexts. This is done by addressing fundamental issues and themes at practical levels, for example, access to abortion and minority rights, and at conceptual levels, for instance, social and political understandings of women, reproduction and motherhood.

What are reproductive rights?

One might expect a book on 'Women's Reproductive Rights' to begin by listing the reproductive rights currently in force and able to be exercised by women. Perhaps the book would then proceed to analyse whether these rights were properly implemented – whether women were aware of their rights, willing to claim them and whether the resources and infrastructure (economical, social and legal) was there to support such rights. Such a book would then be likely to conclude with a discussion on whether this bundle of rights was adequate and if not which rights should women's groups be attempting to add to the bundle of reproductive rights. However, in the case of reproductive rights the terrain is not this easy to traverse. This is primarily for the simple reason that reproductive rights are not easy to define – they are absent from the Universal Declaration of Human Rights and at a European level there is no consensus; although all bodies agree on the importance of reproductive health. Thus, it is not clear what reproductive rights are, who is responsible for providing such rights and even to whom they pertain – are reproductive rights by definition gendered or do they apply equally to men as to women? There are no simple answers to any of these questions. Indeed the fact that these questions are not easy to answer is one of the reasons why reproductive rights continue to be such a fundamental issue in attempting to formulate a conception of women's rights.

Nevertheless, while one cannot provide a clear and concise list of reproductive rights, one can assert the primacy of this 'bundle' of rights (however reproductive rights are ultimately constructed). If a woman does not have a right to control her own reproductive life – who she has sex with, when she gets pregnant, when to continue and when to end a pregnancy – how can she meaningfully hold other rights? For example, employment rights – how can a woman make choices regarding the trajectory of her career if she cannot make decisions about if and when she will have children? Arguably even political rights are dependent upon reproductive rights, for while a women may have the right to vote and attendant civil rights, if her reproductive rights and choices are not her own, her ability to make independent political choices may be diminished. For example, if a woman is not permitted to make autonomous choices regarding contraception and abortion, decisions which are connected to her own bodily integrity, one has to wonder whether in these other issues she will be able to act independently of (and potentially in contradiction to) the wishes of her partner or family.

However, while clearly reproductive and political rights are connected, it is not necessary or desirable to assert the primacy of reproductive rights – nor is it likely that such a claim could be successful as chronologically speaking political rights long pre-date concepts of reproductive rights and without political rights it is hard to imagine women's rights (including reproductive rights). Fortunately, the task of this volume is not to untangle the ascendancy of women's rights, nor to define the place of reproductive rights in any hierarchy of such rights. Rather it is to assert that reproductive rights are a fundamental piece of any women's rights puzzle and if one wishes to talk about women's rights in the economic, social or political sphere one would do well to do, as the NEWR project did, to include reproductive rights. Thus, while focusing on reproductive rights in this volume, it is important to recognise that such rights are linked to other rights, to political, social and economic rights. For example, women's rights to economic stability depend upon whether a woman can postpone childbirth (if she wishes) until she is established in a career or in a stable relationship (rights to contraception and abortion and reproductive autonomy) as well as to social situations and institutions (such as state provision of childcare and social assumptions about the role of women). Thus, reproductive rights are central to any concept of women's rights and interconnected with political, economic and social rights.

Reproductive rights as women's rights

Having said that there is no consensus on what constitutes women's rights, an obvious limitation on the way reproductive rights have been defined in this volume stems from the perspective of the project as a whole which sets the debate about reproductive rights in the context of women's rights as human rights. Thus women, and women's rights, are the lenses through which reproductive rights are considered. From one perspective this might seem obvious – how could reproductive rights, which are ultimately concerned with choosing when, if and how to give birth (decisions which concern women and their bodies) fail to be women-centred? Yet, many regard this starting point as flawed and deny that women have any special claim to reproductive rights. For example, in discussions about couples' reproductive rights or men's reproductive rights, women are not the central agents in reproductive decisions; indeed in many communities and cultures women are not at the centre of these decisions, rather they are made for women by their partners or families.

Women disappear further from the centre of the picture in debates about reproductive rights which focus on the moral status of the embryo as the primary ethical and legal concern. From such perspectives, women's social and economic freedom and reproductive autonomy is explicitly not the central issue and, if women are considered at all (which they are increasingly not, for example, in the debate about the ethics of stem cell technology) women's rights are presented as being in conflict with the rights of the embryo. Most commonly, the woman's right to reproductive autonomy is placed in opposition to the foetus' right to life (e.g. in the abortion debate). However, although the moral status of the embryo continues to be an important concern in both ethics and law it is not the central issue of this volume (although the moral status of the embryo is mentioned in many chapters, including Chapters 3, 6, 7, 8, 10 and 11). The reason for this is, in part, because of the women's rights focus of this volume, but also for the conceptual reason that in most (although not all) jurisdictions the embryo is not usually considered a 'person' and therefore is not a bearer of human rights (only becoming a rights bearer at birth). Thus the embryo is most often considered to have 'interests' which are given increased weight as it develops and the nearer to birth and to the possibility of 'viability'.

Therefore at the outset, this particular bias – of conceiving reproductive rights through the lens of women's rights – of this volume should be acknowledged, yet this granted, how reproductive rights should be conceived is very much an open question and one with which this volume directly engages and about which contributors to the volume differ. The project and this volume have treated the definition of reproductive rights as one of the research questions and it is addressed by many chapters – both directly and indirectly. While recognising that there is no consensus on this matter (even among those who adopt a women's rights perspective on the reproductive rights debate) the authors of the volume wrestle with this issue, in both the issue-based chapters (such as Chapters 3 and 6), where the concept is problematised and in chapters which address the normative issue directly (Chapters 7, 10 and 11). Not surprisingly, the issue of what are and what should be reproductive rights is central to all the chapters of this volume. Therefore, while it would be wrong of this volume (and misrepresentative of the project) to endorse any one definition of reproductive rights, the issue is not neglected by any of the authors but is a central and ongoing concern throughout the volume.

In addition to wrestling with broad themes, such as the definition of women's rights (explicitly discussed in Chapters 10, 11 and 12) this project addresses many of the practical issues facing women today as they attempt to exercise reproductive rights and reproductive autonomy. Issues addressed in this volume cross the spectrum of women's concerns from basic demands for education and information as well as access to contraception (Chapters 3 and 4), to being able to make autonomous reproductive decisions (Chapters 1, 2 and 5), to the issues raised by New Reproductive Technologies (NRTs) (Chapters 6, 7, 8 and 9). In addition to such specific concerns there are many cross-cutting themes which can be traced through many chapters, such as the continued struggle by women for basic reproductive rights as a means to equality (Chapters 3, 4 and 6), to questions of justice, not only with regard to equality with men but between privileged and less privileged women (Chapters 5 and 12), to broader concerns about the social construction of women and the way such constructions impact upon the real possibilities open to women (Chapters 7, 9, 10 and 11).

Addressing women's reproductive rights

In order to best discuss women's reproductive rights this volume has been divided into three sections – 'Tensions in Europe: Critical issues in reproductive rights', 'The impact of technology: Scientific advances and reproductive rights' and 'Into the future: Projections for reproductive rights' – and moves from specific current issues, through more conceptual questions raised by the innovations in science and technology to the final section which addresses the broadest issues of what reproductive rights are and what they should be.

The first section 'Tensions in Europe: Critical issues in reproductive rights' address, five of the most fundamental issues in reproductive rights in the contemporary context, those of, abortion, adoption, birth rate, teenage pregnancy and the rights of minority groups.

Catherine Kenny, in her chapter 'Abortion – a reproductive right?', addresses the issue of access to abortion. Access to abortion is perhaps 'the' reproductive right, as without the ability to refuse to carry an unwanted child to term not just reproductive autonomy, but women's autonomy in general, is brought into question. Kenny describes the situation vis-à-vis access to abortion in contemporary Europe. She describes the erosion of the 'right' to abortion across Eastern Europe in the post-communist period and the continual pressure to restrict and rescind abortion rights in Western Europe. In so doing, she uses examples from many countries and traces some of the causes for these trends, such as the increased influence of nationalistic and religious groups (particularly, but not exclusively in Eastern Europe) as well as the effects of current US attitudes and policies regarding abortion.

The next chapter, 'Adoption: Practices and regulations' moves from the right not to be a parent to those who wish to be parents but for some reason cannot, or choose not to, have biologically related offspring. Fiona MacCallum traces the historical development of adoption, from its establishment in ancient civilisations through to current adoption practice and regulation. MacCallum outlines the differences between adoption and the NRTs as roots to family creation, particularly those surrounding parent selection. She explores issues of inter-country adoption and the varieties of adoptive legislation across Europe in light of the latest psychological evidence about adoptive parenting. MacCallum's chapter is important as it highlights an issue which is too often ignored – that adoption too is a means of family creation for infertile women or couples. This recognition is crucial for the women's rights debate, because it brings into question many of the assumptions surrounding reproductive rights, particularly assumptions about the biological nature of reproductive rights and essentialist conceptions of women (issues which are taken up explicitly elsewhere, for example, Chapters 9 and 10). Thus, this chapter reveals through the practical issue of adoption the inherent bias in much of the debate and ensures the recognition of the non-biological aspects of reproductive rights.

The next two chapters provide and analyse information on birth rates. Paloma de Villota discusses declining birth rates and the reasons for them in her chapter on 'Birth rates and women's rights in Europe'. Her focus is primarily on Spain in comparison to other European countries, although, the tendency she describes is evident across industrialised countries and the chapter includes a survey of many European countries. In accounting for this tendency, de Villota cites the economic and social influences and concludes with a summary of the pubic policy implications which arise from such a study. In Chapter 4, Olga Toth focuses specifically on teenage birth rates, comparing in this chapter the birth rates, abortion rates, policies, trends and attitudes across Europe and with the United States. She discusses factors which influence teenage pregnancy rates including, access and attitudes to contraception and abortion, levels of sex education as well as the social position of young women and divergent cultural attitudes to teen pregnancy. Like de Villota, Toth concludes by highlighting policy issues, and to this end she lists a number of ethical and practical issues that should be addressed with regard to teen pregnancy.

Together these chapters by de Villota and Toth show the fundamental integration between different aspects of women's rights. de Villota forcibly argues that women's autonomy is undermined if women do not have the economic stability necessary to enable them to decide to have children. This point is brought home by her discussion of the impact public childcare policies have (either directly or indirectly) on birth rates – in other words on whether having children is a 'real' possibility. The interdependence of women's rights is further emphasised by Toth in her claims that the social status of women is one of the key factors influencing the teenage birth rate and that in addition to providing free contraception and ensuring that young women have the information they need to make decisions about their own reproductive health, women should be supported in continuing their education in an attempt to improve their social standing. Together these chapters show the inter-relationship between reproductive rights and women's rights broadly conceived, including social, economic and political rights.

The last chapter in this section, by Nidhi Trehan and Isabel Crowhurst, is concerned with minority groups and reproductive rights. This issue, like adoption, is too often forgotten in contemporary discussions of reproductive rights and therefore, not surprisingly and as the authors point out, it is an area which is under-researched and under-theorised. This chapter focuses on two practices – that of forced sterilisation of minority women (in this case Romani women) and that of 'female circumcision' or 'female genital mutilation' occurring among immigrant populations. In the course of this chapter the history of forced sterilisation is considered across Europe, and current practices of both forced sterilisation and female genital mutilation or female circumcision are described and assessed. The response to women who undergo such practices is analysed from the perspectives of gender and ethnicity, and the roles of state regulators and non-state actors, in particular NGO advocates of minority women, are discussed with emphasis on their influence on attitudes to such women and the challenging of current injustices. The inclusion of this chapter adds to the volume as a whole not only by pointing to areas in which reproductive rights of women are most abused and ignored – something which is compounded by cultural norms and constraints – but also by illustrating the dilemma of all women in a dramatic way.

All women struggle from being conceived as 'the other', from being 'different' and thus in danger of being invisible. If this were not the case there would be no need for a project about women's rights as human rights, for women's rights would be impossible to distinguish from human rights. The very fact that women's rights can, at least in some areas, be differentiated from Human Rights illustrates the bias in 'Human Rights' towards 'man' as the 'norm' of 'Human' not women. The plight of minority women shows that while all women may suffer from being differentiated from the norm, these minority women are twice removed from the 'norm' – by gender and then again by culture and ethnicity. Thus, these women suffer from 'double jeopardy' and the test of whether women's rights can be seen as human rights will be whether these women's rights are asserted and upheld.

This first section is followed by a section of four chapters under the title of 'The impact of technology: Scientific advances and reproductive rights'. Choosing to do a separate section and devote four chapters to the effect of technology on reproductive rights, at first glance, may seem in conflict with the aims of the project – to be representative and to highlight the most fundamental areas of concern for reproductive rights. Certainly, it is the case that NRTs affect only the smallest minority of women and consequently one could argue that debates about NRTs are only relevant to relatively rich and highly privileged women and thus do not merit one-third of a book devoted to reproductive rights conceived of from the perspective of women's rights. For most women in Europe, and not only those who are obviously in the margins (such as the minority women discussed in the last chapter), the issues surrounding NRTs will not directly affect whether or not women are able to exercise their day to day reproductive rights. However, NRTs are important with regard to the new issues they raise and in terms of how women are (and can be) conceived. In these ways NRTs do impact upon all women – a subject which is directly addressed in two of the chapters in this section (Chapters 7 and 9). In addition, much of the debate about NRTs in legal terms is connected to other legislation surrounding women's rights, and very much situated in the context of women's and embryo's rights – hence, legislation about NRTs may well impact upon other regulations connected to reproductive rights; particularly with abortion regulation. Thus taken together, the conceptual and legal issues do impact upon all women, whether or not they have direct contact with NRTs.

Given the interrelation between NRT regulation and regulation regarding other reproductive rights this section begins with a chapter by Itziar Alkorta which provides an overview of fertility medicine regulation in Europe. Alkorta uses this overview as a means by which to draw out the main tendencies currently evident in such regulation in order to provide a deeper critique of how reproductive rights are actually conceived and actualised in contemporary Europe. In uncovering these underlying trends, Alkorta focuses on a number of issues, such as the place of women as patients and the return to emphasising the interests and rights of the embryo. In light of the tendencies she uncovers she considers broader conceptual issues, such as traditional family structures and concepts of infertility.

These broader issues, which are introduced by Alkorta in the context of current regulation of NRTs, are taken up by Lori Andrews in the next chapter. Andrews directly addresses the conceptual issues of social and cultural significance brought about by NRTs in her chapter entitled 'How is technology changing the meaning of motherhood for western women?' Here Anderws explicitly addresses the wider conceptual issues raised by NRTs and their potential impact on the way that women are conceived of and the social roles which they occupy, for example, whether NRTs encourage and reinforce the view that women are merely vessels to produce healthy babies. She also addresses the potentially darker side of reproductive technology asking whether, in the guise of giving a couple or a woman a baby, women are undergoing experimental treatment, unacceptable in other spheres of medicine. In addition, she considers issues of commodification and commercialisation implicit in many aspects of these technologies, and considers whether the laws surrounding NRTs and genetic technologies, in general, are really adequate to protect women.

Having raised general questions about the impact of NRTs on many aspects of social conventions and norms, the next two chapters by Aitziber Emaldi and Heather Widdows, proceed to examine more specific issues in the debate and so illustrate the current situation and dilemmas surrounding NRTs in a more concrete manner. Emaldi considers one practice – that of PGD (preimplantation genetic diagnosis) – while Widdows considers one conceptual issue – that of genetic relatedness.

Emaldi's chapter, 'Preimplantation genetic diagnosis: Problems and future perspectives' provides an analysis of the ethical–legal problems that surround preimplantation genetic diagnosis as well as a pan-European overview of the existing legislation on preimplantation diagnosis. Thus, this chapter provides an in-depth ethical and legal assessment of one NRT including, discussions of the potentially eugenic nature of the practice and controversial issues, such as embryo selection, sex selection and embryo experimentation. The chapter concludes by advocating the availability of preimplantation genetic diagnosis to couples who could benefit from its use, however, given the inherent dangers it suggests that the practice should be closely regulated (suggesting the Spanish model of regulation). In this manner, this chapter discusses the ethical and legal aspects of a one procedure from the perspectives of both practice and regulation.

Widdows's chapter moves from considering the ethical and legal issues surrounding one particular practice to addressing one conceptual issue that of 'The impact of New Reproductive Technologies on concepts of genetic relatedness and non relatedness'. In this chapter, Widdows explores the hypothesis that NRTs support and promote concepts of genetic relatedness. In examining this issue Widdows engages with the broader debate about how women and relationships are (and can be) conceptualised, and thus, in turn, contributes to the debate on whether access to NRTs should be a reproductive right. In assessing this claim she considers a number of NRTs: first, *in vitro* fertilisation (IVF); and second, third-party NRTs, particularly, donor insemination (DI) and embryo donation. Widdows, highlights the double-edged nature of NRTs (which have the potential to both liberate and enslave) and advocates the recognition of these potentialities in considering whether to claim access to NRTs as a reproductive right. She is primarily concerned to show that these wider social and political effects must be central to the reproductive rights debate in all its forms: The debate must not only consider the ethical issues as they affect individual women or couples on a case by case basis, but must also take a broader perspective and consider how the use of such technologies affect concepts, assumptions and worldviews and so impact upon all women.

This discussion about the dual-edged nature of NRTs and the importance of addressing the social and political context as well as the wishes and needs of individuals overtly returns the debate to the fundamental question of this volume, that of defining what reproductive rights are and what they should be. It is this topic which is taken up in the final section of this volume, 'Into the future: Projections for reproductive rights'. This section contains three chapters all of which look at different elements of the future of reproductive rights: considering how they are, could be and should be conceived and implemented.

Chapter 10 by Hille Haker directly explores the issues raised in the last chapter by Widdows, those of essentialism and the dual nature of reproductive rights. Haker addresses this issue in the broadest possible manner in the context of what reproductive rights both are and should be. She begins this comprehensive and detailed chapter by considering the history of ethical reasoning from which reproductive rights have emerged, considering fundamental issues for women – such as individual autonomy from a feminist perspective and concepts of parenthood. Such analysis of ethical concepts leads Haker to discuss the foundations of reproductive rights, and thus she considers how to assert reproductive rights without advocating an essentialist picture of women; an issue she explores using a relational framework which draws on the ethics of responsibility. By such means she asserts the social and political context of reproductive rights and argues that those advocating reproductive rights must consider how these rights (and their implications for women) are conceptualised. In addition, she argues that reproductive rights and autonomy must be set in the global context and be fundamentally linked to basic healthcare and other social and economic rights. Thus Haker presents a vision of reproductive rights which is broader and more demanding of both the women's movement and society: a vision which, as the women's movement has traditionally asserted, fundamentally connects the individual with the wider society and the personal with the political. Thus, besides exploring and setting out possible constructions of reproductive rights (including the theoretical difference between positive and negative constructions) this chapter, like the chapters of de Villota and Toth in the first section, forcibly asserts the interconnectedness of women's rights and the necessity of always conceiving of reproductive rights in economic and social contexts.

One of the issues raised by Haker is the increasing commercialisation of women's bodies (a trend which she suggests should be opposed). This issue is overtly addressed in the next chapter by Donna Dickenson in her chapter entitled 'Ownership, property and women's bodies'. Dickenson problematises the issue of ownership arguing against those who wish to assert that women have property rights in their bodies. She claims that while the claim that women own their own bodies (and thus have the power to decide what to do with them) seems appealing for the women's movement and has polemical and political utility, it is incoherent in philosophy and law. Dickenson's suggestion is that we should not conflate the 'entirely plausible concept of women's reproductive rights' and the 'implausible notion of property in the body', but rather should keep these two concepts separate. Dickenson argues that there are better arguments by which to provide a firm foundation for women's reproductive rights and in this chapter she proceeds to outline such an argument. She argues that reproductive rights can be based on the claim that women possess a right in the labour of their bodies (not in their bodies themselves). Moreover she presents this right as gendered, unique to women's labour in childbirth and pregnancy, and not capable of providing a similar foundation for men – because men simply do not labour to the same extent in the process of human reproduction. From this conception of property rights Dickenson argues that women possess an absolute and inviolable right to determine whether or not they will undergo pregnancy, submit to hormone stimulation in IVF, retain the children they bear in contract motherhood or allow their ova to be used for other people's ends. This chapter thus offers one solution to the basis of reproductive rights which avoids some of the difficulties raised in the last chapter by Haker as Dickenson's model does not suggest an essentialist view of women, and yet, it does provide a gendered definition of reproductive rights.

The volume concludes with a chapter by Sirkku Hellsten entitled 'Beyond Europe: Rhetoric of reproductive rights in global population policies'. In this chapter, Hellsten, following Haker's recommendations, moves beyond the European context and considers reproductive rights in the global sphere. She critiques this issue from vantage point of population growth and suggests that in the rhetoric surrounding population control programmes the differences in how women (and women's reproductive rights) are conceived in poor and rich countries are apparent. She suggests that the language of population policies, such as human rights, often conceals structural global injustices and thus denies the same 'reproductive rights' to rich and poor women. This final chapter fundamentally reminds the reader of the importance of reproductive rights for all women – whether in the rich or the poor counties – and powerfully advocates the broadest possible perspective when one conceives of women's rights as human rights.

Conclusion

What is clear from all the chapters in the volume is that reproductive rights continue to be highly contested concepts and women's reproductive rights and autonomy are by no means guaranteed. Furthermore, from a women's rights perspective, many chapters indicate that reproductive rights are under threat and in many instances are being eroded; in both 'high tech' areas of NRTs and the 'low tech' traditional areas of access to abortion and contraception. Moreover, these changes are in danger of exacerbating each other as changes in one area affect already established women's rights in another (e.g. the impact of NRT regulation on abortion regulation). Thus, one conclusion which arises from the volume as a whole is that reproductive rights as women's rights are far from firmly established, in either law or practice, at both practical and theoretical levels and perhaps even more importantly there is little consensus about how those who wish to endorse women's rights should respond. Such a conclusion serves to show the timely and important nature of this topic and the pressing need to define, endorse and ultimately establish a conception of reproductive rights from a women's rights perspective.

Part I

Tensions in Europe: Critical Issues in Reproductive Rights

1
Abortion – A Reproductive Right

Catherine Kenny

Introduction

Access to both abortion and contraception is being threatened by religious and other ideological forces. This is the case not only in Eastern Europe, where access to abortion is being systematically eroded, but also in the West, as exemplified in the recent changes to the abortion laws in Italy. In this chapter, these threats, in particular, the rise of nationalist movements, the role of Churches and the strength and sophistication of the anti-choice movement are discussed and analysed. The paper provides a comparative study across Europe, analyses the changes in national laws and identifies the factors behind such changes. The chapter is divided into two sections, concerned first with Eastern Europe and then Western Europe and using examples from Croatia, Serbia, Poland, Hungary, Russia, Ireland, Malta, Italy, the United Kingdom, Northern Ireland, Spain and Portugal.

Abortion as a reproductive right

In 1994, 172 countries agreed on a programme of action at the Cairo United Nations International Conference on Population and Development (ICPD). This Programme of Action defined reproductive health as 'a state of complete physical, mental and social well-being ... in all matters related to the reproductive system and to its functions and processes' (ICPD Programme for Action, 1994, Ch. 7.2). It goes on to state:

> Reproductive rights embrace certain human rights that are already recognised in national laws, international human rights documents and other consensus documents. These rights rest on the recognition

of the basic right of all couples and individuals to decide freely and responsibly the number, spacing and timing of their children and to have the information and means to do so, and the right to attain the highest standard of sexual and reproductive health. It also includes their right to make decisions concerning reproduction free of discrimination, coercion and violence, as expressed in human rights documents. (ICPD Programme for Action, 1994, Ch. 7.3)

The 1995 Beijing Declaration and Platform for Action agreed at the UN World Conference on Women, affirms that the right of a woman to control her own sexuality and reproduction is a human right (Beijing Declaration, 1995, para. 14). In addition, it urged states to remove criminal sanctions against women who have had illegal abortions and to take measures to understand and address the causes and consequences of illegal abortions (Beijing Platform for Action, 1995, para 107(j)).

As one commentator has noted 'this limited recognition of women's reproductive rights has been difficult to secure and is the subject of ongoing struggle, both at national and international levels' (Mullally, 2005, p. 79). This struggle is a daily reality for many European women. According to the United Nations Population Fund, ensuring that there is access to comprehensive contraceptive services at a reasonable price still presents a 'critical challenge' in many parts of Central and Eastern Europe. Under the socialist system, reproductive health care, although inadequate in many cases, was available free of charge as part of the general health service in these states. With the exception of Romania and Albania, abortion was available in all the Central and Eastern European countries during the Communist era.

Reduction in government spending on health services, reductions in subsidies on health care products and privatisation have meant that modern contraceptives are proving too expensive for many people (Center for Reproductive Rights, 2001). This is exacerbated by the lack of information available, in particular for young people in relation to reproductive health. Attempts by governments in Central and Eastern Europe to restrict women's rights to abortion backed by nationalist and religious groups serves to remove from many women in these states, the ability to exercise any control over their own reproductive health.

The European Women's Lobby (EWL) in a position paper entitled *Women's Sexual Rights in Europe*, has noted that in several European Countries very strict abortion laws remain in place, in particular, Poland, Slovakia, Malta, Ireland and also Spain and Portugal. Women living in these states must either travel to another country to terminate their pregnancy or undergo an illegal abortion. The EWL paper also describes the increasing influence of anti-abortion movements and religious groups in many countries and conscientious objection of medical staff in relation to performing abortions (European Women's Lobby, 2005).

The situation in Eastern Europe is compounded by the influence of the United States, which is highly significant in the Eastern European context. The impact of the United States Supreme Court in *Roe* v. *Wade* was not limited to the United States. The decision in *Roe*, which acknowledged that a woman's right to terminate her pregnancy was a fundamental right, encouraged groups working for reproductive rights around the world (Ernst *et al.*, 2004, p. 753). However, since the Roe judgment, the 'gradual backsliding in the legal framework and jurisprudence affecting women's right to abortion, together with an increasingly anti-choice U.S. foreign policy, pose serious threats to women's ability to exercise their right to reproductive choice, not only in the United States but around the globe' (Ernst *et al.*, 2004, pp. 753–4). The Bush administration reinstated the 'global gag rule' (also known as the 'Mexico City Policy') which prohibits organisations worldwide that receive US funding from providing abortion services, even if these services are provided from other funding sources (Stephenson, 2005). According to a report carried out on behalf of the Council of Europe Parliamentary Assembly, this policy has had a negative impact on reproductive health in Council of Europe Member States including Albania, Serbia, Montenegro and Moldova. As the report demonstrates, the reduction of funding, results paradoxically in some of the poorest women in Europe having no choice but to undergo illegal abortions (Council of Europe Parliamentary Assembly, 2003).

The US administration's opposition to international instruments that could be vehicles for granting reproductive rights is most recently illustrated in the review of the Beijing Platform for Action. The United Nations Commission on the Status of Women conducted a review of the Beijing Platform for Action from 28 February to 11 March 2005. The United States sought to amend the declaration adopted by the delegates reaffirming international support for the Beijing Declaration and Platform for Action and to ensure international agreement, that the Platform for Action did not create any new human rights (including the right to abortion). However, the Platform states clearly that 'any measures or changes related to abortion within the health system can only be determined at the national or local level according to the national legislative process' (Beijing Platform for Action, 1995, para 107(k)).

Some US anti-choice groups have established branches in Europe, particularly in Eastern European States. The tactics employed by

US anti-choice groups in their attempts to undermine reproductive rights in the United States have been followed by anti-choice groups in Europe. Such groups in the United States, where majority public opinion favours abortion have turned their attention to 'more incremental tactics to erode women's ability to exercise their right to abortion' (Ernst *et al.*, 2004, p. 754). Similar strategies are being utilised in the United Kingdom, where issues such as 'emergency' contraception, 'late' abortions and the rights of young women to abortion without parental consent are the focus of campaigns and legal proceedings, rather than the right to abortion itself, which is generally accepted by the majority of British people. Anti-choice groups have also become involved in the assisted fertility debate and have supported the inclusion of rights for the embryo in legislation governing assisted fertility.

Access to abortion in Eastern Europe

The political changes that took place in Eastern Europe in the early 1990s diminished women's rights rather than strengthened them (Mertus, 1998, p. 370). Women had achieved formal equality under the Communist system, however, this masked to a large extent the level of gender inequality in the private sphere. According to one report on the position of women in Eastern and Central Europe, under the communist system, 'there was a symbiotic co-existence of a radically modern legislation aiming at social equality of opportunities and of a deeply sexist practice in the private realm' (Council of Europe, 2004, para 13). Since the fall of Communism, inequalities between men and women have increased, participation of women in the workplace has decreased and the levels of violence against women have worsened considerably. Some commentators have noted that 'The emancipation of women has been regarded as a Communist tactic to be resisted by the resort to traditional values' (Charlesworth *et al.*, 1991, pp. 621–2). Therefore, in these contexts it would seem fair to say that opponents of communism are, in general, also opposed to women's equality.

The emergence of Eastern and Central Europe from decades of communist rule has given rise to strong religious and nationalist movements frequently sharing a traditional view of the role of women as mothers and carers. It has been argued that Central and Eastern Europe is 'under the sway of an increasingly powerful anti-choice movement, fuelled by a post-Communist rush of religious fundamentalism and nationalism' (Ernst *et al.*, 2004, p. 762). It is these movements and their impact upon reproductive rights, and in particular, access to abortion, which we will now explore.

Nationalist movements often seek to return to what they perceive as the traditional values of their country. For women, this means a reversion to their traditional roles as mothers and carers. As Halliday has argued, 'nationalist movements subordinate women in particular, definition of their role and place in society, [and] enforce conformity to values that are often male defined' (Halliday, 1988, p. 424).

In the early 1990s the former Yugoslavia became engulfed in nationalist struggles. Women were required to play their part by reverting to traditional roles of mothers. Julie Mertus has noted that in these nationalist struggles, 'Women's bodies become the vessels for new foot soldiers for the national cause; women's homes become the training ground in which dutiful members of the nation are nurtured and indoctrinated' (Mertus, 1998, pp. 385–6). Nationalist ideology favoured a high birth rate and women were encouraged to have large families. Although both contraception and abortion were, and continue to be, legal, in the States of the former Yugoslavia, their use was discouraged by nationalists, who considered women who refused to bow to nationalist pressures and bear children as not fulfilling their national duty.

In Croatia, anti-choice and nationalist groups combined and succeeded in putting pressure on the Parliament to adopt a 'National Programme for Demographic Development', a programme that emphasises the protection of the family and rewards Croatian families with three or more children (Mertus, 1998, p. 386). The 1978 Yugoslav *Law on Abortion* was carried forward into Croatian law on independence and permits abortion up to 10 weeks after conception. Thereafter, women requiring terminations must obtain the permission of a special commission, which is comprised of two doctors and a nurse or a social worker. However, many hospitals will not perform abortions after 22 weeks and some hospitals impose a 14 week limit (Mertus, 1998, p. 442). Both hospitals and individual doctors are vulnerable to the reactions of and pressure from anti-choice groups and the Catholic Church (Mertus, 1998, p. 442).

In Serbia, women were similarly expected to bear children for the nation and those that refused to accept this role were described as unpatriotic. Nationalist movements were supported by the Serbian Orthodox Church who couched their anti-abortion stance in the language of nationalism. For example, analogies were drawn between Serbs dying on the battlefield and the killing of Serbs by abortion (Mertus, 1998, pp. 455, 456).

Nationalist movements have also emerged in states that had a peaceful transition to democracy. In Russia, a significant decrease in population and the rise of nationalism have led to a desire to increase the birth rate.

Women have been the target for much of the blame for declining birth rates in recent years (Stewart, 2004, p. 52). In Hungary, the nationalist movement seeks to restore the 'Hungarian nation' and its Christian heritage (Mertus, 1998, p. 448). A central element of the nationalist philosophy is the return of women to their traditional role as mothers, and nationalists have joined with other anti-choice groups in attempting to bring about a restriction of women's reproductive rights (Mertus, 1998, p. 448).

In addition to the increasing influence of nationalistic groups, the influence of religion has been paramount in restricting access to abortion in these countries. It can be argued that the influence of the Roman Catholic Church on world affairs exceeds that of other religious denominations. It is the only religion with permanent observer status at the United Nations. The Vatican (or Holy See) is recognised as an independent state with diplomatic relations with nations throughout the world. While the Church's role in advocating for social justice may be regarded as progressive, it maintains a traditional view of the role and the rights of women. Frances Kissling of 'Catholics for a Free Choice', has argued that the role model the Church offers to women is that of Mary, the Virgin Mother and 'and, unable to be both virgins and mothers, women must be one or the other' (Kissling, 1998).

In the States of the former Soviet Union and in some Eastern European States, the Orthodox faith is the dominant religion. Orthodoxy shares many of the Roman Catholic Church's views regarding the role of women and their right to reproductive choice. It regards abortion as 'murder' and disapproves of contraception as interfering with reproduction which it regards as the principle function of marriage (Stewart, 2004, p. 52). Since the early 1990s evangelical groups have made substantial inroads into Eastern Europe (Danchin, 2002, p. 49). These groups share the same anti-choice position as the more established religious denominations.

The Catholic Church in Poland continued to play a major role in Poland in the Communist era and the 'collaboration between Catholic institutions and Polish society increased during the last decade of the communist regime' (Czerwinski, 2004, p. 656). The close association between the Church and the Solidarity movement and the Church's opposition to Communism, ensured a dominant position for the Church in post-Communist Poland. Since the emergence of democracy, the Church has used its position to influence government policy, in particular, policies relating to 'moral' issues. It has supported efforts to undermine women's rights and to reinforce women's traditional role in the family as mothers and carers (Mertus, 1998, p. 387).

During the Communist era, women in Poland were entitled to abortion on demand. However, within four years of democratic rule, legislation was passed which restricted the right to abortion to circumstances where the pregnancy threatened the woman's life or health, the pregnancy was as a result of rape or incest or if the foetus was damaged (Czerwinski, 2004, p. 658). In 1996, the Polish Parliament approved legislation, which gave Polish women additional rights to abortion. Under the new law, abortion could take place until the twelfth week of pregnancy where there were compelling social or financial reasons, in cases of rape or incest and in the case of serious foetal abnormalities.

This law was challenged before the Constitutional Tribunal, which ruled that it was unconstitutional (Cholewinski, 1998, p. 263). According to Cholewinski, this decision was the most recent of a number of restrictive decisions taken by the Tribunal, which would appear to limit the powers of the Polish Parliament to legislate in relation to abortion (Cholewinski, 1998, p. 262). In 1991, it upheld a regulation issued by the Health Ministry allowing doctors to refuse to carry out abortions as conforming to freedom of conscience provisions in the Polish Constitution. The following year it dismissed a petition by the Ombudsman which challenged the Polish Medical Association's code of ethics which prohibited doctors from performing abortions except in certain limited cases.

In the 1997 decision, the Tribunal held that the law violated the Constitutional provisions on the right to life, which it interpreted as requiring the protection of life from beginning to end (Mertus, 1998, p. 450). Recent attempts by the Polish Government to liberalise its abortion law have been thwarted by anti-choice members of the Polish Parliament supported by the Catholic Church. Parliament voted in February 2005 not to consider a proposal by the ruling Democratic Left Alliance, which would allow abortions up to 12 weeks. In addition, the Government's proposal to allow abortions for minors without the consent of their parents was defeated by the lobbying of anti-choice groups and the Church. One anti-choice group is reported to have sent dolls which they claimed resembled a foetus at 10 weeks to legislators and journalists (Morning Star, 2005). The Catholic Church wrote to all members of parliament and claimed the proposed changes in the abortion law 'would be a crime against the nation, especially in the light of the very low birth rate' (Morning Star, 2005). The problems encountered by women in Poland in availing themselves of abortion services are further compounded by the difficulties regarding access to, and the cost of, contraceptives which are often prohibitively expensive for the average person. In addition, the lack of comprehensive sex education in schools and the lack of family planning in rural areas mean that a considerable number of people lack awareness about contraception (Mertus, 1998, p. 451). Thus, even with a relatively liberal government access to abortion and contraception are severely limited. Commentators predict that the forthcoming general election will result in a conservative government coming to power (Economist, 2005). Consequently it would seem unlikely that Polish women will realise their right to reproductive choice in the near future.

The position of the Catholic Church in Hungary has traditionally been weaker than in Poland. Nonetheless, its anti-choice position, has influenced government policy towards abortion in Hungary. Hungarian pro-choice groups, in their submission to the UN Human Rights Committee have noted that women who wish to terminate their pregnancy must undergo 'biased' counselling which attempts to persuade them to proceed with their pregnancy (Center for Reproductive Law and Policy and NANE, 2002). In addition, the groups confirm that the Hungarian Government has abolished subsidies on abortion services and will not provide funding unless the abortion is a medical necessity, where there is a social or financial situation or where the pregnancy is the result of a crime (Center for Reproductive Law and Policy and NANE, 2002).

While Russia's abortion laws remain liberal by comparison with those of Poland and Hungary, recent legislation seeks to roll back women's reproductive rights while granting rights to the foetus. In an amendment to the *Family Code* in 2003, introduced with the aim of 'safeguarding children's rights before birth', a 'viable foetus' is considered as an 'unborn child' with identical rights to those of children, including the right to life (Stewart, 2004, pp. 51–2). Legislation adopted later the same year, reduced the number of 'social' reasons according to which an abortion would be permitted (for women from 12 to 22 weeks pregnant) from 13 to 4. These reasons include being in prison, and pregnancy as a result of rape. Women are also required to have the permission of a doctor and a local welfare organisation in order to terminate their pregnancy (Stewart, 2004, pp. 51–2).

Access to abortion in Western Europe

Although there has been a progressive liberalisation of abortion laws in Western Europe in recent years, abortion rights are nonetheless very limited in a number of states and often women are forced to leave their own country to terminate their pregnancies. In addition, women who have no choice but to resort to illegal abortion, face the possibility of imprisonment. Moreover, attempts are being made in states that have a well-established reproductive health services to undermine the reproductive autonomy of women as the strategies utilised by anti-choice groups become more sophisticated.

The role of religious groups in attempting to roll back the rights of women, in particular, in relation to reproduction, is not limited to Eastern Europe. Countries like Ireland, Malta, Spain and Portugal, where the Catholic Church has traditionally been dominant, have prohibited abortion or have very strict limits on abortion. Italy, which has a more liberal abortion law than those of the other Catholic states, has adopted legislation which has recognised the rights of the embryo, which anti-choice groups hope will eventually pave the way for at least a restriction on Italy's existing abortion law.

The unique position of the Catholic Church in Ireland may be contrasted with other north-west European states. It played a significant role in nation-building including in the formulation of the 1937 Irish Constitution and could be regarded as having a monopoly over key public functions including education and health (Deane and Lodge, 2000, p. 2). Close relationships developed between church and political leaders and the church did not hesitate to use its influence over legislators. As one leading commentator noted 'there can be no doubt (...) that when the church deemed it vital to its interests, its intervention was conclusive and there was no doubt either about the direction in which its weight was cast' (Chubb, 1992, p. 14). The sale of contraceptives became legal for all persons over 18 in 1985 and divorce was prohibited until as recently as 1995 when, after a divisive campaign, the Irish people voted by a small majority to lift the constitutional ban on divorce.

Although the influence of the Catholic Church in Ireland has declined considerably in recent years, Ireland continues to have one of the most restrictive abortion laws in Europe. The prohibition on abortion in the UK, *Offences Against the Person Act* (OASA) of 1961, was carried forward into Irish law on independence. A combination of factors led anti-choice groups to push for a referendum to insert a provision into the Irish Constitution protecting the life of the 'unborn'. These included Ireland's entry into the European Community in 1973 and decisions by courts both domestically and in other jurisdictions to strike down legislation that conflicted with the right to privacy (Bouclin, 2002, p. 137). The Irish Supreme Court held in *McGee* v. *Attorney General* that the prosecution of a woman under the OASA for importing contraceptives infringed her right to privacy. The US decision in *Roe* v. *Wade* permitting abortions in the first three months of pregnancy was based in part on previous decisions permitting the use of contraceptives on privacy grounds. However, the fears of anti-choice groups that abortion would be legalised on the basis of privacy proved to be, groundless. The Supreme Court in *McGee* affirmed that the judgment was confined only to contraception and it was not 'intended to apply to abortifacients, though called contraceptives, as in the case of abortifacients entirely different considerations may arise' (*McGee* v. *Attorney General* [1974] I.R. 284). Despite this, anti-choice groups with the support of the Catholic Church campaigned successfully for a referendum, which was carried by a two-to-one majority. The Eighth Amendment inserted the following provision in the Irish Constitution at Article 40.3.3. : 'That the State acknowledges the right to life of the unborn and, with due regard to the equal right to life of the mother, guarantees in its laws to respect, as far as practicable, by its laws to defend and vindicate that right' (Constitution of Ireland, 1937, Article 40.3.3).

Since the legalisation of abortion in the United Kingdom in 1967, Irish women have travelled to the United Kingdom to have their pregnancies terminated. Many women were concerned that the Constitutional provision could be used to prevent them from travelling to the United Kingdom for the purpose of terminating their pregnancy or to prosecute them on return to Ireland (Miller, 1999, pp. 199–200). Their concern was justified, not satisfied that women in Ireland could not avail themselves of abortion services in their own country, anti-choice groups sought to prevent women travelling to the United Kingdom in order to terminate their pregnancies there. Proceedings were successfully instituted to restrain a counselling service from providing the names of clinics in the United Kingdom providing abortions; to stop financial assistance to women travelling to the United Kingdom for abortions and to prevent a students union from providing information about abortion services available in the United Kingdom. In the first case, an application was brought to the European Court of Human Rights, alleging that the right of the counselling service to privacy and freedom of expression under the *European Convention on Human Rights* had been violated (*Open Door Counselling and Dublin Well Woman* v. *Ireland*, 1992). The Court found that the injunction against the applicants, which had forced them to cease providing a non-directive pregnancy counselling service, violated their freedom of expression.

In a case that appalled the Irish public (and led to a softening of attitudes regarding the prohibition of abortion) the High Court issued an order compelling a 14-year-old girl, pregnant as a result of rape, to return to Ireland from the United Kingdom where she had gone to have her pregnancy terminated (*Attorney General* v. *X* [1992] 1 I.R.). The Supreme Court later overturned the High Court's decision after evidence was produced showing that the girl was suicidal. According to the Court, abortion could only be permitted, 'if it could be established as a matter of probability that there is a real and substantial risk to the life as distinct from the health of the mother, which can only be avoided by the termination of her pregnancy'. After the X case, considerable uncertainty existed regarding the legal status of abortion and a woman's right to travel to other jurisdictions for terminations. Two further amendments dealing with the right to travel and access to information regarding abortion services legally available in other jurisdictions were made to the *Constitution* as a result of referendums held in 1992. A third proposal was put before the Irish people permitting abortion if the continuing pregnancy would result in harm to the life or health of the mother, excluding suicide. This was rejected. However, in a later case involving a young rape victim who wished to have her pregnancy terminated in the United Kingdom, and who was suicidal, the Court held that she could travel to the United Kingdom since the termination '... is a medical procedure, is clearly in my view also a medical treatment for her mental condition' (*A. and B.* v. *Eastern Health Board and C.* [1998] 1 I.R. 464). The Court also noted that there was no right to travel outside the State for abortion rather the Constitution 'merely prevents injunctions against travelling for that purpose'.

Despite the increasing secularisation of Irish society and support for at least limited abortion rights, politicians are unwilling to incur the hostility of the substantial anti-choice lobby and the Catholic Church, in particular, in the run-up to the next general election. Ireland's report to the CEDAW Committee will be examined in June and no doubt the Committee will reaffirm its previous criticisms of Ireland's failure to acknowledge the reproductive rights of women. However, women in Ireland will for foreseeable future travel to the United Kingdom to terminate their pregnancies. Those who lack financial or other resources to travel to the United Kingdom, including women living in poverty, young women, women with disabilities and migrant women, are left with no choice but to continue unwanted pregnancies.

Similarly another new EU Member State, Malta is intent on preserving its absolute prohibition on abortion, and consequently women in Malta are forced to travel abroad to terminate their pregnancies (although for some this is not an option). In 2003, a Russian woman was taken into custody in Malta in order to prevent her from travelling abroad to have an abortion after her partner complained to the authorities that she was travelling abroad for that purpose (Malta Today, 2004). The *Criminal Code* of Malta prohibits abortion in all circumstances and women that are convicted of having an abortion are liable for a term of imprisonment, as is any person who assisted the woman (UN Population Division, 2002). Prior to Malta's membership of the European Union, it negotiated a protocol to protect its prohibition on abortion from any change that may be required as a result of EU membership.

While Italy may be regarded as having liberal abortion policies in comparison to either Ireland or Malta, conservative politicians, anti-choice groups and the Catholic Church have attempted to undermine reproductive health provision. In August 2004, a proposal by a politician from the governing Forza Italia Party to limit free abortions in Italy to one for each women angered women's advocacy groups and opposition politicians. The proposal came just a week after the Vatican reiterated the Catholic Church's position on the role of women, which relegated them to the roles of 'wife' and 'mother'. According to Italian MEP, Emma Bonino, 'More and more, we Italians are not European citizens, we are Vatican citizens. Every day we wake up and find there is something new designed to take away women's right to choose' (Arie, 2004).

Earlier the same year a controversial law governing assisted fertility was passed by the Italian Parliament, due mainly to a cross-party alliance of Catholic members of parliament (ANSA, 2005). The law prohibits the use of donor sperm and eggs, embryo freezing and experimentation and surrogate motherhood. The law discriminated against single women and same sex couples by prohibiting them from availing of assisted fertility services. Women may not refuse implantation once their eggs are fertilized and screening of embryos for abnormality is not permitted (ANSA, 2005). Although the law did not specifically refer to abortion, it recognised the right to life of the embryo and gave it protection from conception (Hooper, 2003).

Italian pro-choice advocates fear that the assisted fertility law will pave the way for limitations on the right to abortion, with parliament now appearing to be under the influence of the Catholic Church. Before the assisted fertility law was passed, Pope John Paul II directly intervened and urged legislators to approve the Bill. According to one MP, this provision 'made necessary a profound revision of the abortion law' (Hooper, 2003). In addition, the Church has also condemned moves to overturn the law (ANSA, 2005).

The United Kingdom is one of the most secular states in Europe and it was one of the first to liberalise its abortion laws through the *Abortion Act* 1967. While it may seem unlikely that the United Kingdom will change its abortion laws following the forthcoming general election, the prime minister and the leader of the main opposition Conservative Party have both expressed some reservations regarding abortion. Although both leaders are anxious to ensure abortion does not become an election issue, the Conservative leader indicated that he wished to see a lowering of the time limit for terminations of pregnancy. This has received the backing of the Catholic Church and anti-choice groups (Tempest, 2005). The prime minister has said that he has personal difficulties with abortion and, of course, he is keen to appeal to Christian groups in the run-up to the election, but he has not supported lowering the time limit (Tempest, 2005).

The majority of abortions in the United Kingdom are performed on women who are less than 12 weeks pregnant. In 2002, figures available from the British Pregnancy Advisory Service show that 87 per cent of women terminated their pregnancies at less than 12 weeks. Less than 0.1 per cent of all abortions were carried out after 24 weeks. Therefore the 'late' abortion debate could prove to be a pretext for those who wish to undermine women's reproductive choice in the United Kingdom. Any attempt to further restrict the time limit is likely to impact most heavily on vulnerable women, especially young women and women travelling from other countries to have abortions in the United Kingdom.

Three high profile cases are due to come before the courts which will keep the focus on abortion rights and may lead to a gradual erosion of reproductive autonomy in the United Kingdom. The first case does not directly deal with the issue of abortion. It concerns an attempt to overturn the Human Fertility and Embryology Authority's decision to permit a child to be born through IVF to parents of children with certain serious illnesses to ensure the birth of a child which is compatible with the elder sibling: popularly referred to as 'saviour siblings'. The technique relies on PGD (Preimplantation Genetic Diagnosis) to identify compatible embryos which are then implanted, non-implanted embryos are destroyed and for this reason the technique is opposed by 'Pro-life' groups (Hinsliff, 2005).

In the second case, a mother of five is challenging the policy to permit young women under 16 to terminate their pregnancies without the consent of their parents. In the third case, a Church of England clergywoman is seeking judicial review of a decision taken in 2001 to permit a woman who was more than 24 weeks pregnant and carrying a foetus with a cleft lip and palate to have an abortion. It is argued that this did not constitute a serious handicap within the meaning of the *Abortion Act* (Hinsliff, 2005).

The law on abortion in Northern Ireland is more restrictive than in the rest of the United Kingdom. The *Abortion Act* 1967 does not apply to Northern Ireland and abortions carried out there are done on the basis of *R. v. Bourne*. In this 1938 case, the Court held that 'the law permits the termination of pregnancy for the purposes of preserving the life of the mother ... if the doctor is of the opinion ... that the probable consequence of the pregnancy will be to make a woman a physical wreck' (*R. v. Bourne* [1938] 3 All E.R. 615). When the UK Parliament passed the *Abortion Act*, Northern Ireland had its own parliament, which had the competence to decide on such issues. However, the overwhelmingly male parliament did not take up the issue. In 1984, the Northern Ireland Assembly voted not to extend the *Abortion Act* to Northern Ireland. Although some abortions are carried out in Northern Ireland, women wishing to terminate their pregnancy usually travel to Britain.

During the Franco era in Spain, both contraception and abortion were prohibited. Spanish women who had sufficient resources travelled abroad for abortions. After Franco's death, the Catholic Church tried to maintain its position of the established church in Spain and its influence on government. Therefore, although the Church no longer has the status of being the State religion, the Constitution does oblige 'public powers' to 'cooperate with the Catholic Church and other faiths'. It has been suggested that, 'the words "Catholic Church" in the Spanish Constitution symbolises the influence that the Church maintains even today in a Spain that is moving towards a more secular political process' (Fleishman, 2000, p. 292).

In 1985, the Socialist Government introduced a Bill before parliament aimed at legalising abortion. The first draft was found to be unconstitutional by the Spanish Constitutional Court. The government amended the bill and it was finally passed by the Spanish Parliament. The law is one of the most restrictive in Europe and only permits abortion in cases of rape, foetal damage or danger to the mother's physical or mental health (Fleishman, 2000, p. 296). Abortion in any other circumstances is a criminal offence and women face imprisonment for up to 6 years. In addition, any person who assists the woman in having an abortion also risks imprisonment. Although this said, in 1991, the Spanish Supreme Court dismissed a criminal case taken against a woman, her partner and a friend of the couple who assisted with arrangements for the abortion. The Court found that the couple could not support another child and that if she had been forced to give birth the woman would have suffered mentally and physically.

Several unsuccessful attempts have been made to liberalise Spanish law. In 1996, a proposed law was rejected by only ten votes. Two years later, a bill which would have permitted abortion up to 12 weeks 'if it created a personal, social or family conflict for the woman' (Fleishman, 2000, p. 298) was defeated only after four rounds of votes in parliament; three times the vote was tied and the fourth time the bill was defeated by only one vote. The proposed legislation was strongly opposed by the Catholic Church which issued a communique entitled *Even Broader License to Kill Children*, organised demonstrations and gave sermons concerning the Bill (Fleishman, 2000, p. 299). Although the proposed law was defeated at this time, the influence of the Church in Spain regarding reproductive choice is diminishing.

While most states where abortion is restricted, do not actively prosecute women who terminate their pregnancies illegally or the medical staff or others who assist them, Portuguese women who have abortions outside the terms of the country's strict abortion law are constantly at risk of prosecution. They face the humiliation and publicity of a trial and may receive a prison sentence. A nurse was sentenced to 7.5 years imprisonment for performing illegal abortions. In 2004, 17 people including 7 women, who it was alleged had illegal abortions, were acquitted of all charges (Feminist Majority Foundation, 2004b). Thus, while the right to abortion might not be eroded in the West in the dramatic way it is being eroded in Eastern Europe, it is by no means guaranteed. The examples we have used have shown that in Malta and Ireland there is no right, or a very restricted right to abortion, while in countries where abortion has long been regarded as a reproductive right groups continue to lobby to overturn this right.

Conclusion

Today across Europe from Russia to Ireland, millions of women are denied a comprehensive reproductive health care service, including education and information. A dangerous trend has emerged where, under the influence of anti-choice, nationalist and religious movements, the right to abortion – a fundamental reproductive right – is being undermined.

Yet, despite this relatively bleak picture, there are some grounds for optimism. For example, in Italy, 1.5 million signatures have been collected requesting a referendum aimed at overturning the assisted fertility law. In Portugal, the recently elected Socialist government has given an undertaking to hold a referendum on its restrictive abortion laws in 2006. Similarly, the Spanish Government has committed itself to placing women's equality at the top of its agenda and, as part of this commitment, to liberalise Spain's abortion law. However, although most European states continue to have relatively liberal abortion laws by comparison with other parts of the world, there is no room for complacency. The examples we have considered from Eastern and Western Europe show that access to abortion (the most basic of reproductive rights) is under threat across Europe – they are disappearing in the East and continually contested in the West.

2
Adoption: Practices and Regulations

Fiona MacCallum

Introduction

This chapter looks at the practice of adoption, a method of parenthood sometimes overlooked when considering women's reproductive options. Starting by summarising the evolution of adoption practice through history, it then explores the current state of adoption in the United Kingdom, with particular reference to the selection criteria required for acceptance as adoptive parents in the United Kingdom and the growing number of adoptions of children from overseas. Comparisons are made with regulations and practices in other European countries. The justification of imposing conditions on women and men who wish to adopt is investigated by considering the psychological challenges faced by adoptive parents, and by reviewing research on adoption outcomes.

History and development of adoption

Adoption is the oldest form of creating families through a means other than natural conception, having been around since antiquity. It is still popular amongst childless couples, with about 25 per cent of infertile couples eventually attempting to adopt (Brodzinsky, 1997). In Britain, the number of adoptions by non-relatives in 2002 was approximately 4000 (British Association for Adoption and Fostering, 2003). Over time, adoption practice has changed in line with the prevailing beliefs and social attitudes of the period. Examining the historical development reveals four distinct stages in the evolution of adoption (particularly regarding its regulation and its focus) in Western culture (Triseliotis *et al.*, 1997).

In its first inception, adoption was for the most part instrumental in nature. In ancient Greece and Rome, young males were adopted to perform religious ceremonies, to provide an heir to perpetuate the family or to enable candidates to meet the criteria for political office. Roman law introduced the concept of adoption as absolute and irreversible, with birth parents having no legal rights over the child following the adoption (Cole and Donley, 1990). In general, both Roman and Greek laws were concerned with the role of the adopting adults, with the intent of securing the succession of property and land for the benefit of wealthy families. Thus, during this first period of adoption, emphasis was on the interests of and benefits to adults, with the benefits to children being of secondary importance.

The second stage of adoption practice came about from the need to provide secure homes for increasing numbers of parentless children. Although Roman law served as the basis for many British laws, adoption was not legally recognised by statute in the United Kingdom until the 1926 *Adoption Act* in England. Prior to this, some orphaned or illegitimate children were cared for in institutions, such as almshouses, or in orphanages established by religious groups and philanthropists. Other children in need of homes were placed with families. For example, in some Scottish parishes, schemes were established where farmers were paid a small allowance for each foster child they took in; a situation similar to adoption evolved but this was an informal affair with no legal security for the child, or for the 'adopting' parents should the birth parents wish to retrieve the child (Triseliotis *et al.*,1995).

Development of the 1926 *Adoption Act* advanced in response to the First World War, and the need to find homes for the increased numbers of illegitimate and orphaned children. In particular, the importance of proper regulation of adoption was recognised and the Act placed emphasis on the need for supervision of adoption in order to protect the child. Agencies dedicated solely to adoption were established, in order to monitor the proper observation of adoption statutes and to investigate prospective adopters. In addition, adoption records were sealed and the practice of secrecy and anonymity in adoption was founded. The second period of adoption was thus more concerned with the welfare of the child than had been the case previously. However, the usefulness of adopted children as extra labour was still stressed, leading to adoption being mainly practiced by the rural working classes.

The third stage in the evolution of adoption occurred after the Second World War, when there was renewed public interest in adoption with a particular demand for healthy 'adoptable' infants. Adoption came to be seen as a solution to infertility and became popular with the middle classes. The aim of the adoption agencies was to select the 'perfect baby' for the 'perfect couple' (Triseliotis *et al.*, 1997) and was influenced by two psychological movements. First, the development of psychoanalytic theory led to intensive psychological assessment of adoptive couples. Second, Bowlby's theory of attachment predicted that after age three, children would not be able to bond effectively to adoptive parents (Bowlby, 1969). This led to the concentration on the placement of infants, with older children being considered 'un-adoptable' and raised in residential care homes.

Over this period, the number of couples applying for adoption began to exceed the number of available infants. Consequently, agencies further restricted their eligibility criteria for adoption, specifying factors such as age limits, socio-economic status and often religion. Despite this, the focus was on finding 'a child for a home' rather than the most suitable home for that particular child. There was no recognition of the need for post-adoptive services, with the assumption being that once the adoption was finalised the adoptive family would be 'normal'. In line with this position, adoption records remained sealed and adopters were discouraged from sharing the fact of the adoption with the child.

The fourth period of adoption can be seen as beginning in the 1960s and carrying on through the 1970s. During this phase, there was a shift in the nature of adoption towards a more child-centred structure. This was prompted in part by alterations in the characteristics of children available for adoption. Single parenthood became increasingly socially acceptable due to changes in attitudes towards illegitimacy (Cole and Donley, 1990). Coupled with a rise in the availability of contraception and abortion, this resulted in a drastic reduction in the numbers of young healthy infants placed for adoption. Partly as a consequence of this, the annual number of Adoption Orders made in England and Wales fell through the 1970s from 25,000 in 1968 to 11,000 in 1980 (Warman and Roberts, 2003). Social services and adoption agencies broadened their concept of an 'adoptable child' to include older children, those with disabilities, mixed-race children and sibling groups, all of whom were classed as 'special needs' or 'hard to place' children. The demands of these children could not always be met by young, middle-class, childless couples. Therefore, the definition of a suitable adoptive family was broadened to include single parents, older parents and those who had biological children already, and restrictions on socio-economic status were relaxed (Brodzinsky and Pinderhughes, 2002). Emphasis was placed on finding 'a home for a child' and applicants were assessed not just on parenting per se, but on how they would provide the right environment to support a particular child. Adoptive parents were encouraged to be open with the child about the adoption, and the *Children's Act* 1975 in England and Wales legislated that adopted children could have access to their birth records, allowing them to know the names of their birth parents. The primary concern was now considered to be 'the best interests of the child', including the child's need for knowledge of its origins.

Current adoption practice

The developments that had begun in the fourth stage of adoption have continued in recent years. By 1999, the number of Adoption Orders had fallen still further to 4100 (Warman and Roberts, 2003), with a large proportion of these being adoptions involving family members, especially step-parents. Rather than being a service for placing babies with childless couples, adoption is now viewed primarily as a means of finding families for older children who would otherwise be in the care of the state. Infertile couples wishing to become parents are opting in increasing numbers for this type of 'special needs' adoption rather than waiting years for an infant to become available for placement. Since those children who are in need of adoptive families tend to be exactly those once classed as 'hard to place', the policy of screening-in rather than excluding different types of adoptive applicants has been sustained and expanded. The recent *Adoption and Children Act* (2002) in the United Kingdom permitted the placing of adoptive children with unmarried couples, including same-sex couples (HMSO, 2002). This Act also aligned adoption law with the *Children Act* of 1989, thus stipulating that the child's welfare be the paramount consideration in all decisions to do with adoption, necessitating the continued application of rigorous selection criteria for prospective adoptive parents.

Selection criteria for adoption

If an infertile woman and her partner wish to be considered as adoptive parents, they face a selection and preparation process that is lengthy and detailed, focusing on social factors and intimate emotional details. In the United Kingdom, prospective adopters will be assigned a social worker who will visit their home several times over a period of months. A two-part form (Form F) must be completed; Part I asks first for factual information concerning characteristics, such as age, marital status, ethnic origin, occupation, income, and hours of work. It then asks for two personal references for the applicants, and assesses the referees' views of the applicants' parenting capacity. Part II of the form is a descriptive report made by the social worker, based on observations of the household members during the home visits. A great amount of detail is obtained about the applicants, including their present relationship, their previous relationships, their attitudes towards being childless, their understanding of child development and their own childhood experiences. Issues ranging from the self-image of the applicants to specific problems that may be encountered in the child's upbringing are explicitly considered. Emphasis is placed on the personalities of the individual applicants and the nature and quality of their relationships (British Association for Adoption and Fostering, 1991). If, having completed Form F, the social worker considers the applicants to be suitable to become adopters, their recommendation is then put to an adoption panel of independent assessors who have the final say on whether the applicants should be approved for consideration as adoptive parents. Prospective adopters must also attend courses with other couples with the aim of preparing themselves for all possible aspects of adoption. Although the contemporary emphasis of this process is supposedly to educate rather than to evaluate, many couples feel that they are being judged and find the procedure intrusive and anxiety-provoking. It is also highly time-consuming, both for the couple and for the social services agency. In addition to this lengthy procedure, couples must be matched with children according to the specific needs of the child, and thus, even having been approved by the panel, a couple may have to wait for a long time to be considered suitable for an available child. The focus is very much on the needs of the child and on finding parents appropriate to fulfil those needs, with the in-depth assessment procedure considered as essential to protect the child.

Adoption is thus by no means an 'easy option' for infertile women who wish to become mothers. In comparison, an infertile couple who pursue the option of assisted reproduction face a much less intensive selection process, which focuses on medical criteria, with the emphasis on whether the mother is 'medically suitable' to become pregnant and carry the child rather than on whether the couple are psychologically suitable to be parents (Widdows and MacCallum, 2002). Decisions on who should be allowed access to the treatment are made by medical practitioners, rather than by someone trained to consider the social and psychological factors. In the United Kingdom, the only social criteria couples applying for assisted reproduction treatment are expected to meet are those laid down by the *Human Fertilisation and Embryology Act* (1990). The Act states that a woman 'shall not be provided with treatment services unless account has been taken of the welfare of any child born as a result of the treatments (including the need of that child for a father)' (HFEA, 1990). This places providers of assisted conception services under an obligation to consider the prospective parents in terms of the child's future well-being. However, the HFEA *Code of Practice* asserts that clinics must consider both the 'wishes and needs of those seeking treatment *and* the needs of any children involved' (HFEA, 2004, emphasis added). Unlike adoption where the child's needs are of primary importance, fertility clinics must give equal weight to the prospective parents' wishes.

Regarding the collection of information relevant to the future 'welfare of the child', the *Code of Practice* suggests that this should be done by taking medical and family histories, and seeing the couple together and separately. Counselling should be available but is not mandatory. The clinic is also required to contact the couple's GP to check if there is any reason why they should not be offered treatment. If the result of any of these inquiries causes concern, the clinic should approach the relevant authority or agency, such as the police or social services, for further information. However, an approach can only be made with the consent of the couple. In effect, the psychological components of the selection process are relatively superficial, and it seems that only couples who are at risk of actually harming the child will be refused on social grounds (this applies only to heterosexual couples, and not to single women or lesbian couples for whom selection may be more complicated). Those couples who are medically unfit or for whom successful conception is doubtful are more likely to be refused, especially given the need of clinics to increase their 'take-home' baby rate.

Thus, the selection of adoptive parents is far more complicated, and more concerned with psychological issues, than the requirements for fertility treatment: 'Selection for adoption is concerned with whether an applicant will be a fit parent and every effort is made to discover this, for medically assisted reproduction the effort is fairly minimal and is designed to exclude only those who might seem grossly unfit' (Campion, 1995, p. 107). The fundamental principle in adoption is that the child is the client, whereas in assisted conception the client is the would-be parent and the child is a product of a service created to meet the needs of these clients.

Inter-country adoption

Possibly due to the change in the nature of adoption over the last 30 years, the biggest growth area in the United Kingdom and other

Western countries has been that of inter-country adoption, which is now estimated to involve over 30,000 children per year worldwide moving between countries (Selman, 2000). It is particularly popular with childless couples who want a baby since many children available for international adoption, unlike in domestic adoption, are infants. Additionally couples who do not wish to be placed on a long waiting list for a domestic adoption or who fear (rightly or wrongly) they would not be allowed to adopt in their own country, for example, because of their age, go overseas where the selection criteria may be less stringent. Inter-country adoption generally involves movement of children to rich countries, mainly the USA and Western Europe, from poor countries, such as Russia, or those where a humanitarian crisis has been widely publicised, such as in the Romanian orphanages following the fall of the Ceausescu regime, or the girls abandoned in China partly as a result of the 'one-child' policy. Overall, around 4 per cent of all Adoption Orders in England and Wales are for inter-country adoptions (Warman and Roberts, 2003).

Previously in the United Kingdom, it was suggested that safeguards surrounding inter-country adoption were not as stringent as those applied to domestic adoptions, leading to the danger of a 'two-tier' service (Department of Health, 1998). Critiques claim that there has been a shift in the focus of international adoption from child-centred humanitarian justifications to meeting the adult-centred needs of infertile couples (Bridge and Swindells, 2003). This can be seen as resulting in a lack of consideration of the rights of the children concerned, and in the abuses, such as abduction or trafficking of children, which are occurring in order to meet the needs of infertile couples in the West who subscribe to the viewpoint that they have 'a right to have a child' (Saclier, 2000). Concerns about the possibility of the exploitation of vulnerable birth parents have also been raised. Attempts were made in the United Kingdom throughout the 1990s to address the inequalities between domestic and inter-country adoption, in particular, to ensure that the needs of the child were at the centre of policies regarding adoption from overseas. This culminated in the inclusion of revised provisions relating to inter-country adoption in the *Adoption and Children Act* (2002). For example, reports on those planning to adopt overseas must now be made by qualified social workers employed by a local authority or voluntary adoption agency and approved by an adoption panel, and prospective adopters should attend preparation and training courses as for domestic adoptions but with extra information on the specific challenges of adopting from overseas. The list of countries from which inter-country adoption is allowed is to be reviewed by the Government, with the aim of approving only those meeting certain criteria, such as, where informed consent for the adoption has been given by birth parents and measures are in place to prevent improper financial gain as a result of the adoption (Department for Education and Skills, 2005).

Adoption practices across Europe

Across Europe, trends have been similar with the number of infants needing adoption declining while the number of adoptions involving children from other countries has increased. However, the precise nature and implementation of adoption legislation differs across EU countries. In the majority of EU member states, adoption law is based on the principle of the best interests of the child, and prospective adoptive parents must undergo some form of psychological investigation before authorisation to adopt is given. Precise selection criteria vary between countries, for example, regarding age limits, in Italy, adoptive parents must be less than 40 years old, whereas in the Netherlands they must be between 18 and 50 years, and in Portugal one partner must be over 25 (Ruxton, 1996). Similarly, restrictions regarding marital status vary, with the Netherlands allowing unmarried couples, including those in gay relationships, to adopt (Warman and Roberts, 2003), contrasting with Portugal where the couple must have been married for four years before adoption is permitted. No European country imposes conditions of the same magnitude on couples who wish to become parents through assisted conception. Even in countries, such as France or Germany, which restrict access to assisted conception to those in 'stable relationships' (Jones and Cohen, 2001), intensive psychosocial evaluation is not conducted.

With regard to inter-country adoption, its prevalence is higher in certain European countries than in others. For example the numbers of inter-country adoptions in Denmark, Sweden and the Netherlands are rising steadily, whilst in France inter-country adoptions now make up 40 per cent of all Adoption Orders (Warman and Roberts, 2003). In fact, in terms of absolute numbers of children adopted from overseas, France is second worldwide, next only to the United States. One possible explanation for the proliferation of such adoptions in these countries lies in their policies regarding the adoption of older children in care. This is encouraged in the United Kingdom but is relatively uncommon in France where birth parents retain parental responsibility for children in long-term care unless there are very strong grounds for removing it. In the Netherlands, children over six years old cannot be adopted, and in Sweden, the parental rights of birth parents cannot be terminated. Therefore, the emphasis in the welfare provisions in these countries for older children in long-term care is on placement with foster families or in small residential units rather than attempting to find matched adoptive parents. In combination with the lack of babies needing adoptive parents, this means that childless couples look elsewhere when attempting to adopt. As in the United Kingdom, concerns have been raised in other European countries about the regulation of inter-country adoptions. Many now demand the adoption to go through an approved agency in order for the adoption to be ratified, and impose conditions as to which countries children can be adopted from. The criteria for acceptance as adopters of overseas children have also been tightened, for example, in the Netherlands, adopters have to undertake eligibility evaluations and preparation programmes analogous with those required for domestic adoption.

Every country in Europe has some form of law relating to adoption. Although there are variations, any couple wishing to adopt has to prove themselves as fit to be parents, in a manner which is not obligatory for becoming parents either through natural conception or through assisted reproduction. In order to address the question of whether such psychosocial assessment of prospective adoptive parents is justifiable, it is useful to consider the psychological challenges faced by adoptive parents.

Challenges of adoption

The first factor to take account of is the possible effect of infertility on the adoptive parents. Usually, prospective adopters will have undergone a lengthy period of infertility prior to considering adoption, possibly including invasive fertility tests and failed treatments. Any couple wishing to have children will experience some degree of stress when faced with infertility (Burns, 1990). Reviews identify common reactions including grief and depression following the diagnosis, feelings of self-blame and guilt, loss of self-esteem (Robinson and Stewart, 1996), anxiety during treatment and depression when the treatment is unsuccessful (Golombok, 1992). If any of these symptoms of emotional distress were to persist, difficulties would be predicted for adjustment to adoptive parenting and for the parents' future psychological well-being (Brodzinsky and Huffman, 1988).

Furthermore, the feelings arising from infertility differ to some extent between the genders. Women take infertility particularly hard, with 48 per cent of women in one study describing it as the worst experience of their lives compared to only 15 per cent of men (Freeman *et al.*, 1985). Women are also more likely to attribute the responsibility for the infertility to themselves, even when the diagnosis is of a male problem (Mason, 1993; Robinson and Stewart, 1996). These gender differences may result in relationship difficulties; for example, in Burns's study, infertile couples reported a disruption in their normal sexual relationship, lack of communication and difficulties in understanding each other's perspective (Burns, 1990). There may also be a discrepancy in the desires of the couple to embark upon an uncertain procedure, such as adoption. However, other studies using standardised questionnaires have found no significant marital or sexual difficulties in couples undergoing infertility evaluations or treatment (Cook *et al.*, 1989; Raval *et al.*, 1987). Insofar as infertile couples do experience marital problems, if these are not resolved prior to the adoption, it has been suggested that parents may become child-centred in order to avoid conflict with their spouse, which may place a great deal of pressure on the child to stabilise the family unit (Burns, 1990). Parents may expect the child to be a 'cure' for the psychological stresses of the infertility experience. Thus, unrealistic expectations may be created, both of themselves as parents, and of the child's own behaviours and achievements.

In addition to the concerns about the effects of infertility on parenting, there are concerns that relate more specifically to adoption. Unlike parents who conceive through assisted reproduction, adoptive parents have to accept that there will be no form of biological parenthood possible for them, either genetic or gestational. The traditional social work philosophy was that a couple's suitability to adopt depended on their having fully resolved their own feelings about infertility and 'let go' of the ideal of themselves as biological parents. However, Daly pointed out that while some couples have to relinquish the biological parenthood identity before pursuing adoption, other couples are able to identify as adoptive parents whilst still pursuing the possibility of having a biological child (Daly, 1988, 1990). This may depend on how strongly the couple value genetic connectedness in parenting, compared to how they value the social and emotional components of parenthood. Although it is no longer assumed that complete resolution is a necessary prerequisite for adoption, failure to confront this issue adequately, for example, when adoptive parents still mourn the loss of the longed-for biological child, could affect parental bonding with the adopted child (Brodzinsky, 1997).

The lack of the gestational link in adoption may also affect parent–child relationships. It has been argued that immediate post-delivery contact between mothers and infants is important for maternal bonding (Klaus and Kennell, 1976), although this is not now seen as so significant. In addition, recent studies have shown that mothers form attachments to their babies whilst the child is in the womb, and that maternal–foetal attachment styles are correlated, albeit modestly, with post-natal attachment styles (Laxton-Kane and Slade, 2002; Muller, 1996). An adopting mother does not experience pregnancy and does not have an opportunity for post-delivery bonding. Therefore, adoptive mothers may find it more difficult to bond with the child.

Despite adoption being an established method of family creation, there is still some social stigma surrounding becoming an adopted parent (Miall, 1987). Adopters may feel that adoption is still regarded as having 'second-class status' to biological parenthood, and may be concerned about support for their choice to adopt, and about acceptance of the child by their extended family and friends. This, coupled with the uncertain timing of the expectancy period in adoption, may make prospective adopters reluctant to announce their decision or anxious about doing so. Therefore, they may feel a lack of social support from those around them, compared to biological parents (Levy-Shiff *et al.*, 1990).

The challenges faced by adoptive parents are not over after the placement, but continue throughout the child's life. From a psychological perspective, the adopted child will have a number of tasks to accomplish which are not faced by children being raised by their biological parents (Triseliotis *et al.*, 1997). Unless the child is in the rare situation of having been placed directly at birth with the adoptive parents, they will have spent some time living either with the birth parents, with foster parents or in residential care. Uprooting the child from this placement and setting them in a new family environment may make it difficult for some children to form secure attachments to their adoptive parents. Children with insecure attachments will be at greater risk for problems with their future psychological adjustment over a range of domains (Cohn, 1990; Greenberg, 1999). The ease of attachment formation is likely to depend upon the age of the child at adoption and their pre-adoption history, as well as on the quality of parenting provided by the adoptive parents.

A further, and possibly more complex, task for the adopted child is that of coping with the awareness that they are adopted. The current practice advocated by social work practitioners and adoption agency workers is to start the adoption disclosure as young as possible, usually from the time the child first starts to ask about where babies come from. Disclosure is then seen as a process, rather than a one-off event, with parents adding more information to the adoption story as the child's cognitive capacities increase. Pre-school children may know that they are 'adopted' with little understanding of the implications of this statement. However, by the time children are between 5 and 7 years of age, their comprehension of adoption grows, particularly the understanding that they have a biological family whom they do not live with. It is at this age that children may begin to experience feelings of loss and stigma related to the adoption, and may feel somewhat ambivalent about being adopted (Brodzinsky, 1990). This can create stress and confusion for adopted children, and undermine their feelings of security in the adopted family, or their feelings of self-worth.

With the progression from childhood into adolescence, all individuals face the developmental task of establishing a coherent sense of identity (Erikson, 1968). This may be more complex for the adopted adolescent, who must integrate the adoption into their growing sense of self. Erikson defined a positive identity as 'a sense of psychological well-being, a feeling of being at home in one's body, of knowing where one is going, an inner assuredness of anticipated recognition from those who count' (Erikson, 1968, p. 168). All of these aspects may be complicated by the fact of adoption; for example, an adopted teenager may find it more difficult to become 'at home' in their body due to the lack of physical similarity between themselves and their adoptive family (Brodzinsky *et al.*, 1998). Part of identity formation for non-adopted individuals involves incorporating knowledge about their past and their family. An adoptee lacks this genealogical continuity and may find it more difficult to develop a secure and healthy sense of ego identity.

To successfully integrate the child into the family and promote security of attachment and positive identity development, the adoptive parents must be sensitive to the specific needs of their child, which will vary according to the pre-placement history, and the circumstances of the adoption. As the child grows older, the parents must communicate with the child about the adoption in an age-appropriate manner. This involves the parents recognising their own feelings about the child's birth families, and may give rise to parental anxiety or insecurity in their parenting role (Brodzinsky and Pinderhughes, 2002). In particular, adoptive parents involved in inter-country or domestic transracial adoptions are advised to openly acknowledge the child's racial, historical and/or cultural background, and the ways in which this may differ from their own.

Clearly, adoptive parents are presented with several challenges that are not present in other forms of families. The challenges do seem to justify the inclusion of many components in the selection process applied to adoptive parents. Since parental psychological and marital state may be affected by infertility and adoption, and may in turn affect the social and emotional development of children, it seems reasonable for these to be assessed when evaluating a couple's readiness to adopt. Couples need to have confronted their feelings about their own infertility to some extent, so this should be addressed by the social worker during the evaluation. Preparation for possible future adoption-related topics seems helpful, for example, how to approach the issue of disclosure. Overall, the intensive evaluation appears justifiable. However, the remaining question is of whether adoption is actually a successful method of creating families, in regard to the psychological development of the parents and children involved.

Adoption outcomes

With respect to the couple's relationship, the concern that adoptive parents will experience marital dysfunction does not seem to be borne out by the evidence. One study compared first-time adoptive parents-to-be with first-time biological parents-to-be on a scale of marital adjustment, interviewing both groups of parents between two and four months before the child's arrival (Levy-Shiff *et al.*, 1990). Prospective adoptive parents expressed significantly higher marital satisfaction than prospective biological parents. Similarly, Humphrey (1975) found that adopting couples were rated higher on measures of affection given and received between partners than a matched sample of non-adoptive couples. When these couples were followed up nine years later, group comparisons still showed the adopting couples to have the superior marital adjustment. Although infertility and adoption can put a strain on a marriage, the fact that adoptive parents are generally older than biological parents, and have often been married for a longer period of time, may act as a buffer against this stress (Brodzinsky and Huffman, 1988). It is possible that the increased duration of the relationship enables them to better understand and communicate with their partner. Having gone through the process of adoption together, with all the accompanying emotional highs and lows, may also strengthen the couple's relationship, promoting more sensitivity towards and discussion of each other's feelings (Levy-Shiff *et al.*, 1990). On the other hand, it may be that only those couples that already have a strong, stable relationship make it through the adoption process.

Regarding other areas of parental well-being, there has been little empirical research on the psychological adjustment of adoptive parents.

Levy-Shiff and colleagues found that adoptive mothers-to-be showed significantly lower levels of depression than pregnant mothers (Levy-Shiff *et al.*, 1990). Contrary to assumptions related to social stigma associated with adoption, the adopters reported more satisfaction with social support from the community and from friends than the biological parents. Other studies have also found adoptive parents to be as psychologically well-adjusted as their non-adoptive counterparts, and where differences were seen, they tended to favour the adoptive parents (Hoopes, 1982; Plomin and DeFries, 1985). It has been suggested that since adoptive parents achieve parenthood after a long time of trying, becoming parents gives them a sense of fulfilment that outweighs not only the specific stresses associated with adoption, but also the universal stresses of parenting (Levy-Shiff *et al.*, 1990). However, as with the findings for marital relationships, it is possible that only those individuals who are psychologically stable to begin with are able to go through the difficult process of becoming adoptive parents.

Early studies of the quality of parent–child relationships in adoptive families suggested that there was a long-term adverse effect. Two studies by Yarrow and associates (Yarrow and Goodwin, 1973; Yarrow *et al.*, 1973) looked at the the impact of a change in mother figure on infants. They found that all infants who were separated from their biological parents after 6–7 months of age showed socioemotional difficulties due to the separation, in line with Bowlby's theory of early attachment (Bowlby, 1969). When these samples were followed up 10 years later, a large number of the adopted children placed after 6 months were still exhibiting psychological problems, particularly in their ability to form attachments to family members and others. However, there were methodological weaknesses in these studies, particularly the absence of a control group of non-adopted infants. A controlled study of relationships in adoptive families was conducted by Singer and colleagues, comparing adopted infants to non-adopted infants at the age of 13–18 months. Contrary to the concerns that adoptive parents may have difficulty in bonding with the child, the authors concluded that 'most adoptive mothers and their infants develop warm and secure attachment relationships' (Singer *et al.*, 1985, p. 1550), especially if the adoption is of an infant of the same racial/ethnic background as the adopters.

Some studies have looked at the effects of adoption on other aspects of family life. As children move into the pre-school and early childhood stages, positive parent–child relationships persist with adoptive parents providing high quality home environments (Plomin and DeFries, 1985).

Research has found that adoptive parents show more affection, warmth and acceptance of their child in early childhood, and interact with them more than do biological parents (Golombok *et al.*, 1995; Hoopes, 1982). Adoptive parents exhibit some signs of over-involvement in terms of protection of, and anxiety about, their pre-school child. These more anxious attitudes to parenting may be due to the stress experienced by the adoptive parents as a result of the infertility diagnosis and the adoption process, or the fact that the adopted children were 'likely to be especially cherished and protected because they were not easily acquired' (Hoopes, 1982). However, by the early school years, adoptive parents show less intrusive and controlling behaviour than non-adoptive parents.

There is now a large body of research on the outcomes for children of early adoption. In terms of the proportions of adopted children classified as having social or psychiatric problems, a series of studies have found that adoptees are over-represented in psychiatric hospital populations and other mental health settings (Hershov, 1990). It is possible that this is due to the genetic inheritance of psychological problems from their biological parents (Cadoret, 1990). Alternatively, the stress of the adoption process and the nature of adoptive family life may increase adopted children's vulnerability to psychological dysfunction. It is important to note that caution must be taken when generalising the results of clinical studies to the outcomes for adopted children as a whole, since the samples involved are small and the age at placement and circumstances of the adoption are not always specified. For this reason, there is a growing body of research examining the psychological development and adjustment of adopted children compared with non-adopted children in non-clinical community settings.

Non-clinical studies of adopted children do not find them to be at risk of problems with temperament or development in the early years (Carey *et al.*, 1974; Plomin and DeFries, 1985; Thompson and Plomin, 1988). However, in middle-to-late childhood, adopted children do seem to show higher levels of adjustment problems than non-adopted children, with respect to domains, such as social competence, school success and behavioural problems (Brand and Brinich, 1999; Brodzinsky *et al.*, 1984). These problems persist as adoptees progress into early adolescence (Bohman and Sigvardsson, 1990; Brand and Brinich, 1999). By late adolescence, adoptees are still exhibiting higher levels of negative behaviour in some areas (Fergusson *et al.*, 1995; Miller *et al.*, 2000), but longitudinal studies show that the magnitude of the differences between adoptees and non-adoptees diminishes across the adolescent period (Bohman and

Sigvardsson, 1990; Maughan and Pickles, 1990). Adjustment problems in adopted children thus emerge from around age 7, become most marked at around age 11–12 and decrease by age 16–18.

Inter-country adoptions have been studied separately from domestic adoptions, since they raise different issues, in that internationally adopted children have the additional task of dealing with the fact that they come from a country culturally different to that in which they are being raised (Juffer and Rosenboom, 1997). They may also have a racially different appearance from their adoptive parents, which could cause further problems regarding identity. Looking at the results for psychological development of children involved in inter-country adoption, the outcomes are generally positive, with functioning at average or above-average levels compared to the general population (Brodzinsky *et al.*, 1998). Some studies have found higher levels of problems in internationally adopted children as compared to their non-adopted counterparts (Rutter *et al.*, 2000; Verhulst, 2000). To some extent, this increase can be attributed to the early deprivations experienced by these children, for example, as exhibited by children from Romanian orphanages. However, even taking this into account, internationally adopted children are still at increased risk of maladjustment, particularly as they move into adolescence.

It is important, however, to bear a few caveats in mind. First, there is a great deal of variability in the patterns of adjustment exhibited by adoptees, with contributing factors including age, pre-placement history and the quality of the adoptive family relationships. Second, the vast majority of adoptees, from both domestic and inter-country adoptions, are as well-adjusted as non-adopted individuals. Third, most adopted children are more socio-economically advantaged than they would have been if they had been raised by their biological parents, and are also placed in more secure, nurturing and stable environments than would be found in foster homes or residential care (Brodzinsky and Pinderhughes, 2002). This is supported by the findings that adopted children have lower levels of maladjustment than children in foster care or deprived biological families (Bohman and Sigvardsson, 1990; Brand and Brinich, 1999; Collishaw *et al.*, 1998; Fergusson *et al.*, 1995; Maughan and Pickles, 1990). Also, adopted children have been found to have higher IQ scores and scholastic achievement than would be expected on the basis of their biological background (Lambert and Streather, 1980). Thus, adoption can serve as a protective measure for children who would otherwise be raised in deprived or damaging environments (Brodzinsky *et al.*, 1998).

Conclusions

Women who are unable to become pregnant naturally, and who cannot or do not wish to conceive through assisted reproduction, may choose the option of adoption. Throughout history, parents have raised non-biological children as their own, although it is only in the last century or so that legal provisions have been made for this process. The current climate surrounding adoption in Europe places the child at the centre, with his/her needs as the primary and paramount consideration. In line with this, prospective adoptive parents face an arduous procedure of evaluation and education before a child will be placed with them. The rigour of the selection process does not seem out of proportion in light of the fact that adoption undeniably presents challenges for both parents and children, which may affect the quality of parenting and the psychological development of children in adoptive families. However, to meet the rights of infertile women, it should be ensured that the selection criteria within a country are both transparent and justifiable, and are applied consistently to all couples. Care should also be taken when considering inter-country adoptions, since these open up the possibility of violation of rights of birth parents and children in poorer countries in order to meet the desires of infertile couples in wealthier countries. Placements should only be permitted from countries which meet ethical requirements regarding the regulation of adoption. When these conditions are met, the evidence suggests that adoption is a successful solution to the problem of children whose biological parents are unable or unwilling to raise them, in addition to fulfilling the wishes of infertile couples who desire to become parents.

3
Birth Rate and Women's Rights in Europe

Paloma de Villota

Women are having fewer children than before. This chapter explores the reasons for the decline in birth rate and addresses issues that might be perceived as contributing to such a decline. In addressing this topic, I will consider first the different levels of women's labour force participation in different industrialised countries because during the last two decades, a crucial demographic change has taken place. On the one hand, fertility rates have sharply decreased in most developed countries to levels below replacement rates, and, on the other, there is now a positive correlation between fertility and female labour participation rates throughout the OECD countries. Economic security for young women and men seems to have a positive effect on having children, and correspondingly, a high unemployment rate or the lack of social arrangements for childcare has a negative effect (as the cases of Italy and Spain show). In the last section, I focus on the evolution of social expenditure for childcare in relation to Gross Domestic Product in different EU countries in an attempt to offer another reason by which to explain the demographic changes outlined in the chapter.

Combining employment and family life in Europe in different countries

Women's marital and parental status profoundly affect their rate of employment. Marriage alone causes some women to completely withdraw from the labour market or to leave the labour market for a significant period of time. This occurs most frequently in the southern European countries of the European Union, primarily Greece and Spain. In these two countries the extent of the withdrawal from the labour market due to marriage can be observed by comparing the activity

50

rates of single and married women in similar family circumstances, that is, with no children or with children aged 15 or over. Single women's activity rates reach 80.6 and 77.1 per cent in Greece and Spain, respectively, and decline to 58.8 and 57.2 per cent, respectively, for married women (a difference of over 20 percentage points) (European Commission, 1998a). Motherhood clearly influences the employment decisions of women, particularly the decision to withdraw from the labour market. In EU countries, the most pronounced drop into inactivity takes place in Ireland, followed by the United Kingdom and Luxembourg. In the rest of OECD countries, a similar decline in employment occurs with the onset of motherhood, for example, in New Zealand and Australia. Therefore, decisions on social and employment policies should take into account whether welfare allowances lead to women's withdrawal from the labour market or, conversely, whether they effectively reconcile employment and motherhood, as appears to be the case with policies in Northern Europe (Denmark, Finland, Norway and Sweden).

However, while the impact of motherhood on employment is negative, this does not imply, as the OECD report points out (see Figure 3.1):

> that employment rates of women without children are high in all countries: they range from a low of just 53% in Italy to a maximum of 89% in Iceland. Furthermore, some of the countries with low overall female employment rates (Greece, Italy, Spain) do not display an above-average size of the impact of parenthood rates on employment rates. Accordingly, cross national differences in employment rates of women are not only due to variation in the extent of labour market integration of mothers. (OECD, 2002, p. 77)

This phenomenon seems to confirm the existence of socio-economic and cultural behaviour patterns that dissuade married women from reconciling motherhood and employment. Also, in some countries certain tax disincentives exist that lead to the economic penalisation of spouses who return to work. Luxembourg, with its system of compulsory joint taxation, is an example. Figure 3.2 reflects the extent of the divergence due to marital status (a difference of 40 per cent between married and single mothers with at least one child between the ages of 10 and 14).

At this point, it is extremely interesting to note that, an in-depth examination of the survival of traditional cultural patterns reveals that 50 per cent of European public opinion considers that a mother's work outside the home is detrimental to the welfare of her children (European

52

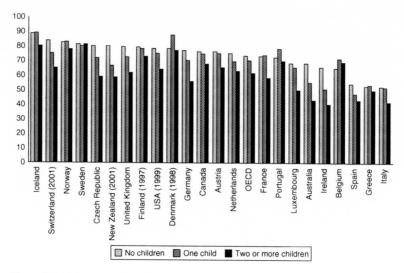

Figure 3.1 Women's employment rates by presence of children, 2000 (aged 25–54)

Source: Own elaboration from data OECD *Employment Outlook*, July 2002, p. 77.

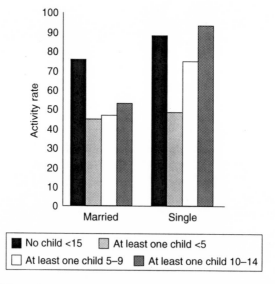

Figure 3.2 Women's activity rate by civil status and number of children – Luxembourg

Source: Author's research from Employment Rates Report 1998. Employment Performance in the Member States. European Commission.

Commission, 1998b, p. 43). However, the southern-most countries of the European Union – Greece, Spain and Italy – do not consider work outside the home to be negative. This is demonstrated by the results of a survey carried out in the spring of 1996, compiled in Eurobarometer – a result which surprised the investigators:

> It comes as a surprise that the southern countries – Greece, Spain, Portugal and Italy have the highest percentages of people who think that the fact of the woman going out to work 'tends to be positive' for the wellbeing of the child. While the male respondents also take this view, they are less positive than women, with the difference being greatest in Spain, and especially in Greece. The views in most other countries are close to the average for the Community apart from the former FRG and Austria, where no more than one fifth of women take this view. Sweden is the only country in which men outnumber women in thinking that it is a good thing for the children if their mother goes out to work, but the difference between the views of men and women is only 2%. (European Commission, 1998b, p. 40)

Figure 3.3 outlines the results obtained from the survey when asked: 'If the mother goes out to work, does this tend to have a positive effect on the well-being of the children?' It is reasonable to consider that cultural trends should not be underestimated, especially in certain countries, for example, Luxembourg, former West Germany and France. In light of this, policymakers should advocate measures that attempt to counteract such cultural effects and so encourage the harmonising of professional and family life for women and men.

Figure 3.4 showing the female activity rate represented by age group, indicates to what extent reconciliation is possible and how often it is unattainable for many women of the European Union.

Life cycle influences whether or not women are employed (in the sense of performing paid work). While men enter the labour market once they have finished their studies and remain in employment without interruption, throughout their working lives (unless they are forced to take early retirement after they reach the age of 50, as is happening with increasing frequency), women often abandon the labour force when they marry or have children. In a number of countries in the European Union women leave the labour market primarily when they decide to have children and raise them themselves and they do not always return to work once this stage of their lives is over. Motherhood and the presence of young children

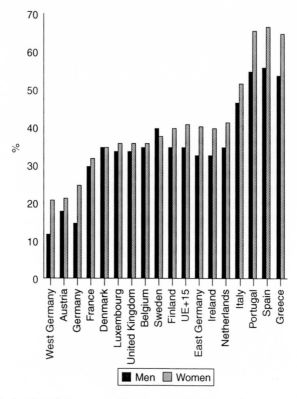

Figure 3.3   Results of the survey (% of men and women who consider mothers who go out to work to have a positive effect on their children's well-being)

Source: European Commission, 1998b: *Equal opportunities for women and men in Europe. Eurobarometer 44.3*. Brussels, p. 40.

cause an empirically demonstrable decline in women's participation in the labour force, and even their total absence. This can be attributed to many factors, especially the lack of adequate childcare services and the fact that society continues to consider children the responsibility of the mother, and not of both parents.

Consequently, a graph representative of men's working life throughout their vital cycle shows important differences from that of women. There are three main patterns of activity for women depending on the country they live in. In some countries, there is a well-defined maximum of paid activity between the ages of 21 and 29 that drops sharply as a result of marriage and child rearing. This is still the situation in

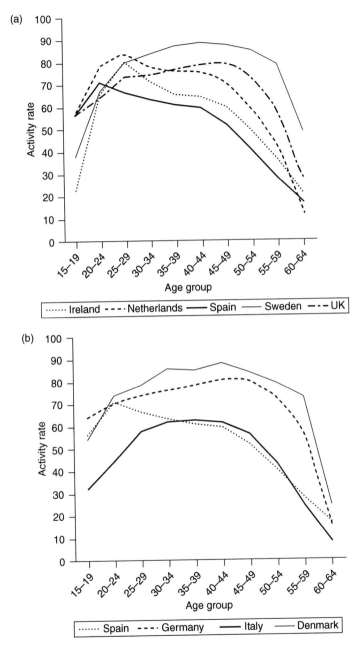

Figure 3.4 Women's activity rate and vital cycle (2001)

Source: Author's research from European Social Statistics. EU Labour force survey results 2001. Data taken during 2nd term of 2001.

Ireland and Spain today, without any appreciable number of women returning to work at a later date – see Figure 3.4. The result of this behaviour is that women, overall, have a low rate of activity. For a second group of countries, an 'M' pattern appears on the graph, where the dip down to lowest rate coincides with the period of maximum childcare (e.g., Germany and United Kingdom). This indicates that simultaneous employment and child rearing continue to be incompatible and that a subsequent reincorporation into the labour world is only viable when children are old enough to attend school. In a third group of countries (e.g., Denmark), the pattern forms a curve in the shape of an inverted 'U' or plateau that is very similar to that of men. The configuration of each of these profiles is closely related to whether or not a social policy exists that facilitates the reconciliation of a professional or working life for women and men with caring for dependant family members; for example, through the adequate provision of nursery and kindergarten services for children and care for the elderly and the disabled. These factors contribute to making motherhood and the care of other family members compatible with employment, along with institutional and legal factors relating to parental leave, working hours and school hours. The combination of all these factors is of fundamental importance in explaining the profile of women's paid activity. They condition whether women withdraw, partially or definitively, from the labour market or manage to integrate their professional and family life throughout the different phases of their life cycle.

Examining differences based on gender tells us that the female workforce profile offered by Ireland and Spain is highly distinct from that of the male workforce (see Figure 3.5). The latter presents a curve in the shape of an inverted 'U', with an activity rate of over 80 per cent between the ages of 20 and 55 (at which point the number of workers diminishes as a consequence of early retirement). Meanwhile, that of women shows a far lower level of labour market participation. The maximum rate of activity is concentrated between the ages of 25 and 27, followed by a massive withdrawal from the labour market from the age of 29 onwards, without any sign of a subsequent return to work in either of these countries.

Before concluding this section, I would like to suggest that the effect of taxation should be linked to the effect of public expenditure on family transfers and childcare in order to assess their combined effect when offering explanatory hypotheses about the changes in female behaviour observed in different countries.

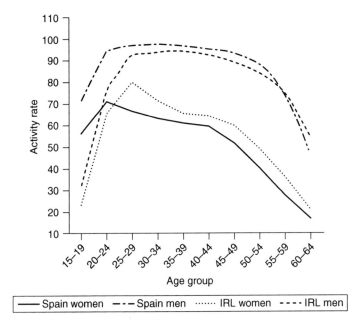

Figure 3.5 Activity rate and vital cycle men and women, 2001

Source: Author's research from European Social Statistics. EU Labour force survey results 2001. Data taken during 2nd term of 2001.

The demographic changes observed during recent years in developed countries

From a demographic point of view, it can be pointed out that recently various empirical studies have observed a changing trend and a positive correlation between fertility rate and women's employment from the mid-1980s onwards in several industrialised OECD countries. That is, it can be empirically noted that fertility has increased in countries where there is a high rate of female activity. This is emphasised by the OECD in the report entitled, *A Caring World. The New Social Policy Agenda*:

Furthermore, the cross-country relationship between the two has changed. Up until the 1970s, the level of completed fertility was negatively related to the level of women's labour force participation. Now, completed family size is lowest in countries where women's labour force participation rate is lowest. Although such simple comparisons do not prove that increasing female labour force participation will inevitably increase fertility rates, they do suggest that child-rearing and paid work are complementary, rather than alternative activities. Indeed, the exception proves the rule – the sharp fall in fertility in Sweden in recent years following a steep rise in unemployment does not seem to be coincidental. (OECD, 1999, p. 16)

Figures 3.6 and 3.7 show the empirical basis on which the OECD based this statement. Furthermore, Namkee Ahn and Pedro Mira in a study entitled *A note on the changing relationship between fertility and female employment rates in developed countries* (1999), reach a similar conclusion

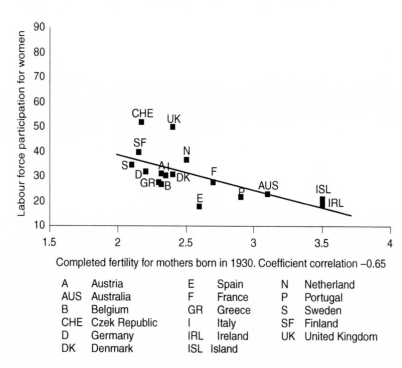

A	Austria	E	Spain	N	Netherland
AUS	Australia	F	France	P	Portugal
B	Belgium	GR	Greece	S	Sweden
CHE	Czek Republic	I	Italy	SF	Finland
D	Germany	IRL	Ireland	UK	United Kingdom
DK	Denmark	ISL	Island		

Figure 3.6 Relationship between fertility and female labour force participation (1964)

Source: OECD (1999) *A Caring World. The New Social Policy Agenda*. Paris, p. 17.

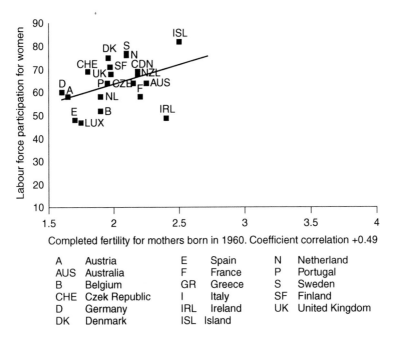

A   Austria   E   Spain   N   Netherland
AUS   Australia   F   France   P   Portugal
B   Belgium   GR   Greece   S   Sweden
CHE Czek Republic   I   Italy   SF Finland
D   Germany   IRL   Ireland   UK United Kingdom
DK   Denmark   ISL   Island

Figure 3.7 Relationship between fertility and female labour force participation (1994)
Source: OECD (1999) *A Caring World. The New Social Policy Agenda*. Paris, p. 17.

after observing, in different countries, the change experienced from the mid-1980s and the appearance of a positive correlation from that time onwards in both variables:

> Total Fertility Rates (TFR) were falling and Female Participation Rates (FPR) were increasing, conforming to a well known long-run trend. Along the cross-sectional dimension, the correlation between TFR and FPR was negative and significant during the 1970's and up to the early 1980's. This seemed consistent with secular movements. However, by the late 1980's the correlation had become positive and equally significant. (Ahn and Mira, 1999, p. 1)

According to their conclusions, women's economic security – enjoying enough income or enough personal autonomy – builds up slowly and is an indispensable condition for making autonomous decisions regarding future motherhood: It is a necessary prerequisite, but it is not enough in and by itself. Also important are participating in employment and receiving income in an economic sense, as well as being part of a welfare state designed to be favourable, or at least not unfavourable, towards managing work and family life, as these authors point out:

> since the mid 1980s the OECD average unemployment rate has been close to 8% with many countries experiencing a double-digit unemployment rate. In this context the business cycle is likely to work through the employment state .... Unemployment (i.e., a 'zero' wage) induces a strong income effect for households in which the husband is unemployed, while it should yield both income and substitution effects if a participating wife becomes unemployed. When the female participation rate is low, income effects due to the loss of the husband's income should be relatively more important. In particular, countries with lower wages and female participation rates experience a higher incidence of households in the 'zero-earnings' state, with devastating effects on fertility. This should contribute to a positive correlation between fertility and participation. (Ahn and Mira, 1999, p. 13)

These authors consider specifically the cases of Spain, Italy, Greece and Ireland where the dramatic decline in fertility throughout the 1980s and 1990s, in their opinion, has been caused partly by high unemployment rates during this period:

> The negative effect of unemployment on fertility must have been stronger in these southern European countries since young males and females have been affected most acutely by it and most unemployed youths usually do not receive unemployment subsidies due to the lack of previous employment. Further negative effects of unemployment on fertility are likely to be seen if we think in a dynamic context ... The greater the uncertainty in the labour market or the higher the unemployment rate, the more severe are these negative effects. (Ahn and Mira, 1999, pp. 13–14)

This changing trend and positive correlation between fertility rate and women's employment from the mid-1980s onwards in several industrialised countries is also underlined by Alicia Adsera who stresses that during the 'last two decades a silent demographic transformation with important economic and political consequences has taken place' (Adsera, 2004, p. 38). The two most important aspects of this change are:

1. That fertility rates have sharply decreased in most developed countries to levels below replacement rates, and
2. That the correlation between fertility and female labour participation rates across the OECD countries has become positive.

She also insists on the importance and interrelation between economic insecurity and childbirth observed in some countries from the south of Europe and empirically observed in Spain and Italy:

> the reversal of the fertility and participation correlation occurred precisely at the time when unemployment rates climbed to stubbornly high levels, mainly in Southern Europe, where participation rates had traditionally been lower. In Southern Europe, high unemployment rates and unstable contractual arrangements for young workers entailed a negative income effect stemming from a lower expected income not only for women but, critically, for young men also. The employment insecurity of young men delayed marriage and childbearing even for women outside of the labor force. Of course other institutional characteristics of those countries, absence of part time schemes, dual markets, moderate maternity benefits, intensified the depressing effect of unemployment. (Adsera, 2004, p. 37)

On the other hand, this author extols the virtues of what occurs in northern European countries, where income tax and 'child dependent benefits encourage fertility and a career lifetime commitment to labour market for women' (Adsera, 2004, p. 38).

Before moving on, it must be asserted that fertility rates also differ according to the ethnicity of each country as Joëlle E. Sleebos notes:

> Some OECD countries where total fertility rates are comparatively high also have large proportions of ethnic minorities, whose younger age profile and higher fertility contribute to sustain their total population ... . In the United States, Hispanic women have a fertility rate of 3'0 children, which is higher than in many developing countries, as compared to levels of 2'1 for black women and 1'8 among non-Hispanic whites. (Sleebos, 2003, p. 30)

According to Sleebos, the effect of migration flows on fertility rates is of vital importance to change the trend towards ageing populations in some countries of the European Union, and contribute to the future sustainability of social security pension system.

Reconciling paid work and unpaid work and social expenditure

It is undeniable that a higher or lower rate of female participation in the labour force is related to the introduction of adequate social policy that provides the support infrastructures necessary for reconciling the professional and working lives of women and men, such as nurseries and kindergartens. These are key factors that contribute to making motherhood compatible with employment, so too are the institutional and legal factors relating to parental leave, working hours and school hours. All of these are of fundamental importance in explaining the profile representative of paid activity by mothers, whether they withdraw partially or definitively from the labour market or combine a professional career with motherhood, as occurs in some countries, where there is no longer an appreciable difference between the rate of male and female activity throughout the vital cycle.

We believe that an analysis of the evolution of the economic effort undertaken in this respect can help to explain how public policies have moved in one direction or another. Table 3.1 shows the option chosen by each country and the evolution of social expenditure for the care of family members in relation to Gross Domestic Product.

In the Spanish case it is clear that there has been a drastic reduction in this kind of social expenditure, with a sharp drop occurring during the first five years of the 1980s, and continuing to the present. Italy has a profile similar to Spain's, but without sinking to the level represented by the Spanish percentage.

It is undeniable that public expenditure on childcare in the European Union for the purpose of promoting a specific social policy works in favour of women's incorporation into the labour force. However, the results differ when the preferred option is economic transfers, as opposed to the provision of childcare either in nurseries or by qualified childminders in the home.

State recognition of the importance of childcare in the European Union as a whole is reflected in social spending priorities, both in terms of their temporal evolution and the sums allocated. The relative importance that each country attaches to this function can be

Table 3.1 Social benefits provided for the family and children (as a % of GDP)

	1980	1985	1991	1992	1993	1994	1995	1996	1997	1998	1999	2000
Belgium	3.1	2.7	2.3	2.3	2.4	2.3	2.3	2.3	2.4	2.4	2.4	2.3
Denmark			3.4	3.5	3.7	3.9	3.9	3.8	3.7	3.8	3.8	3.7
Germany	2.5	1.9	2.1	2.2	2.2	2.1	2.1	2.7	2.9	2.8	3.0	3.0
Greece			1.7	1.7	1.7	1.9	1.9	1.9	1.8	1.9	1.8	1.9
Spain	0.7	0.4	0.3	0.4	0.4	0.4	0.4	0.5	0.5	0.5	0.5	0.5
France	2.9	2.8	2.7	2.7	2.9	2.9	2.9	2.9	3.0	2.8	2.8	2.7
Ireland	1.7	2.4	2.1	2.2	2.2	2.2	2.2	2.2	2.1	1.9	1.8	1.7
Italy	1.4	1.2	0.9	0.8	0.8	0.8	0.8	0.8	0.9	0.9	0.9	0.9
Luxembourg	2.6	2.1	2.3	2.4	2.8	2.9	3.0	3.0	2.8	3.0	3.3	3.4
Holland	2.6	2.2	1.7	1.6	1.6	1.4	1.3	1.3	1.3	1.2	1.1	1.2
Austria	3.3	3.0	2.7	3.0	3.2	3.5	3.3	3.1	2.9	2.7	2.9	3.0
Portugal			1.0	1.0	1.1	1.0	1.0	1.0	1.0	1.0	1.0	1.1
Finland	1.9	2.6	3.9	4.2	4.1	4.5	4.1	3.8	3.6	3.4	3.3	3.1
Sweden				—	4.6	4.5	4.0	3.7	3.5	3.5	3.4	3.4
United Kingdom	1.9	2.6	2.1	2.3	2.4	2.4	2.4	2.4	2.3	2.3	2.0	1.8

Source: EUROSTAT (2003) for data 1980 and 1985 *Social Protection Expenditure and Receipts, Data 1980–97*, Brussels, 2000, p. 58; for 1991 to 2000 *Social Protection Expenditure and Receipts, Data 1991–2000*, Brussels, p. 77.

measured, as is shown in Figure 3.8. There are six countries in which the sum spent on family/childcare equals or exceeds 10 per cent of all social expenditure, while in Spain and Italy by 2000 it was only 2.7 and 3.8 per cent of overall spending, respectively. In relation to the GDP of each country, a quick glance at Figure 3.9 is sufficient to perceive the options chosen by the different countries. Leaders in this regard are Denmark, Sweden, Luxembourg and Finland, which devote the highest level of social expenditure to family and children, over 3 per cent of GDP in 2000. In the second place, we have Germany, Austria and France, at between 3 per cent and 2.7 per cent. The next four countries occupy an intermediate position, with spending between 2.3 per cent and 1.7 per cent of GDP. The four countries are, in decreasing order of expenditure, Belgium, Greece, United Kingdom and Ireland. They are followed by the Netherlands and Portugal, both with 1.2 per cent and 1.1 per cent respectively. Particularly striking are the insignificant figures of 0.9 per cent and 0.5 per cent of GDP corresponding to Italy and Spain, respectively. Coincidentally, they are the countries that in 2000 presented the lowest birth rates in the world.

The OECD report *A Caring World. The New Social Policy Agenda*, underlines that:

> Expenditure on family services (which includes childcare) is generally small in most OECD countries with the notable exception of the Nordic countries. However, these gross totals are difficult to interpret as childcare is supported in many ways. In France, tax expenditures are important (see OECD, 1996j); Australia pays a cash benefit for child-care services; the United Kingdom provides a 'free-area' in most in-work benefits, so reducing the net cost of child care. (OECD, 1999, p. 88)

It is undeniable that public expenditure on child rearing can facilitate the incorporation of women into the labour market. However, it is highly relevant, from the gender perspective, whether the funds are earmarked for economic transfers (parental leave) or allocated to childcare services, day-care centres for the elderly or care in the home from trained providers. Nor is prevailing public opinion among women and men homogeneous throughout the European Union. In 1996, for example, there was widespread public demand for more nursery places in Spain and the United Kingdom, whereas economic transfers were the preferred option in Finland, Sweden, Luxembourg, Denmark, Austria,

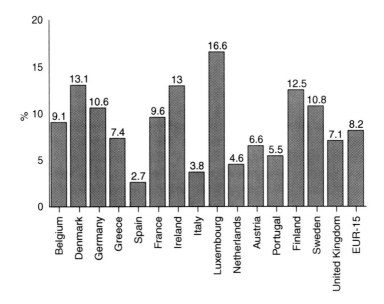

Figure 3.8   Family/children benefits as % of total benefits (2000)

Source: Own elaboration from European Commission (2003). *European Social Statistics, Social Protection, Expenditure and Receipts*. 2003 Edition. Data 1991–2000, p. 65.

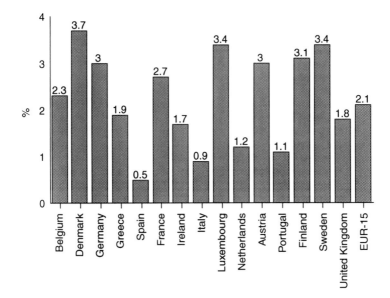

Figure 3.9   Family/children benefits as % of GDP (2000)

Source: Author's research from EUROSTAT (2000) *Social Protection Expenditure and Receipts*, Data 1980–97. Brussels, p. 58.

Portugal and Italy in response to the question 'Would you prefer more child care facilities and services or financial help?' (European Commission, 1998b, p. 48).

It is unfortunately true that in some countries, social policy has not been designed in line with prevailing public opinion and the gender perspective has been ignored. In Spain, the provision of places in schools for children starting at age three has been a praiseworthy effort furthered by the educational reform of the 1990s, although there is still a vacuum to be filled for those younger than three years old. If one compares the level of nursery services provision by the public services in the European Union, the comparison is highly disadvantageous for Spain – see Table 3.2. In Denmark, for example, according to the data produced by the group of experts in the report *Care in Europe*, carried out for the

Table 3.2 Provision of publicly funded childcare services

Country (year)	% of children availing of publicly funded[1] services[2] (age in years)		
	0–3	*3–6*	*6–10*
Austria (1994)	3	75	6
Belgium (1993)	30	95	
Denmark (1994)	48	82	80
Finland (1994)	21	53	65
France (1993)	23	99	30
Germany (1996)			
– West	2.2	85.2	5.1
– East	41.3	116.8	34.1
Greece (1993)	3	70	6.5
Iceland (1995)	37	64	0
Ireland (1993)	2	55	5
Italy (1991)	6	91	
Netherlands (1993)	8	71	5
Norway (1995)	31	72	31
Portugal (1993)	12	48	10
Spain (1993)	2	84	
Sweden (1994)	33	72	64
United Kingdom (1993)	2	60	5

[1] 'Publicly funded' is defined as funded to the proportion of at least 75 per cent.
[2] Services providing care and recreation to school-aged children.

Source: European Commission (1998), p. 27. Reproduced from Deven *et al.*, 1997: table 1.1.

Equal Opportunities Unit for women and men and matters regarding families and children of the Directorate General V (DGV1015) of the European Commission, 48 per cent of children aged two attended state nurseries in 1994; a proportion that drops to 33 and 30 per cent in Sweden, Belgium, Norway and France, while in Ireland and Spain it barely reaches 2 per cent.[1] The most outstanding case is Germany, thanks to its recent history. In 1996, for instance, there was an enormous territorial difference in the provision of nursery services in this country, with coverage of 2.2 per cent in the West and 41.3 per cent in the East. In this respect, there is a close relationship between widespread public childcare services and the higher participation of women in employment. This is readily seen in the experience of countries like Norway where:

> good publicly funded provisions for childcare tend to associate with higher female participation (e.g. in Scandinavian countries). In theory, a 'virtuous circle' is at work whereby more services create demand for women's jobs at the same time as they 'free' women from domestic responsibilities. In practice, the exact relationship between services and female employment may be more complex. The Norwegian experts, for example, point out that female participation in Norway was high before the country started to significantly expand services for young children. (European Commission, 1998a, p. 28)

Nevertheless, regardless of whether or not the relationship between these two variables is casual, the group of experts agrees on the importance of nursery services as 'one of the least controversial measures to support full integration of women in the labour market' (European Commission, 1998a, p. 29), and they particularly emphasise the continuing lack of these services in almost all the member states, even in those that offer better coverage:

> Despite its welfare improving potential, the current supply of care services for children still falls short of demand in almost all countries. While this is hardly surprising for countries that have chosen to be low providers in the past, unmet demand surfaces even in countries that figure as relatively good providers, like Denmark. A few years ago a 'day-care guarantee' was introduced by the Danish government promising parents public care for their children within a specified

period of time. The municipalities to attract good taxpayers use the guarantee, but in some local communities there are still queues of up to one and a half years long for very small children. (European Commission, 1998a, p. 29)

Likewise, the experts highlight the lack of interest shown by some countries in providing these social services:

> While some poor providers of public childcare services are taking steps to increase supply, some of the relatively good providers are threatening cuts. In Austria, Luxembourg, Germany, the Netherlands and Spain, the availability of public places for small children is slowly increasing or is set to increase, although demand still falls far short of supply. (European Commission 1998a, p. 29)

The group of European (childcare) experts point to the imminent danger of a social policy aimed primarily at economic transfers owing to the possible reduction in the female labour supply that this entails and the tacit encouragement it gives to women to stay at home to take care of their children, while the provision of adequate social services is abandoned:

> Financial benefits are fully used as a rule, but they often respond to rationales, which differ across different countries or even within the same country. A woman-centred pattern of childcare where the working mother uses leave provisions to stay at home or to work part-time, and financial benefits make up for foregone earnings, wholly or in part; Austria typifies this model. Not only are Austrian leave provisions generous and generously compensated but also expenditure on family and child-related allowances is among the highest in Europe (European Commission, 1995). In contrast, services for children have been neglected until recently and are still quite underdeveloped in the country. Germany also follows this pattern, having given priority to financial resources and leave provisions rather than public child care services. (European Commission, 1998a, p. 23)

In conclusion, I offer a general, panoramic vision of the different nations' social transfers for childcare (see Figure 3.10); the amounts involved must be compared and contrasted in order to measure the economic effort of each country and the direction in which their efforts are leading.

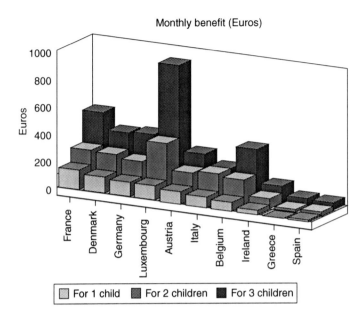

Figure 3.10 Transfers for the care of one, two or three children in the European Union

Source: Author's research from European Commission (2000).

It should be emphasised that some measures serve more to reward higher fertility rather than to reconcile the working and family lives of women and men. For example, the public provision of nursery places by the different members of the European Union shows a political will for the reconciliation of the family and employment to a larger extent than the concession of economic transfers that may serve to bolster the traditional family model.

Conclusion

There is no doubt that the evolution of the birth rate in different OECD countries witnessed in recent years makes it impossible to continue to hold that motherhood is an obstacle to the integration and permanence of women in the workplace. It has been empirically demonstrated that in some countries motherhood is not an obstacle to continuous membership of the workforce. Furthermore, if it were, the low rates of participation, particularly of Spanish and Italian women, should have been accompanied by a higher birth rate, however, this was not the case.

Other analytical parameters can explain the dramatic decline in the Spanish birth rate. Among them are the rates of male and female employment, which Ahn and Mira emphasise, and the lack of publicly subsidised services to care for people throughout all phases of the life cycle. Lack of subsidised care hinders the kind of monetisation of care that occurred in Sweden in earlier decades.

Therefore it does not seem reasonable to continue attributing the birth rate decline to an increase in female participation in the labour market, nor to maintain beliefs based on a negative correlation between the two variables, when empirically tested data have shown that, since the 1980s, the opposite is true in many OECD countries.

Note

1   For more information on this, see de Villota and Ferrari (2001).

4
Teenage Pregnancy
Olga Tóth

Introduction

The number of teenage pregnancies varies greatly across Europe: the difference between the lowest and the highest rate is up to eightfold. However, decreasing numbers of teenage pregnancy is a universal tendency across Europe: a decrease of 27–84 per cent between 1980 and 2000. We find only three countries (Republic of Moldova, Lithuania and Belarus) where the number of teenage pregnacies has risen during this period and only one European country (United Kingdom) where the rate remained the same. The decrease of teenage pregnancy can be explained by some complex, mutually related demographic, social and educational reasons.

This chapter presents comparative demographic data on teenage fertility rates and abortion rates from European countries and the United States. Using the available data the changes that have occurred with regard to teenage pregnancy are documented across time. The chaper draws some preliminary conclusions from the data, but does not engage in deeper sociological analysis.

The demographic background

The so-called second demographic transition marks a change in marital and fertility behaviour across Europe (Van de Kaa, 1999). Shortly after the 'baby-boom' period in the 1950s, fertility rates started to decrease in all European countries. By the 1990s this decrease had become so considerable in some Eastern Europen countries that researchers named the phenomenon as a 'demographic crisis'(Cornia-Paniccia, 1996 cited in Dányi, 2001, p. 437). During the same period cohabitation became an acceptable alternative to marriage and the mean age of entry into first marriage increased. Likewise, births out of wedlock also became acceptable and the mean age of women at the birth of their first child also increased. These changes in demographic behaviour, which caused anxiety to a greater or lesser extent in every European country, had a positive side effect, namely, a decrease in the number of teenage births.

In addition to these demographic changes, changes in health systems and services also contributed to the general decrease of teenage pregnancy. In particular, the use of modern contraceptive methods made it possible for broad social groups to prevent unwanted pregnancy. Likewise, most of the European countries legalised abortion and provided at least partial financial support, making it possible for unwanted pregnancies to be terminated. Furthermore, in many countries sex education and preventive programs were started in order to teach teenagers how to control their sexual lives and avoid unwanted pregnancy.

However, perhaps the most important change with regard to the decline in teenage pregnacies, has been in the social position of young women. Most notably, during this period, taking part in secondary and higher education became more important for young women in every European country. Young women not only spend more years in education but also wish to have a job and to embark on a career. Thus, educational and career opportunities and aspirations have played an important role in preventing teenage pregnancy.

In attempting, to understand these changes and to explore the moral and ethical consequences of teenage pregnancy we have to take into consideration the complex nature of this issue. We must understand that there are very different connotations of teenage pregnancy (especially birth) in countries with different traditions and culture. In addition, social class and ethnic background are also important factors in assessing this phenomenon.

The social demographer, John Hajnal, suggested that an imaginary line can be drawn on the map of Europe from St Petersburgh to Triest, dividing Europe into two with regard to marriage and fertility (Hajnal, 1965). Marriage customs in territories lying west of this 'line' are characterised as 'European marriage type' and territories lying east characterised as 'non-European marriage type' as shown in Table 4.1. The main features of these two marriage models are as follows.

This picture, although useful, has been shown by many later historical and demographic studies, not to be uniform in either the 'West' or the 'East', since deviations from the basic type are found both among regions and over time (Andorka and Balázs-Kovács, 1986; Wrigley and

Table 4.1 The main features of 'European marriage type' and 'non-European marriage type'

'European marriage type'	'Non-European marriage type'
Late marriage (late twenties)	Early marriage (teens to early twenties)
Relatively high proportion of people who never marry	Relatively small proportion of people who never marry
Low fertility rate	High fertility rate
After marriage couple live independently	After marriage couple may live with their parents, founding an independent household is not necessary

Schofield, 1981), and striking differences between countries remain. However, the effect of the traditional marriage patterns are still visible even in the present period. Ukraine is a good example for this as even in 2001, 24 per cent of brides were under 20 years (Zhurzhenko, 2004, p. 194). It also means that in some Eastern European countries a significant number of teenage pregnancies happen after marriage. In these cases teenage pregnancy is not a 'deviant' behaviour, but it is traditional and 'norm-following'. Similarly, teenage pregnacy is also normal and expected in some ethnic groups (for instance, in traditional Roma communities).

In the light of the variability of traditional demographic behaviour, it is important to analyse whether the pregnancy of a teenage woman is wanted and planned or unintentional. Another important question is whether the young mother decided to have a child alone or whether the couple planned the child together. Clearly, how one considers a teenage pregnancy will be different if the conception happened in a stable partnership or as a result of a one-night-stand. Of course a stable relationship does not mean in any case that the young mother made the optimal decision to give birth to the baby. However, in this case there is a better chance that the child will grow up with both parents. It is also important to know whether the extended family and the community accept or refuse the pregnancy of a teenage woman, as supporting backgrounds give the mother and child better social and health outcomes.

In order to analyse the phenomenon of teenage pregnancy, we should not limit our attention to the births only. Legal and illegal abortion, miscarriage and birth all raise different social, moral and health consequences. Unfortunately, we have no accurate data on teenage pregnancies that end in miscarriage. However, we are justified in supposing that the health risks of pregnancy at very young age are higher and so too are the levels of stress experienced during the period of pregnancy, also increasing the risk of miscarriage. Access to legal abortion is not available in some European countries (Ireland, Poland and Portugal). In these countries unwanted pregnancy causes an insoluble problem for a teenager. 'Pro-choice' activists campaign for legal abortion in these countries, but strong opposition continues to exist. While we lack data, we can only suppose that illegal abortion is practiced in these countries, as too is 'abortion tourism'. In countries where legal abortion is available, decisions about abortion raise moral issues. Including questions, such as whether the teenager has truly been able to consider different options?; whether her decision was made freely, without coercion from parents and the community? and whether she was helped in making her decision and by whom – were they pro- or anti- abortion?

In the next part of the chapter, we present available data on teenage fertility rates and abortion rates in European countries and in the United States.

Data sources

Given the complex nature of teenage pregnancy it is very difficult to find accurate data. Data on the fertility rates of teenagers and on the percentage of births to teenage mothers are available from every European country. However, fewer countries provide data on the number of legal abortions performed on teenagers and no data has been collected on the number of teen pregnancies which end in miscarriage. In the light of these facts, our ability to make comparisons between different countries is limited; the only effective comparison we can make is regarding the number of births to teenagers.

In this chapter, official statistical data from the United Nations, Council of Europe and Eurostat were used along with data taken from an article by Singh and Darroch (S. Singh and J. E. Darroch, 2000).[1]

Indexes used in this article:

- Teenage birth rate = number of live births per 1000 women (aged 15–19) per year.
- Teenage abortion rate = number of (legal) abortions per 1000 women (aged 15–19) per year.
- Total fertility rate = number of live births per 1000 women per year.
- Percentage of births to women under 20 years per year = number of live births to women under 20 years per total number of live births.
- Percentage of abortions to women under 20 years per year = number of abortions to women under 20 years per total number of abortions.

Births

Table 4.2 shows that there are significant differences in the number of teenage births across Europe. In Switzerland, the Netherlands and Sweden the teenage birth rate started to decrease as early as the mid-1970s and by the end of the century was the lowest in Europe. Some of the factors discussed in the first section of this paper, such as education, availability of modern contraception and changing gender roles, may have contributed to the low teenage birth rate in these countries. Italy and Spain also have a low teenage birth rate, however, these countries follow a different model. In these countries, the teenage birth rate began to decrease in the mid-1990s, at the same time as the age for entry into marriage was increasing and the total fertility rate was falling. Some Eastern European countries and the United States witness very high level of teenage birth rate. In these Eastern European countries the marriage traditions, the poverty, the deep economic crisis, the high price of contraceptives and the marketised health system may contribute to the high level of teenage birth rate (see Robila, 2004). In the case of United States one can find a substantial racial variaton in the prevalence of teenage pregnancy. As Futris and Pasley state, whites were nearly 2.5 times less likely to become pregnant than Hispanics and African Americans (Futris and Pasley, 2003, p. 26). They also stress that poverty, lower socio-economic status and traditions together with other factors can elevate the risk of teenage pregnancy.

Table 4.3 shows the changes in the level of teenage birth rate in different countries from 1980–2000, using the data of Singh and Darroch (S. Singh and J. E. Darroch, 2000).

From this table we can see that there have been dramatic changes in teenage birth rate in some European countries. For example, in Moldova there has been a significant increase in the teenage birth rate and it has moved from the category of 'moderate' to that of 'very high'; the only European country, in the year 2000, to share this status with the United States. In general, Eastern European countries, along with the United States and United Kingdom, have the highest teenage birth rate, both in 1980 and 2000. The only exceptions are Slovenia and the Czech Republic, which show a significant decline in the teenage birth rate, moving to 'very low rate' and 'low rate' from 'very high rate' categories by 2000. The main reason for this move could be explained by the fact that these two countries are the most culturally 'western' of the Eastern European countries. However, given the dramatic shift in the teenage birth rate, other 'high rate' countries may find the policies and

Table 4.2 Rates of teenage birth per year (per 1000 women aged 15–19), in the European countries and the United States, for 1980, 1995–6 and 2000

Country	Birth rate			% of change 1980–2000
	1980	1995–6	2000*	
Low teenage birth rate in 1996–2000				
Netherlands	9.2	8.2	5	−46
Switzerland	10.2	5.7	6	−41
Italy	20.9	6.9	7	−67
Spain	25.8	7.8	7	−73
Sweden	15.8	7.7	7	−66
Denmark	16.8	8.3	8	−52
Belgium	20.3	9.1	9	−56
Finland	18.9	9.8	9	−52
Slovenia	56.3	9.3	9	−84
France	25.4	10	10	−61
Greece	53.1	13	12	−77
Germany	19.5	12.5	13	−33
Norway	25.2	13.5	13	−48
Austria	34.5	15.6	15	−47
Albania	21.9	15.4	16	−27
Ireland	23	15	17	−26
Czech Republic	53.1	20.1	19	−64
Poland	32.9	21.1	19	−42
Moderate teenage birth rate in 1996–2000				
Croatia	45.4	19.9	21	−54
Portugal	41	20.9	21	−49
Iceland	57.7	22.1	23	−60
Latvia	39.9	25.5	23	−42
Bosnia-Herzegovina	36.8	38	26	−29
Hungary	68	29.5	26	−62
Slovak Republic	48.2	32.3	29	−39
United Kingdom	29.6	28.4	30	1
Yugoslavia	52.7	32.1	30	−43
Estonia	44.6	33.4	31	−30
Belarus	31.4	39	34	8
Lithuania	28.0	36.7	34	21
High teenage birth rate in 1996–2000				
Russian Federation	43.6	45.6	38	−13
Romania	72.3	42	40	−45
Bulgaria	81.2	49.6	47	−42
Ukraine	49.4	54.3	49	−1
United States	53.0	54.4	54	1
Republic Moldova	34.7	53.2	55	59

Note: *Birth rate 2000 = average for the preceding 5-year period.

Source: For 1980 and 1995/6: S. Singh and J. E. Darroch 2000, for 2000: National Population Policies 2001.

Table 4.3 Change in the level of teenage birth rate in European countries and in the United States, 1980–2000

1980	Very low rate >10	Low rate 10.0–19.9	2000 Moderate rate 20.0–34.9	High rate 35.0–49.9	Very high rate >50
Very low rate >10	the Netherlands				
Low rate 10.0–19.9	Denmark Finland Sweden Switzerland	Germany			
Moderate rate 20.0–34.9	Belgium Italy Spain	Albania Austria Ireland France Norway	Belarus Lithuania United Kingdom		Republic of Moldova
High rate 35.0–49.9		Poland	Bosnia-Herzegovina Croatia Estonia Latvia Portugal Slovak Republic	Russian Federation Ukraine	
Very high rate >50	Slovenia	Czech Republic Greece	Hungary Iceland Yugoslavia	Bulgaria Romania	United States

practices adopted by these two countires for preventing teenage pregnancy useful.

Abortions

Figure 4.1 shows the abortion rate among teenagers in few European countries and the United States. There are very few European countries that provide data on the teenage abortion rate for both years of reference (1980 and 1995–96). Moreover, international statistical sources do not contain data on teenage abortions for 2000. Therefore, comparison between countries is limited both with regard to which countries can be compared and over what time frame.

In most of the countries for which we have data, the abortion rate among teenagers has decreased. However, the decrease in the abortion rate was not as significant as the decrease in the fertility rate; the exemption being Finland, where the abortion rate halved during the 15-year

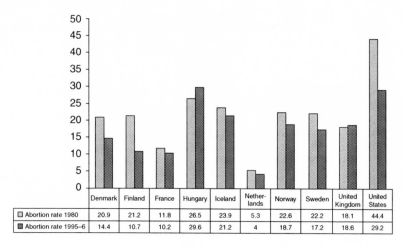

Figure 4.1   Abortion rate among teenagers per year (per 1000 women aged 15–19)
Source: Few European countries and the United States, for 1980 and 1995–6 (where data is available).

period. Some of the results are surprising, for example, the case of Hungary. In Hungary, while the fertility rate of teeangers decreased, fitting with European trends, the abortion rate increased. Such an increase in the teenage abortion rate is alarming, especially as, during this period, the absolute number of abortions showed a significant decrease. The rise in the teenage abortion rate suggests that teeangers do not have enough information about how to prevent unintended pregnancy, as well as the high cost of contraception: pills are very expensive and generally are not supported by health care coverage. Thus, lack of knowledge and responsibility, along with the practical difficulties of attaining contraception, play an important role in accounting for the growing rate of teenage abortions in Hungary.

Proportion of births and abortions in women under 20 is shown in Table 4.4.

Another means of gaining data on teenage pregnancies is to compare the proportion of total births that is accounted for by teenagers. The Table 4.5 compares, by country, the changes in this proportion over a 20-year period, 1980–2000.

Using this data it is possible to divide European countries into four groups according to the proportion of the total birth rate that is accounted for by teenage births. Most of the Western and Southern European countries as well as Albania and Slovenia belong to the first

Table 4.4 Proportion of births and abortions in women under 20 (For European countries and the United States, 1980, 1995–6 and 2000 (where data is available), ranked by 2000 data)

Country	% of births to teenagers			% of abortions to teenagers	
	1980	*1995*	*2000*	*1980*	*1995*
Netherlands	3.1	1.9	1	16.5	9.4
Switzerland	3.3	1.3	1		
Belgium	6.3	2.4	2		11.4
Denmark	5.5	2	2	18.3	12.8
Italy	6.9	2.9	2	7.8	6.6
Sweden	4.5	2	2	17.7	13.2
Albania	4.4	2.9	3		
Finland	5.6	2.6	3	26.4	16.5
France	6.7	2.6	3	14.5	12.2
Norway	7.6	2.9	3	26.5	16.8
Spain	7	3.3	3		13.9
Austria	12.3	3.9	4		
Germany	10	3.4	4	12	6.6
Greece	12.2	4.7	4	10.1	
Slovenia	12.8	3.6	4		7.6
Ireland	4.9	5.1	5		
Croatia	10.4	6.3	6		
Iceland	13.8	5.3	6	20.1	25.9
Portugal	11.6	7.1	7		
United Kingdom	9.3	6.4	7	27.6	17.7
Czech Republic	11.6	9	8	6.6	10.8
Poland	6.4	7.8	8		
Bosnia-Herzegovina	10.5	11	9		
Yugoslavia	10.7	9	9		
Hungary	14.3	10.8	10	10.3	14.9
Latvia	10.2	10.5	10		10.3
Slovak Republic	10.1	12.2	11	4.1	8.9
Lithuania	7.8	12.1	12		
United States	15.3	12.6	12	29.2	19.3
Estonia	10	12.9	13		10
Belarus	8.5	14.3	14		6.7
Romania	12.7	17	15		4.6
Russian Federation	11.2	17.2	16		13.2
Republic Moldova	8.3	18.6	20		7.9
Ukraine	12.8	19.5	20		
Bulgaria	19	20.5	21	7.8	12.5

Source: For 1980 and 1995–6: S. Singh and J. E. Darroch, 2000, for 2000: National Population Policies 2001.

Table 4.5   Change in the proportion of teenage births in European countries and in the United States, 1980–2000

| 1980 | 2000 | | | |
	Low rate <5%	Moderate rate 5–10%	High rate 10–15%	Very high rate >15%
Low rate <5%	Albania Ireland Netherland Sweden Switzerland			
Moderate rate 5–10%	Belgium Denmark Finland Germany Italy Norway Spain	Poland United Kingdom	Belarus Estonia Lithuania	Republic Moldova
High rate 10–15%	Austria Grece Solvenia	Bosnia- Herzegovina Croatia Czech Republic Hungary Iceland Latvia Portugal Yugoslavia	Romania Slovak Republic Ukraine	Russian Federation
Very high rate >15%			United States	Bulgaria

group where this proportion is under 5 per cent. Some countries in this group, like the Netherlands and Switzerland, had a very low proportion of teenage births even in 1980, at the beginning of the period in question, while others, especially Austria, Greece and Slovenia showed a significant improvement over the period. In these three countries, every eighth birth was to teenagers in 1980 falling to only 4 per cent of all births by 2000.

The second group is composed of countries in which the proportion of births to teenagers is between 5 and 10 per cent. These countries are mostly Eastern European countries, but the United Kingdom, Portugal and Iceland also belong to this 'moderate level' group. Although it is important to note that the proportion of total births to teenagers was higher in all of these countries in the 1980s, therefore, at least a moderate decrease has occurred by the year 2000.

The third group of countries, 10–15 per cent of total births, and the fourth one, more than 15 per cent of all births, are made up from Eastern European countries and the United States. All of these countries traditionally have a high level of teenage births, however, some of these Eastern European countries, especially Moldova, show significant changes over the time period. In Moldova, Bulgaria and Ukraine, by 2000, every fifth birth was to a teenager. As discussed above in relation to Moldova, economic difficulties, lack of perspective of teenage girls, lack of cheap contraceptives and lack of information all contribute to the high percentage of teenage births in these countries.

As we have already discussed, lack of adequate data means that it is impossible to present a full picture of the proportion of abortions which are performed on teenagers. Therefore, all we can do is to note that simply because there is a decrease in births to teenagers it does not necessarily follow that the percentage of abortions performed on teenagers also decreases. However, in most of the Western European countries (where data is available) both the proportion of teenage births and the proportion of teenage abortions showed a parallel decrease; the most significant changes occurring in Norway and Finland. The only exception is Iceland, where we find a significant decrease in propotion of births to teenagers, but an increase in propotion of abortions. The situation in Iceland is repeated in Eastern European countries, where the proportion of abortions to teenagers was higher in 1995 than it was in 1980. This situation is explained by the growing social inequalities in these countries, particularly, the increasing poverty and lack of opportunties which followed the collapse of Communist regimes.

Multivariate analysis – some factors that influence the level of teenage pregnancy

Teenage fertility shows a strong, significant negative connection to the level of GDP both in 1995–6 and in 2000, although the connection is stronger in 1995–6. The higher the GDP in a country the lower the level of the teenage birth rate. The two important exceptions are United Kingdom and the United States where the level of teenage birth rate – and we may suppose, the level of teenage pregnancy – is much higher than would be predicted by the GDP of the countries. However, in these countries the teenage pregnancy rate varies across a wide range. Economically, underdeveloped regions have higher rates compared to more developed regions (Singh and Darroch, 2000, p. 21). There is no significant correlation between the level of GDP and total fertility rate in

1995–6 and we find only a slight positive correlation in 2000, suggesting that by the year 2000 countries with higher levels of GDP had a slightly higher total fertility rates. It is important to mention that we did not find either a positive or negative correlation between the total fertility rate and the teenage fertility rate.

However, overall the teenage fertility rate has decreased from 1980 to 2000. And those with a high rate for teenage fertility at the beginning of the period are likely to have high teenage fertility rate in 2000, as very few countries have changed their position in comparison to other countries. Only in Eastern European countries does the proportion of births to teenagers exceed 10 per cent, and in some countries this proportion is significantly increasing. We may suppose that inadequate availability of contraceptives, increasing social inequalitites, poverty and the disadvantageous position of (young) women together contribute to these data.

We find a strong negative correlation in every examined year between the teenage birth rate and the mean age of first marriage (.74 at 0.01 level); the higher the age of entry into first marriage in a country the lower the teenage birth rate. There are two different, but interconnected, factors which account for this correlation. First, in some countries (especially in Eastern Europe) early marriage means that many young women start family life young and therefore give birth to their first child during their teenage years. In these countries, and especially in special social or ethnic groups (for instance in Roma communities), teenage pregnancies are not 'deviant' behaviour. Second, in Western European countries, where cultural traditions do not support early marriage and early motherhood, more is done to prevent unplanned teenage pregnancies. However, this said, there does not seem to be a connection between the teenage birth rate and the presence of government policies to prevent teenage pregnancies. This is a surprising result, suggesting that – at least at the level of countries – the traditions and practices surrounding marriage, parenthood and poverty, play a more important role in the level of teenage pregnancy than government action.

Governmental concerns and policies

Although our data did not prove that government policy has a direct effect on the teenage fertility rate, it could be seen as having an indirect effect. Therefore, it is informative to consider which countries have implemented special programs for reducing the number of teenage pregnancies and what these programs entail. Tables 4.6 and 4.7, present

Table 4.6 Level of government concern and existence of policies towards teenage pregnancy in European countries and in the United States for 1995 and 2000

Country	Government concern		Government policy	
	1995	*2000*	*1995*	*2000*
Countries with no or minor concern and no policies				
Albania				
Austria	minor			
Bosnia-Herzegovina				
Bulgaria				
Czech Republic				
Estonia				
Finland	minor	minor		
Germany	—	minor		
Hungary		minor		
Italy				
Latvia	minor	major		
Poland	minor	minor		
Republic Moldova				
Slovakia				
Slovenia				
Switzerland				
Countries with moderate level of concern and existing policies				
Belgium	minor	minor	—	yes
Croatia	no	minor	—	yes
Denmark	minor	minor	yes	yes
Ireland	—	—	yes	yes
Norway	minor	minor	yes	yes
Romania	no	minor	yes	no
Sweden	minor	minor	yes	yes
Yugoslavia	minor	minor	yes	no
Countries with high level of concern and existing policies				
Belarus	major	major	no	no
France	major	major	yes	yes
Germany	no	major	no	yes
Lithuania	no	major	no	yes
Netherlands	major	no	yes	no
Portugal	major	major	yes	yes
Russia	minor	major	yes	yes
Spain	—	major	—	yes
Turkey	no	major	no	yes
Ukraine	major	major	yes	yes
United Kingdom	major	major	yes	yes
United States	major	major	yes	yes

Source: National Population Policies 2001.

Table 4.7 Special government programmes to curtail the number of teenage pregnancies

Country	Programmes	
	1996	*2001*
Belgium		In Wallonie: providing information in schools; licensing of subsidies to homes for unwed mothers; facilitating access to consultation centers
Croatia		Health education; access to contraceptives
Denmark	Not specified	
France	Information, education and communication in school	
Germany		Educational materials on fertility
Ireland	Pilot school projects	
Lithuania		National programme on a healthy lifestyle
Malta		Educational programmes on responsible and safe sexual practices
Netherlands	Information, education and communication; sex education in school by NGOs	
Norway	Family-life and family planning education in school	Knowledge, attitude and practice activities
Portugal	Training of health staff; providing at specific services for youth health centres; sex education; facilitating the access of the young to contraception; information, education and communication	Not specified

Continued

Table 4.7 Continued

Country	Programmes	
	1996	*2001*
Romania	Information, education and communication	
Russian Federation	Family planning programme; family planning and health association; regional family planning centres	
Spain		Regional programmes on pregnancy prevention among adolescents
Sweden	Information, education and communication in schools	Health education on sexuality and human relations; special youth clinics; reduced cost of contraceptive pills to young women
Ukraine	Not specified	
United Kingdom		National programme on reducing teenage pregnancies, consisting of sex and relationship education, health services, research and development
Yugoslavia	Family planning programme	
United States	Family-life programme for adolescents; family planning and Medicaid programmes; maternal and child health block grant	Programmes on adolescents' family life; prevention of teenage pregnancy; abstinence; family planning; maternal and child health and social services

Source: National Population Policies 2001.

this data. Table 4.6 shows the level of governmental concern regarding teenage pregnancy, the period examined is from 1995–2000. The data, taken from the UN Department of Economic and Social Affairs, show that governments may regard teenage pregnancy as a major social problem even when it is at a low level. Conversely, many European countries with high levels of teenage pregnancy are not primarily concerned with this issue, as there are more pressing economic or social problems to address – making teenage pregnancy a minor issue.

Ethical considerations and proposals

As we have seen from the evidence and data presented in this chapter teenage pregnancy is a complex social phenomenon: traditions, levels of GDP, the nature of social and educational policy, political and social tensions all influence the teenage birth rate. However, this said, it is possible to draw some general conclusions from the data and so to point out some shared ethical considerations and there by suggest ways in which the number of teenage pregnancies across Europe could be reduced.

First there are three stages at which ethical and practical issues should be addressed if the number of teenage pregnacies is to be reduced; first, before getting pregnant; second, after getting pregnant and third, after the birth of the child. The issues which need to be addressed at each of these stages will be outlined in turn:

Before getting pregnant:

- Active sexual life at an early age.
- Brief relationships and irregular sex often without contraception.
- Lack of contraception – due to lack of information or the high cost, compouded by a lack of advice from supporting adults.

After getting pregnant:

- The role of young fathers, as, in many cases, young fathers do not take responsibility for the pregnancy, leaving decisions about abortion and birth to the pregnant young women.
- The avaliabilty of alternatives to birth; in some European countries legal abortion is not available.
- Parental and adult support or advice, often teenage girls continue with unplanned pregnacies because of family opposition to abortion.
- Late decisions; lack of information and support can lead pregnant teenagers to decide to have abortions too late.

After giving birth to the baby:

- Social, educational, financial and health disadvantages of teenage births, which affect both the young mother and child.
- The likelihood that teenage pregnancy will result in a one-parent family.
- Public prejudice based on negative views of teenage mothers (and accusations that teenagers have children to secure social security – something for which there is no evidence)
- Accomodating ethnic groups and subgroups which support early motherhood. In these cases improving the levels of young girls' education may reduce teenage pregnancy over time.

Some proposals:

- Ensuring the availability of accurate, non-judgemental information about sex, pregnancy, abortion and parenting for both boys and girls.
- Teaching young people to take the responsibility for their own bodies, for their partner and for the baby.
- Ensuring the availability of cheap (free) contraceptives which can prevent unintended pregnancies.
- Provision of advice and support for teenagers before and after they are pregnant.
- Provision of special training and education for teenage mothers so that they can continue their education and enter the labour market.
- Collection of adequate, up-to-date official statistical data at the European level on the number of births to teenagers, abortions performed on teenagers and – if possible – the number of teenagers who suffer miscarriages.

Note

1 Singh and Darroch while collecting and analysing data in a systematic way, draw attention to the methodological difficulties of attempting statistical analysis in this area too.

5

Minority Groups and Reproductive Rights

Coerced Sterilisation and Female Genital Mutilation in Europe

Nidhi Trehan and Isabel Crowhurst

Governing women's bodies: The experience of ethnic minorities

Examining reproductive rights historically reveals that women's bodies are critically contested sites of governance and regulation by the state and other societal forces. However, key issues of access to reproductive rights and vulnerability to abuse are even more contested in the experiences of minority women, many of whom face the twin realities of their rights being denied, and therefore their agency being thwarted.

While reproductive technologies affect most women to some degree, access to these technologies is determined to a large extent by class and ethnicity. Women with low incomes often depend on government funding for both contraception and prenatal care. Similarly, women from various ethnic minorities frequently find themselves at a disadvantage in exercising their choices either because of cultural constraints that may pose a threat to their reproductive rights or because of popular prejudices from the side of those authorities who govern their bodies (e.g. policymakers, medical practitioners and social workers).

In this chapter, we analyse the significance of two different practices in contemporary Europe – both of which are under-researched and under-theorised – in order to probe contentious ethical dilemmas in the area of reproductive rights for ethnic minority women. The first is the ongoing (though virtually unacknowledged) medical practice of the coercive or involuntary sterilisation of minority women, in this particular case, that of Romani women in Europe. The second concerns the practice of female circumcision or genital mutilation (FC or FGM) within immigrant groups in Europe. During the course of these explorations, we also discuss the importance of state regulation in these areas, as well as the role of private non-governmental organisations (NGOs) in challenging entrenched, antagonistic views in both majority and minority communities.

The eugenic history of the involuntary sterilisation of minority women: The case of Romanies in Europe

The potentially genocidal practice of involuntary sterilisation of people labelled 'unfit' is an egregious phenomenon embedded within modern European societies that is only recently emerging from the shadows of neglect. By the early twentieth century, Western European countries, such as Denmark, Finland, France, Germany, Iceland, Norway, Sweden and Switzerland, began to practise eugenic sterilisation on various groups (persons with mental disabilities or those deemed as such,[1] various Gypsy groups,[2] sexual 'deviants', criminals and others). More recently, with the international spotlight on the coerced sterilisation of Romani women in the Czech Republic, Hungary and Slovakia – a practice dating back from the Communist era[3] – this issue is finally receiving serious attention in Central and Eastern Europe.

Taking Edward Said's understanding of human history as a cue, it is essential to realise that we live in a period of 'misrecognised continuities' rather than ruptures as the modernist fantasy suggests (Brennan, 2004). The history of anti-Gypsyism in Europe is one of these misrecognised continuities. The links between eugenics practices and the medical profession, as well as between sterilisation and anti-Gypsyism are well documented in the literature (Adams, 1990; Broberg and Roll-Hansen, 1996; Friedlander, 1995; Kenrick and Pauxon 1995; Kevles, 1985; Larson, 1995; Müller-Hill, 1988; Seidelman, 1996; Trombley, 1988; Willems, 1997). Though it is difficult to determine how many Romanies and other Gypsy groups were sterilised within various European countries – and indeed, how many Romani women continue to be at risk for this procedure without their consent today – it can be reasonably surmised that a disproportionate number were counted amongst the 'feeble-minded', 'vagrants', 'tramps', 'paupers' and 'criminals'[4] who have been targets of eugenics policies historically (Kevles, 1985, pp. 46–7). An engaging synthesis of the eugenics movement and its legacy vis-à-vis contemporary human genetics by Kevles (1985) reveals how scientists in the early twentieth century began to postulate a biological basis for 'nomadism' and 'shiftlessness' (p. 49). Once (pseudo)scientific eugenics thinking became established within European (and American) scientific discourse, the enactment of various laws on sterilisation and their implementation spread throughout Europe and North America, with even early contraception advocates embracing an openly negative eugenics philosophy. As Ordover emphasises:

> A discussion of the ties between eugenics and birth control is in no way intended to discredit the latter ... a feminist commitment to reproductive rights and freedoms must lay bare the ongoing rever-beration of that early compact, particularly in welfare policies that encroached more and more into the bodies of poor women – especially women of color – as time wore on. (Ordover, 2003, p. xxvi)[5]

The example of early sterilisation laws in the United States in almost 30 states (beginning with the passage of a law in Indiana in 1907) first inspired the Swiss canton of Vaud to pass a sterilisation law in 1928. Subsequently, laws in Denmark (1929), Sweden and Norway (1934), Finland and Danzig (1935), Estonia (1936) and Iceland (1938) were adopted. The individuals targeted under these state provisions were those deemed 'unfit' by the scientific standards of the time. Even persons exhibiting various minor physical impairments, such as poor eyesight, as well as those exhibiting 'asocial' behaviour (criminals, Romanies), were disproportionately selected for sterilisation programmes.[6]

Within Germany, persecution of Roma and Sinti preceded the National Socialist regime. Technically, Romanies enjoyed equal citizen-ship rights under Article 109 of the Weimar Constitution, however, in practice, legislation singled them out for discrimination. For example, a Bavarian law dating from 1926 specified measures for 'combating Gypsies, vagabonds, and the work shy' and required the registration of all Romanies (USHMM, c.2002, pp. 1–2). The law required them to set-tle and provide proof of regular employment or be sent to perform forced labour for two years. This Bavarian legislation became the national standard in 1929 (USHMM, c.2002).

All of these laws were eventually surpassed in their breadth, as well as application by the German sterilisation law of 1933, *The Law for the Prevention of Offspring with Hereditary Defects* promulgated under the Nazis (Adams, 1990; Friedlander, 1995; Broberg and Roll-Hansen, 1996). This new law introduced forced sterilisation for persons suffering from a variety of mental and physical disabilities and in the process, 'defined the groups to be excluded from the national community' (Friedman, 1995, p. 23). Under the auspices of this law, German physicians sterilised an unknown number of Romanies, part-Romanies and Romanies in mixed marriages against their will (USHMM, c.2002). Subsequent laws, such as the *Law against Dangerous Habitual Criminals*,[7] the *Law on Measures of Security and Reform* (1933) and the *Marriage Health Law* (1935) ensured that persons with disabilities, Jews and Romanies would become targets for sterilisation. As Friedman points out, Romanies as a group were 'defined as criminal and antisocial, obviously a categorisation based on race or ethnicity, and thus individual Gypsies, as members of that racially defined group, were automatically classified as antisocial criminals' (Friedlander 1995, p. 25). The fate of Roma and Sinti, as well as other groups designated as 'Gypsies' during the Holocaust is of increasing (though belated) interest to scholars, and although the figures for the number of Romani victims may never be ascertained, current estimates suggest that well over a half million perished in Europe, including the majority of those communities resident for centuries in Austria, the Czech lands, Estonia, Germany, Lithuania, Luxembourg, the Netherlands and Poland (Hancock, 2000; Kenrick and Puxon, 1995; Margalit, 2002).

'Race hygiene' and the welfare state: The Western European experience

> An effective use of the Sterilisation Act toward the Tattare is no doubt desirable and possible ... One step that can be taken ... is that the National Board of Social Welfare is given the task to direct the attention of certain central and local authorities, at least then each and every poor law board and child welfare committee [sic], to the fact that it is important that measures are introduced to sterilize Tattare who, due to mental inferiority or an antisocial way of life alone, are unsuitable for caring for children. (Quoted in Broberg and Roll-Hansen, 1996, p. 127)

State sterilisation programmes targeting 'misfits', such as persons with mental disabilities, Romanies and other Gypsy groups, continued as a practice in Scandinavian countries well into the 1970s – and were viewed as progressive and non-partisan policy by legislators at the time. Sterilisations in Sweden began in 1934, peaked in 1946 and were not discontinued until 1975. According to a recent report, the majority of those sterilised were classified as 'inferior', and grounds for sterilisation included 'unmistakable Gypsy features, psychopathy and vagabond life' (Glasse, 1998), as well as 'displaying undesirable racial characteristics or signs of 'inferiority', poor eyesight or sexual and social deviancy' (Glasse, 1998). These policies eventually led to the sterilisation of over 63,000 citizens, the vast majority of whom (over 95%) were women. While it is difficult to assess to what extent these sterilisations were involuntary, recent research has uncovered that prior to 1955, a majority of these operations were coerced, whilst after that date, women's volition became more apparent in the decisions taken (Runcis, 1998; Tydén, 2002). From the time Sweden's sterilisation policies towards the target groups mentioned above was discontinued in 1976, up until the late 1990s, hardly any acknowledgement, apology or compensation was offered to the victims of sterilisation abuse. It was not until 1997, when reports exposing these practices began to appear in national newspapers, that consciousness-raising began within Swedish society, first as an exposé of past abuses towards those sterilised, and second, as a critical reassessment of the ethos and role of the social welfare state and of the Social Democratic Party of Sweden.[8] As a result, in May 1999, the Swedish Parliament approved compensation for the victims of forced sterilisation. Between 1999 and 2004, the government of Sweden offered compensation amounting to 175,000 Swedish crowns or approximately 9300 Euros (£13,240) to each individual who applied. To date, only about 2300 women have applied for, and have presumably received, compensation.

Swedish dislike for 'vagabonds' was mirrored in other European countries, including Germany, Norway, Denmark, Finland, Estonia and Switzerland (Vaud canton), where sterilisation was also adopted as state policy. In Norway, for example, over 43,000 people were sterilised.[9] Norwegian eugenics policies during the interwar period, as well as coercive measures undertaken against Romanies until the late 1970s, conveyed a rigid intolerance towards a culturally different way of life. The objective of the Norwegian state – similar to Sweden's – was to create a well-functioning society where citizens resided in a fixed abode, were educated within a uniform school system, received identical benefits from the state and were in turn expected to enrich the state economically. Romanies were seen to be problematic social deviants within this social schema, and therefore their active assimilation – including sterilisation in some cases – became state policy.

The Research Council of Norway completed a special report wherein involuntary sterilisation of Romani women was investigated, with '*the research ... show[ing] that this group was overrepresented*' (Kingdom of Norway, 2001, p. 10). A recent Norwegian Government report describing the implementation of the provisions of the Council of Europe's *Framework Convention for the Protection of National Minorities*, specifically mentions Romanies in light of historical state policy:

In 1934, the Storting [Parliament] adopted the Sterilization Act ... The goal was to rid the population of 'inferior genetic material', thereby reducing the extent of such problems as mental retardation, crime and alcoholism. The Romani people were regarded as a group with a high crime rate and a generally 'scandalous way of life'. After World War II, arguments in favour of sterilization shifted away from eugenics and moralization about the way of life of specific persons to focus more on social and socioeconomic aspects. The authorities hoped to be able to correct behaviour through activities such as those run by the Mission [Norwegian Mission for the Homeless]. (Kingdom of Norway, 2001, p. 10)

The gross human rights abuses perpetrated by Norwegian authorities against Romanies were finally publicly acknowledged when in February 1998, the Minister of Local Government and Regional Development at the time, Ragnhild Haarstad, offered an official state apology (Kingdom of Norway, 2001).

Belated apologies for such abuse are a pattern in the treatment of Romani people throughout contemporary Europe, and this was also the case in Switzerland, where the Yenish Gypsies faced involuntary sterilisation. The canton of Vaud practiced forced sterilisation of women with mental and physical disabilities from the 1930s to the 1980s. These included an unknown number of women from the poorer strata of society, including those from the Yenish community. Writing in 1964, Alfred Siegfried, founder and director of the *Oeuvre de l'entraide aux enfants de la grand-route* (Association for Assistance to Traveler Children, set up by a respected Swiss charity *Pro Juventute* in 1926) referred to the Yenish as 'mentally retarded psychopaths', and also misogynistically posited, '[n]omadism, like certain dangerous diseases, is primarily transmitted by women' (Jourdan, 1999). In 1997, though Swiss parliamentarians requested the Federal Council to write a report on the practice itself, as well as the historical, legal, medical and social background of forced sterilisation policies, Parliament ultimately decided against issuing such a report. Strangely, women's organisations in Switzerland were noticeably silent on the issue. Nevertheless, in March 2004, the House of Representatives agreed in a vote 91 to 84 in favour of granting compensation to 100 women survivors of forced sterilisation, and in addition, approved a proposal that would raise the minimum age for authorised sterilisation from 16 to 18, requiring that it be performed under strict conditions with informed consent (*NZZ*, 2004). A ceiling of approximately €52,335 (£36,370) was proposed for the compensation, which interestingly, is far higher – even adjusting for inflation – than the compensation received by children of Yenish and other Gypsies forcibly separated from their parents from 1926 to 1972 by the *Oeuvre* referred to above (NZZ, 2003; Jourdan, 1999).

Coerced sterilisation in Central and Eastern Europe

Moving from our understanding of coerced sterilisation in western and northern Europe, we now consider the relevance of this contentious practice within the central and East European context. Within many post-Second World War Central and Eastern European Communist regimes, Romanies, perceived as mentally deficient, were systematically placed in schools for children with mental disabilities. Anti-Gypsyism in these counties has had its own particular schizophrenic trajectory, coexisting with an ideology of a classless society in which ethnic expression was contained at times and actively suppressed at others. These exclusionary and segregationist practices have been exposed in the past decade or so since the demise of one-party hegemony and subsequent 'democratisation' in the region. Various attempts are currently being made to ameliorate these abuses perpetrated on generations of Romani citizens. The links between perceived mental deficiency and coerced sterilisation will be further explored in this section. Within the region, Romanies continue to be regarded as 'unfit', and evidence suggests that the use of sterilisation as birth control vis-à-vis Romani women remains an alarming practice in state hospitals today.

As discussed above, widespread atavistic concepts associating human behaviour to biology (e.g. criminality and nomadism) within the eugenics movement held sway in European scientific circles from the early twentieth century up until the Second World War. In 1940, a Romanian demographer working for the state, Sabin Manuilă expressed his anti-Gypsy moral panic quite plainly:

> The Gypsy problem is the most important and acute racial problem in Romania ... The anthropological Gypsy type must be defined as an undesirable one which must not influence our racial constitution ... . The types who have reached leadership positions and have committed political crimes, completely foreign to the mental and moral structure of the Romanian soul, are obviously of Gypsy origin ... The Gypsy mix in the Romanian blood is the most dysgenic influence that affects our race. (Bucur, 2002, p. 147)

The imagery of Romanies tainting the pure national body of Romania continues to remain popular and unchallenged to this day. Crime and 'vagrancy' continue to be linked to heredity, and currently take the form of an extreme anti-Gypsyism, whereby Romanies are the repositories of all of society's debasement, and moreover, pose a threat to the 'purity' of the national gene pool (Kohn, 1995). These social constructions, coupled with the fact that a large number of Romani families are impoverished, live in geographically isolated settlements and are disproportionately illiterate, renders them vulnerable to a whole series of abuses by the medical establishment. Currently, there are several cases of coerced sterilisation under investigation (some pending before the courts) in Slovakia, Czech Republic and Hungary. Nevertheless, far more research is needed to see how widespread this practice was under Communism – and continues to be today – as well as to investigate its origins.[10]

Though sterilisation abuse appears to exist throughout the region, and was first brought to public attention by Charter 77 (the Czechoslovak dissident group) back in 1990 with the publication of *On Sterilization of Gypsy Women*,[11] we focus, in particular, on current practice in Slovakia due to the presence of recent empirical research conducted by NGOs, as well as the subsequent international pressure brought to bear on this particular country. The path-breaking research and advocacy report *Body and Soul* (2003), published by the Center for Reproductive Rights (New York) and the Centre for Civil and Human Rights or *Poradna* (Slovakia) revealed an alarming pattern for Romani women living in eastern Slovakia: The pregnant woman goes to hospital to give birth, whilst in labour, when she is already on the surgery table, she is told to sign a consent form; she is then placed under anaesthesia, at which point the doctor promptly performs a caesarean section along with a tubal ligation. At times, the woman is unclear as to what happened to her, and at other times, there is a greater element of coercion involved (e.g. insults made to her person and threats made to her newborn's health) to get her to sign the consent form. *Body and Soul* conclusively documents over a hundred cases of coerced sterilisation on Romani women carried out in this manner in eastern Slovakia. Research uncovered widespread reproductive rights abuse vis-à-vis Romani women including involuntary sterilisation, misinformation in reproductive health matters, racially discriminatory access to health care resources, physical and verbal abuse by health care providers and a denial of access to medical records (CRR/*Poradna*, 2003, p. 13).

The report raises the contentious issue of informed consent, and suggests that a negative eugenics stance, rather than a positive eugenics approach (which would emphasise prenatal care, health and nutrition education and improving life circumstances for Romani women) is prevalent throughout the Slovak health care system today. Apart from the battery of human rights denials that Romanies face, the issue of reproductive rights is emblematic of their oppression within the wider Slovak society. Romanies – particularly those residing in segregated settlements akin to shantytowns in the economically developing world – are seen as pathological and 'socially unadaptable' (Kohn, 1995, pp. 178–9). As the CRR/*Poradna* report notes:

> Hospital administrators, doctors and nurses openly express racist views to their Romani patients, whom they regard as morally defective, unable to provide for their children and unworthy of medical services. Many health-care workers complain about the fertility rates of Romani women and see these birth rates as a direct threat to Slovakia. These stereotypes inform the behaviour of health-care personnel toward Romani patients, who in turn suffer from poor reproductive health care and increased marginalization, with negative repercussions on the overall health status of Romani women. (CRR/*Poradna*, 2003, p. 16).

The antecedents and historical continuities feeding into contemporary sociobiological debates on Romanies have been detailed above. These in turn inform and influence the attitudes of medical scientists and practitioners towards Romani patients who come to them seeking objective advice on their reproductive choices.

Apart from coerced sterilisations where 'informed consent' is rendered meaningless, another critical pattern that emerges when analysing reproductive rights amongst minority women is the use of sterilisation as contraception. Doctors and medical personnel actively encourage Romani women to undergo tubal ligations immediately after delivery as a means to prevent further births of those perceived as 'socially unadaptable'. As referred to in the *Poradna* report, a common belief amongst Slovak doctors was that repeated caesarean births necessitated conducting sterilisations on Romani patients. However, there is no evidence – and certainly *Poradna*'s research does not indicate that it is the case – that non-Romani women were urged to undergo the same procedures.[12] Furthermore, white Slovak women who underwent C-sections were not given vertical cuts, whereas the overwhelming majority of Romani women were.[13]

NGO activism, women's agency?

The activities of NGOs like *Poradna* of Slovakia in safeguarding the reproductive rights of Romani women in the post-Communist era are critical interventions.[14] During 2003, and right up to and beyond the accession of the Slovak Republic to the European Union in May 2004, the efforts of human rights advocates (in particular, *Poradna* and the CRR[15]), brought the issue of sterilisation abuse to the attention of the Slovak Government at the highest levels, as well as the international community (including European and American human rights bodies). In addition to monitoring the ongoing situation, *Poradna* and their colleagues litigated several lawsuits before the Slovak criminal and civil courts, as well as the European Court of Human Rights[16] in an attempt to elicit change at the level of medical practice and to seek compensation for the victims of these abuses.

Furthermore, national and international press coverage generated further awareness and controversy. *Poradna's* director, human rights lawyer Barbora Bukovská, notes that throughout Slovak society, a virulent racism towards the Romani minority is palpable, and the response to media revelations of coerced sterilisation reinforced this observation. Bukovská recounts how Slovak Romanies and their advocates faced opposition in this matter from all sides: many civil society organisations (including feminist groups) were anxious that concern over coerced sterilisations would endanger their efforts to block a recent anti-abortion challenge filed with the Constitutional Court by Christian Democrat members of parliament (ABA, 2003); doctors and other medical personnel were hysterically anti-Gypsy in their defensive public statements and suggested that current sterilisation practices were well within professional norms. Many nationalists as well as (neo)liberals protested, saying that it was not the right time to raise this issue, as *Poradna's* efforts to publicise sterilisation abuse internationally might jeopardise Slovakia's imminent entry to the European Union. However, Bukovská notes that this last point was simply a false concern – the accession treaties had already been signed – and served to mask the deep societal antipathy towards Romanies. In addition, some Slovak leaders claimed that the human rights activists advocating on behalf of the Romani women were all foreigners (despite the fact that Bukovská herself is Slovak) and therefore did not understand Slovak reality. Some detractors went so far as to accuse *Poradna* of having been bribed by the 'Jewish Soros lobby'[17] to work against the interests of Slovakia. Finally, the Roman Catholic Church, normally a strong advocate of pro-life positions was remarkably silent on this issue.[18]

Nevertheless, despite the pressure faced by both the Romani women victims and their advocates in Slovak society, including the enormous harassment by authorities in the law enforcement and medical communities, significant change in Slovak legislation (and practice) is on the horizon. In October 2004, the Slovak Ministry of Health approved a new draft *Law on Health Care and Services Connected to Provision of Health Care (Law No. 576/2004)* that cleared Parliament and entered into effect on 1 January 2005. The new law takes into account many of the recommendations put forward by the Centre for Reproductive Rights and *Poradna*, including a 72-hour waiting period from the time of consent to operation for all future sterilisations. Further impact at the level of practice remains to be seen, though the European Union's monitoring instruments with regard to human rights and women's rights are expected to play a key role in the future (EUMC, 2003). Two other EU member states, Hungary and the Czech Republic, also have had recent cases and/or investigations of coerced sterilisations (ERRC, 2004).

Problematising female sterilisation: Ethnic and gender considerations

As referred to in the above sections, sterilisation as contraception is one of the world's most widespread forms of birth control, accounting for over a third of contraceptive use worldwide, and almost half in economically developing countries. Female sterilisation is much more common than male – by 1992 an estimated 140 million women of reproductive age had been sterilised, in contrast to an estimated 42 million men (Hartmann, 1995, p. 244).[19] The most common complications associated with tubal ligation are anaesthesia-related problems, internal injury, infections, and in some cases, long-term side effects, such as heavier menstrual periods or lower back pain. In addition, the risk of ectopic (tubal) pregnancy increases after sterilisation (Marie Stopes International, 2004). When sterilisations are performed in countries where delivery of health care is not carefully monitored, the risks of post-operative infections and complications are far greater. Although vasectomies are surgically easier to perform with less potential side effects for the patient, the feeling of a 'loss of virility' on the part of men, coupled with the notion by many doctors that female sterilisations are more 'interesting' medically speaking (many sterilisations are performed by resident doctors during their training), ensures that women, in particular, are targeted (Hartmann, 1995, p. 245). This tendency diminishes men's responsibility for contraception, and ultimately reinforces gender hierarchies within society.

Even though female sterilisation is viewed as an effective method of contraception by feminists within the family planning and birth control movements, it is perceived with far greater ambivalence within minority communities. This results from the long history of sterilisation policies in Europe and North America that targeted various minority groups and the poor. Commenting on the history of sterilisation practices, Ordover emphasises:

> the steadfast refusal of liberal organisations, including some liberal feminist organizations, to oppose practices that constitute population control policies and state-sponsored assaults on poor women and girls of colour, even as they espouse reproductive 'choice'. But 'choice' is not a static or immovable construct ... it is bound by race and class, particularly where technology is concerned. (Ordover, 2003, p. xxvii)[20]

With respect to the case of Romani sterilisation in Europe – an egregious human rights violation that some observers suggest may be in contravention of the Genocide convention[21] – we are witnessing a negative eugenics practice within the borders of the European Union today. Although coerced sterilisation of Romani women is not currently state policy *per se* (as it was up until the 1970s in some Western European states and in some Eastern European states during the Communist period), sterilisation abuse remains a problematic practice. Recent investigations in Slovakia, initiated by NGOs, but also followed up by state organs to some extent, appear to be leading to reforms. Nevertheless, denial by the State for complicity in past abuses, and a reluctance to investigate current practices remains intact as the status quo.[22]

Female circumcision/female genital mutilation in the European context

Having looked at the coercive or involuntary sterilisation of Romani women, and in considering the broader question of the treatment of minority women in Europe in the context of reproductive rights, we now examine some issues that surround the practice commonly known as female genital mutilation (FGM) in immigration settings. Specifically, we explore the nature of the response towards this phenomenon in Europe, and the importance of dealing with it through culturally sensitive legal and enforcement instruments.

Various FGM practices comprise either the removal (partial or complete) or alteration of external female genitalia (Gruenbaum, 2001). The World Health Organisation has produced a standardised classification of the various types of female genital alterations – type I, II, III and IV (WHO, 1997), however, evidence indicates the existence of many dozens of types of genital cutting (Gruenbaum, 2001; Shell-Duncan and Hernlund, 2000). The practice is undertaken across varying ages and depends upon the community where it is carried out. In the majority of cases, it has harmful health consequences, including short-term complications, such as 'hemorrhage, severe pain, shock, damage to surrounding organs, and urinary retention and infections' (Jones *et al.*, 1999, p. 220), as well as numerous longer-term, more or less permanent, physical and psychological complications.[23]

Although in the past decade, these procedures have become widely known as FGM, the term 'mutilation' can be perceived as offensive as it entails evil and harmful intent, when this is not necessarily the case (Gruenbaum, 2001; Shell-Duncan and Hernlund, 2000). The other term often adopted – 'circumcision'[24] – is itself problematic, in that it is generally associated with the removal of the male foreskin, an act that does not have the same potential health danger as alterations to female genitalia. Indeed, for males, the equivalent of clitoridectomy, in which all or parts of the clitoris are removed, would be the amputation of most of the penis (Shell-Duncan and Hernlund, 2000). Whilst the United Nations, many governments and international organisations continue to use the term FGM, an increasing number of scholars, NGOs and advocacy groups prefer to use the term 'circumcision', cutting or even surgery. Following Rahman and Toubia, and in light of the above considerations, we adopt here the dual term 'FC/FGM' (Female Circumcision/ Female Genital Mutilation).[25]

FC/FGM practices are widespread in regions of Africa, and to a far lesser extent in Indonesia, the Arab peninsula and India, and only little is known, or reported on the performance of the practice in Latin America and Malaysia (WHO, 1997). It would be incorrect to ascribe the practice to the entire female population of one or more countries, as distribution varies according to ethnic group, as well as socioeconomic class within the same group (Gruenbaum, 2001; Shell-Duncan and Hernlund, 2000).[26] Numerical estimates of the prevalence of this procedure are tentative, although several sources report that 130 million girls and women have undergone some form of circumcision and an additional two million are at risk of undergoing it every year (Rahman and Toubia, 2000).

Despite the growing number of studies on these practices, in particular with a focus on Africa, little is known about its performance, significance and consequence in immigration settings, despite evidence that FC/FGM has been and is an issue within immigrant populations in Europe,

Australia, New Zealand, Canada and the United States (Read, 1998).[27] Again, there are no figures available to quantify how many girls and women are likely to undergo FC/FGM (*in situ* or transported to other countries for this purpose), and how many may have already undergone it in their country of origin.[28]

Legislation within Europe

In Europe, female migrants from countries where FC/FGM is practiced are present in significant numbers in Denmark, Norway, Sweden, the Netherlands, Germany, France, Italy and the United Kingdom. However, amongst these countries, only Norway, Sweden and the United Kingdom have specific legislation against FC/FGM.[29] Sweden was the first European country to criminalise FGM in 1982, and subsequently revised its law in 1998 to make the punishment more severe. As Rahman and Toubia (2000) note, apart from one arrest, no one was prosecuted under the law. FC/FGM has been a criminal offence in the United Kingdom since 1985 under the *Prohibition of Female Circumcision Act*. Nevertheless, as in the case of Sweden, this legislation was considered ineffective and led to no prosecutions. In October 2003, this act was superseded by the *Female Genital Mutilation Act*,[30] which for the first time makes it an offence for UK nationals or permanent residents to perform FGM abroad or 'to aid, abet, counsel or procure the carrying out of FGM abroad, even in countries where the practice is legal' (FGMA, 2003).[31] It also increases the maximum penalty for committing or aiding the offence from 5 to 14 years imprisonment.[32]

The Norwegian law prohibiting FGM was passed in 1995, and again its relative ineffectiveness was due to the fact that it remained virtually unknown, ultimately leading the Norwegian Ministry of Children and Family Affairs in 2001 to enact a three-year *Governmental Action Plan against Female Genital Mutilation* aimed at increasing awareness of FC/FGM practices amongst health personnel, social workers, the wider public and also the various communities most affected by the practice. The plan also detailed some concrete measures to prevent the practice in Norway and in other countries (as part of an international cooperation effort) and to provide adequate support to those girls and women who have undergone the procedure.

The other European countries mentioned above have no specific legislation or national policies addressing the practice, however, they cover and condemn it under other criminal and penal codes. For instance, in 1991, the French Commission for Appeals of Refugees was the first authority to recognise FC/FGM as a form of persecution under the terms of the 1951 *UN Convention Relating to the Status of Refugees*. The latter has set an important precedent for the assessment of claims by women and girls seeking asylum in those countries that have a similar refugee determination process (Oosterveld, 1993).

As literature published by organisations dedicated to improving the health of women and girls affected by FC/FGM indicates (Dorkenoo and Elworthy, 1996; Read, 1998), one of the most delicate aspects in dealing with this phenomenon in immigration settings is the quality of information received by the general public on this complex issue. Indeed, the media in many European countries contribute to the sensationalisation of the issue, as well as the decontextualised criminalisation of the practice by employing provocative and shocking language and imagery, ultimately offering little insight into the nature and significance of the practice itself. One recent study focusing specifically on FC/FGM within immigrant communities was produced by a group of anthropologists who analysed the social construction of the female migrant and the female migrant's body vis-à-vis the practice of FC/FGM in Italy (Pasquinelli, 2000). The findings of this study reveal the repeated use of unsophisticated stereotypes in the national press as well as scholarly literature: terms such as 'monstrous barbarisms' as opposed to 'Western civilisation', (representing Italian society) were found to be commonly used. In line with these representations, the Italian government produced a leaflet entitled *Female genital mutilations: an inhuman tradition with no sense* (2003) which adopts culturally imperialistic language[33] whilst aiming to 'educate' the parents of girls at risk about the senselessness of the practice. It is sufficient to look at the title of the publication which fails to build a base for any form of dialogue – by emphatically implying '*your* tradition makes no sense'. This perspective within European society most recently commanded attention in an editorial in the *International Herald Tribune* by Emma Bonino, a prominent Member of European Parliament who, while making a vigorous statement against FGM, called the practice a 'barbarism ... still justified in the name of "culture" or "tradition" ' (Bonino, 2004).

In reading this article, someone who knows little about FC/FGM will only be exposed to a one-dimensional narrative emphasising just how unjustified this practice is. But one also needs to ask how a woman who has undergone the procedure or is part of a community where this is performed would feel in reading such a polemical perspective. One could argue that it might convince her of the 'barbarism of her cultural practice' and even encourage engagement in its proactive eradication.

Conversely, it might lead to resentment and a consequent further retreat into the silence that already surrounds FC/FGM. Indeed, a more sophisticated and respectful approach needs to be adopted when grappling with this issue. All too frequently, the discursive appropriation and recodification of knowledge about FC/FGM contributes to the presentation of cultures that practise it as backward and oppressive, ultimately placing the minority self within a ghettoised space 'where subjects of the dominant classes, castes, sexuality and colour can look at you, and if possible, "help" you to fight against that which is silently deemed "your problem" ' (Charles, 1992, p. 33). Parallel to this hegemonising process, is the use of representations that generalise the significance of the 'problem' by emptying it of its constitutive complexities, irrespective of the variety of meanings embedded within different cultural and historical contexts where it was generated and where it is currently practiced. Moreover, discourses which construct their '... own authorial subjects as ... the yardstick by which to encode and represent cultural Others' (Mohanty *et al.* 1991, p. 55) inevitably contribute to sharp social dichotomies between those who are represented as full-fledged *subjects* of their lives by virtue of their history, and those who are judged upon as being *objects* of their own cultures and institutions and whose spontaneous will for change is often foreclosed.

No matter how opposed we are to FC/FGM in principle, and how keen we are to eradicate it as efficiently as possible, little will be achieved by employing a patronising approach replete with discursive practices and strategies that are perceived as threatening and disrespectful. As the Population Council[34] states, societal norms that concern 'women's modesty and cultural notions about their sexuality must be respected. Change cannot be simply the product of legislation but requires political support and sensitive education and community development' (Population Council, 1997). Efforts should not be made – as has been the tendency in the Western humanist discourse – to acculturate and designate agency to those women who are represented only as victims of their own cultures (McClintock, 1995). Rather, those who seek to intervene should first of all educate themselves about the variety and complexity of different cultural and historical contexts whereby certain meanings are attached to the practice of FC/FGM. This latter point has been persistently made in the last decade by a number of NGOs, as well as researchers, lawyers and others who emphasise that advice, information and leadership on eradicating such practices should be sought from women themselves in countries where the practice is performed, and who are familiar with their cultural meanings (James and Robertson, 2002).

Interestingly, there is also a 'universalist' counter position, represented by Amnesty International, for example, who assert that 'cultural claims cannot be invoked to justify their violation and those that argue against FC/FGM on human rights grounds cannot be accused of making neo-imperialist attacks on culture' (AI, 1997). Nevertheless, this perspective remains limited as the imposition of correct behaviour on 'wrongdoers' (through the passage of punitive legislation) remains problematic as long as customs and beliefs embedded within cultures are not taken into consideration. A report prepared by FORWARD[35] on FC/FGM in the United Kingdom observed, for instance, that 'the labelling of the practice as child abuse has further driven the practice underground and statutory authorities are viewed with extreme caution by communities who fear that their children might be taken away from them' (Read, 1998, p. 22). Thus, a direct abolitionist approach using criminal legislation to eradicate 'inhuman' practices might look good on the human rights record of countries, but it has little value in achieving the more important goal of concretely addressing and respecting the reproductive rights of women.

It is important to reiterate that actions addressing and challenging FC/FGM *must* originate with the women and communities amongst whom it is practiced, and any intervention from external agents need to be rooted in an appreciation of the cultural and political realities in which the practice is located (Gruenbaum, 2001). Moreover, interventions should take into account not only preventive measures, but also the needs of those individuals who have already undergone the procedure. In this sense, medical practitioners require training to understand the practice itself in a contextualised manner, removed from demeaning stereotypes.[36] Lastly, it needs to be underlined that the interest and proactive initiatives shown in European countries to eradicate FC/FGM should be consistent in a variety of situations. Crucially, these include: international cooperation with the country of origin, a guarantee of the provision of health services to those girls and women, regardless of their immigrant status (i.e. whether they have a residence permit or are undocumented) and a guarantee of refugee status to those who apply for it on the basis that they will probably face FC/FGM if they return to their home country.

Towards visibility: Reproductive rights for minority women

In this chapter, a key focus was placed on the issue of coerced sterilisation of Romani women in part because of the paucity of research in this area. With respect to FC/FGM practices, although there is a greater literature on this subject, it is a relatively new development within European societies today, and one whose evolution continues to be contentious. In the two cases above, both cultural factors as well as the issue of law enforcement were explored.

In discussing the two rather different case studies of coerced sterilisation and FC/FGM practices of minority women within one chapter, we demonstrated how the existence of both phenomena in European settings are either virtually invisible or viewed through the lens of social prejudice. Contemporary forms of denial and distortion explored above are aspects of political intervention that contribute to structuring and systematising social reality in a way that leaves open opportunities for the abuse of the reproductive rights of women, and even more so in the case of women whose minority status render them invisible.

In our view, there is a critical need for more qualitative research on these issues, and also for a contextualised and nuanced exposé of their occurrence and the cultural complexities in which they are embedded. Efforts currently undertaken by a number of local, national or international NGOs should be supported further, and the expertise of people working at the grass-roots level should serve as a privileged source of information for both legislators and those enforcing the law. NGOs serve to challenge entrenched beliefs within society, and therefore can act as catalysts for social change. Second, the angle through which we analysed both cases sought to shed light on the power that the State can have, and has had, on the bodies of its 'subjects', especially of the more vulnerable ones, such as minority women. We have seen the potential for abuse when the State exercises its authority on selective minority 'subjects', and this should serve as a cautionary reminder for future vigilance. Third, both cases have been instructive in pointing to the importance of always taking into account the consequences – intended or unintended – of any intervention.

Notes

The authors would like to thank Barbora Bukovská and Elin Strand-Marsh for their insights into the coerced sterilisation of minority women in their respective countries (Slovakia and Sweden). In addition, Louise Douglas, criminal law policy unit officer at the UK Home Office, provided useful information on the current implementation of *The Female Genital Mutilation Act* (2003).

1　The sterilisation of persons with mental disabilities continues to be an emotive issue in Europe, see Giami (1998).
2　For purposes of this article, we employ the word 'Gypsy' (often an exonym) to encompass a variety of disparate ethnic groups in Europe including various

peripatetic groups, such as the Resande and Tatere of Scandinavia, the Yenish of central Europe, Roma and Sinti (resident in Germany since the fifteenth century), as well as other related groups. The umbrella term 'Romanies' is also used throughout this chapter, and includes Sinti and Scandinavian Resande, but not the aforementioned peripatetic groups.

3 These countries became EU member states in May 2004.

4 All these categories were commonly found in publications by eugenicists of the early twentieth century, reflecting a particular middle-class sensibility embraced by many European professionals of that time.

5 Marie Stopes International, a UK-based charity which provides information on birth control options and performs abortions and sterilisations on-demand for women worldwide, is named after an early British birth control advocate who tied contraception to the eugenic cause (Kevles, 1985, p. 90). Stopes was known for her particular intolerance towards the 'unfit' and her fervent support of their sterilisation (Trombley, 1988, pp. 77–82).

6 The application of compulsory sterilisation as one part of state eugenics policy has been a global phenomenon: in North America and Australia, for example, various indigenous peoples and ethnic minorities have been targeted historically.

7 Under the provisions of this law, German police arrested many Romanies along with other 'asocials' including alcoholics, beggars, homeless persons and prostitutes, eventually placing them in concentration camps.

8 The articles of journalist Maciej Zaremba (1997) were particularly influential.

9 These included castrations, which were also performed in Sweden and Switzerland.

10 Apart from Bucur's book (2002) on Romanian biopolitics in the interwar period, very few studies have been published – at least in English – on the subject of eugenics in Eastern Europe. For an overview of sterilisation of Romani women during Communism in Czechoslovakia, see Tritt/Human Rights Watch (1992). Amongst other things, this report documents how during the Communist regime, financial incentives – such as vouchers for furniture and household appliances – were offered to Romani women who agreed to undergo sterilisation.

11 In 1996, one of the authors herself (Trehan) interviewed Romani women in the Czech Republic who had undergone the procedure during Communist times. With the transition to democracy, the government stopped these financial incentives, however, doctors apparently increased performance of C-sections on Romani women quite dramatically, thus rendering future vaginal births more risky.

12 The vast majority of Romani women sterilised in Slovakia underwent the procedure after one or two C-sections (in some cases after vaginal births). Nevertheless, the contentiousness of this practice is underscored when we realise that within the medical profession itself, advising women who have had emergency caesarean operations to undergo tubal ligations (assuming they have had three or more children if over the age of 30) appears to be a relatively acceptable medical practice in some parts of the world.

13 Vertical cuts are conducted on an active part of the uterus, and women undergoing this procedure cannot give vaginal births afterwards.

14 For a look at some of the ethical dilemmas within the world of Romani NGOs, see N. Trehan (2001).

15 The Budapest-based European Roma Rights Centre also continues to be a visible NGO advocacy group on this issue, see ERRC (2004).

16 *Poradna's* complaint at the ECtHR – concerning the sterilisations of two minors under 18 years of age, as well as a woman who was sterilised after one C-section – was granted priority treatment by the President of the Chambers in 2004; the decision is currently pending. As of October 2004, *Poradna* was continuing to litigate at the level of the civil courts in Slovakia, and in addition, had filed another application to the ECtHR on behalf of nine Romani women.

17 This refers to the Open Society Institute, whose founder George Soros is of Hungarian Jewish parentage. Nationalist diatribes in Slovakia target Soros regularly, combining anti-Semitism with their dislike of Hungarians.

18 Telephone communication with Barbora Bukovská, Director of *Poradna*, 29 October 2004.

19 Apart from tubal ligation, it is important to note that non-surgical sterilisation using the drug Quinacrine has been used to sterilise over 100,000 women worldwide. This method is considered risky due to lack of extensive testing, and has evoked considerable controversy.

20 A seminal article on the reluctance of white middle-class feminists to acknowledge sterilisation abuse within the US context was written by A. Davis (1982).

21 Article 2 (d) of the Genocide Convention states, 'In the present Convention, genocide means any of the following acts committed with intent to destroy, in whole or in part, a national, ethnical, racial or religious group, as such: (d) Imposing measures intended to prevent births within the group.'

22 Indeed, the refusal of the Slovak government to accept political and legal responsibility for sterilisation abuse is troubling; to date, no legal sanctions have been undertaken against the government-employed doctors who performed involuntary sterilisations in state hospitals.

23 For more details on these aspects, consult the WHO report 'Female Genital Mutilation' (1997).

24 Often in quotations, given its imprecise semantic connotations.

25 FC/FGM 'is the collective name given to several different traditional practices that involve the cutting of female genitals' (Rahman and Toubia, 2000, p. 3)

26 Gruenbaum (2001) provides an enlightening examination of the cultural meanings associated with the practice, and notes that it is observed across religious communities, including Muslims, Christians, Jews and amongst followers of traditional African religions; furthermore, she also addresses questions surrounding morality and marriage, especially the issue of virginity and its links to the practice.

27 It is relevant to point out that genital cutting, specifically de-clitorisation was practiced in both Europe and America as a medical 'cure' against vaginal infections, excessive masturbation and lesbianism until the 1950s (Gruenbaum, 2001; Rahman and Toubia, 2000).

28 One of the few sources of statistical data is the UK Home Office which states that there are

> around 74,000 women in the UK who have undergone the procedure, and about 7,000 girls under 16 who are at risk. This estimate is based on the number of immigrants and refugees settled in the UK from countries where FGM is endemic. There are substantial populations from these

countries in London, Liverpool, Birmingham, Sheffield and Cardiff but FGM is not necessarily confined to these areas. (Home Office, 2004)

The data assembled in this report is based on the hypothesis that all female migrants from certain countries have undergone FC/FGM, an assumption that, although not proven incorrect, appears too weak to be definitive.

29   Two more recent developments (2003) in the penal codes of Spain and Denmark make provision for more severe penalties for those who perform FC/FGM (UNFPA, 2004). For specific discussions on other national and international legal provisions against FC/FGM, see Rahman and Toubia (2000).

30   The *Female Genital Mutilation Act* implemented some recommendations of the All-Party Parliamentary Group on Population, Development and Reproductive Health (APPG) on FC/ FGM with the cooperation of relevant UK and overseas NGOs and local authorities. The proceedings shed light on the lack of prosecutions under the 1985 Act, including a lack of awareness of the Act itself, pressure from the family or community to remain silent, denial of the problems associated with FGM and the fear by enforcement agencies of being perceived as racist or culturally insensitive (Louise Douglas, criminal law policy unit officer of UK Home Office, November 2004, email correspondence).

31   Similarly, in December 2004, the lower house of the Spanish Parliament approved modifications to legislation enabling the judiciary to penalise nationals or permanent Spanish residents who carry out FGM abroad (Muheres en Red, 2004).

32   This new act does not however extend to Scotland (FGMA, 2003), for which separate legislation by the Scottish Assembly is necessary.

33   Some examples are visible in the following quotes that were written in the introduction by the Ministry for Equal Opportunities. 'It is believed that they [the populations who practice FGM] blindly respect this millenarian tradition without even knowing why .... Your daughters will live in a new millennium and will live in Italy as Italian citizens. Let's help them to have hope. Let's help them to smile' (2003, p. 2 translation by author).

34   The Population Council is an international NGO conducting biomedical, public health and social science research on population issues.

35   FORWARD (Foundation for Women's Health Research and Development) is a London-based NGO working for the health and human rights needs of African girls and women in the United Kingdom and Africa.

36   In localities with a high density of migrants, this need is particularly important, as reported by HARP (Health for Asylum-seekers and Refugees Portal), a British-based web portal which provides information for health professionals and voluntary agencies working with minority communities. In London, for instance, there are currently three clinics specialised in meeting the needs of women who have undergone FC/FGM.

Part II

The Impact of Technology: Scientific Advances and Reproductive Rights

6
Women's Rights in European Fertility Medicine Regulation

Itziar Alkorta

Introduction

For more than 20 years, Artificial Reproductive Technologies (ART) have focused the attention of gender studies. These studies try to evaluate the impact of Reproductive Medicine mainly on Western women. There is, nonetheless, a perspective that has not been sufficiently explored by the scientific literature on this issue, namely, the analysis of the legal policy models followed by European countries concerning women's rights in the context of reprogenetics. European Fertility Medicine's regulatory texts constitute a unique means to gain insight into the legal status of women's reproductive rights. Therefore, the question that we would like to raise in this paper is this: What purposes do European ART regulations actually serve and what place do women's reproductive rights have within them?

The response to these questions demands that first we draw a map of Reproductive Medicine's regulation in Europe. After that, we will try to identify the main tendencies and values embedded within it, and, finally, we will focus on the legal treatment that women's reproductive rights receive in these regulations and we will try to establish the real weight of these rights and interests in a balance with other rights and interests, such as those of prospective children', researchers' and reproductive centres'.

National regulations

Almost every country in Europe has already issued some statutory regulation on Reproductive Medicine. Solutions offered to problems posed by ART differ from one jurisdiction to another, though if we compare these rules to North American treatment of procreative technology, we realise that European regulations do coincide on one relevant point, namely, on the commitment to set limits for the uses of reproductive technologies. The United States has not yet passed any federal laws on artificial reproduction methods, but the most common understanding of the constitutional privacy principle grants basic freedom to American centres of ART so that they can meet almost any demand.

In contrast with the American *laissez-faire* model, where, as Lori Andrews (1998, p. 208) has put it, laws of supply and demand rule the Reproductive Medicine market, Europe has backed state intervention in the provision and practice of these techniques. From the European point of view, the new reproductive technologies can have an impact on the exercising of some fundamental rights that should be protected from abuse, even though there is no general agreement on what those rights are.

In view of the limits set to Reproductive Medicine, European statutes can be classified into three different groups, even if most of them regard *in vitro* fertilisation and prenatal diagnosis as forms of therapy against infertility and as a means of preventing hereditary diseases. The most restrictive options belong to German speaking countries. Under this model German *Embryo Protection Act* (1990), Austrian *Medically Assisted Procreation Act* (1996) and Swiss *Medically Assisted Reproduction Act* (1998) tend to protect the life and dignity of the human embryo and set severe restrictions on ova donation and preimplantational genetic screening. During the parliamentary discussion of each one of these bills, fears cropped up related to German eugenic history. Interestingly enough, as Olivier Guillod (2002, p. 447) has observed, in Switzerland, where a public referendum was held to pass the bill on Reproductive Medicine, the Latin minority of the country turned out to have more confidence in reproductive technologies than German speaking voters.

However, the 'restrictive' regulation model has recently been surpassed by the new Italian *Assisted Reproduction Act* (2004) regulation on alternative reproductive methods. Unlike the German regulation, largely inspired by the principles of lay humanism, Italy has succumbed to the influence of the Vatican, which condemns Reproductive Medicine on the grounds of the immorality of dissociating sexuality from procreation.

At the other end of the scale, we can find British *Human Fertilisation and Embryology Act* (1990) and Spanish Act no. 35/1988 on *Assisted Reproduction Technologies*, which set some limits to fertility technologies, and at the same time endeavoured to promote Reproductive Medicine in their own countries. Great Britain has clearly favoured the development of ART, as well as research on embryology and genetics. The Spanish

Parliament has, for the most part, followed a similar policy, even if changes of government have provoked some incoherencies on ART regulation.[1]

Finally, most European laws are better understood if taken as lying somewhere between these two extremes. Mainland Europe has enacted much less permissive acts, for example, French Act no. 800/2004 on Bioethics. *Assisted procreation*, Greece Act no. 3089 on *Medically Assisted Human Reproduction* (2002), Norwegian Act no. 56 on *Medical Use of Biotechnology* (1994) and Swedish Act no. 1140 on *Artificial Insemination and Extra corporal Fertilisation* (1984). These laws authorise gamete donation, storage of embryos and preimplantational genetic diagnosis, but they are offered only to infertile heterosexual couples with a parenting project.

International regulation

There is no specific international legal instrument to regulate Reproductive Medicine.[2] However, Europe counts on an important *Convention on Human Rights and Biomedicine* (1997) on the one hand, and also, as Carlos Romeo (2003, p. 15) has remarked, on some international general principles referred to Biomedicine: protection of genetic data, dignity of the human embryo, *extra commertium* nature of human organs and tissue, among others.

The idea of an international agreement on Reproductive Medicine first came about in 1987 promoted by the Council of Europe, which has always shown considerable interest in the subjects related to biomedicine and the law. It turned out to be a premature initiative. At that time, the majority of the member States refused to endorse the draft Recommendation submitted by the Committee of Experts on Progress in Biomedical Sciences arguing that there was no previous national legislation in that field and that, due to rapid progress in the biomedical sciences and the new ethical worries coming to light, the time was not yet ripe for an international codification on new reproductive technologies.

Having taken note of the states' position, the Committee of Ministers decided, as a strategic measure, to make the text of the draft Recommendation available to the national Parliaments. Thanks to this dissemination process, the principles elaborated by the Committee of Experts became influential in the later national bills. These values are still the basis of the common kinship among many European national laws that came afterwards.

Ten years after this first attempt to regulate Reproductive Medicine, the Council of Europe adopted the *Convention on Human Rights and Biomedicine* (1997). Although the Convention addresses ART only in an indirect way, and even if Germany and the United Kingdom declined to endorse it,[3] this is the most important harmonisation instrument enforced until now. More precisely, chapter IV of the Convention, which deals with the human genome, addresses several subjects related to artificial reproductive technologies, such as predictive genetic tests,[4] and also bans selection of sex.[5] Protocols may be concluded in pursuance of Article 32, with a view to developing in specific fields, including Reproductive Medicine, the principles contained in this Convention. Two protocols have been adopted so far on cloning (1998) and organ transplantation (2002), yet, ART has proved once again to be a cumbersome issue for member states to address.[6]

Protected interests and rights

As we have just seen, ART regulation is far from been harmonised within Europe. Nevertheless, national and international regulations of the Reproductive Medicine claim to adhere to some very similar fundamental rights and values. For instance, all of them consider as fundamental the respect for life and human dignity of the embryo, the protection of children's well-being and best interests, and the *extra-commertium* nature of gametes and embryos. Many of the statutes also refer to the informed consent of the patient who undergoes any of these techniques. However, neither national nor international texts make any specific reference to the impact of these new technologies on women's bodies or on their rights.

Thus, the question that remains to be answered is to what extent are those values compatible with women's reproductive rights, and whether this omission implies the failure to protect fundamental reproductive rights of women.

Women as patients of reprogenetic medicine

As stated earlier, European ART statutes view reproductive technology as various therapeutic treatments destined to overcome infertility problems of both men and women.

However, doubts have been cast on the actual performance of Reproductive Medicine, and on the security and efficiency of these practices. On the one hand, ART efficiency rates have been enhanced in recent years, although they continue to be low if compared with other medical procedures and treatments. On the other, the legal vacuum surrounding many routine techniques, such as sperm injection into the ovum (ICSI) and the use of stored oocytes, makes it easy for many

European fertility clinics to offer experimental procedures directly to the patients, without the practices passing security and efficiency tests.[7] Significantly enough, the *European Union Scientific Committee On Medicinal Products And Medical Devices* (2001) has recommended a careful risk analysis of fertility techniques and called for exhaustive tracking of their clinical and experimental uses under the precautionary principle.

Furthermore, within this therapeutic framework, women who undergo IVF are assigned mere patient rights. For example, section 1.2 of the Spanish *Reproductive Technology Act* (1988) refers to the right of access to artificial reproductive methods when other treatments have failed. However, it might be argued that the legal status of 'patient' offers inadequate protection to ART female users. As patients, women have no say in the matter of how many ova are to be extracted, how many embryos should be created and how many of them transferred. While the techniques are considered as therapeutic, no steps are taken to allow the control of the process to be given to the women who undergo it. Women are bound to play a passive role within this framework. The Italian *Medically Assisted Procreation Act* (2004), for instance, goes as far as to oblige women to accept all the embryos being transferred – with the sole exception of the risk to the health of the women – even if some of them are found to be genetically defective.

Protection of the embryo

Since the advent of *in vitro* fertilisation, methods and more so with the discovery of embryonic stem cell properties, the human embryo's moral and legal status has became central to the bioethics debate. European ART laws seem to be also much keener on defining the legal status of the embryo than connecting this issue with the interests of Reproductive Medicine female users.

Italian *Medically Assisted Procreation Act* (2004), to take the most radical example, bans both freezing and destroying embryos, and it also limits to three the number of oocytes that can be fertilised, and states that all the created embryos must be transferred into the woman's body.[8] This act places heavy burdens on IVF users: should a woman who is participating in fertility treatments separate or should her partner die, she will still be obliged to comply with embryo transfer. Recently an Italian judge ordered an IVF doctor to transfer all three embryos obtained by assisted reproduction techniques, despite the fact that the prospective parents, who both carried the recessive gene for Beta-Thalassemia, wanted a preimplantation diagnosis and had declared that they would abort any embryo carrier of the condition. The judge from the Court of Catania added that, according to the new statute, the woman did not have the right to choose to have a healthy baby.

In similar terms of the Italian regulation, the *German Embryo Protection Act* (1990) states as follows:

> Anyone will be liable to up to three years imprisonment or a fine who: ... 2. Fertilizes an egg artificially for any purpose other than inducing pregnancy in the woman from whom the egg cell originates 3. Obtains more than three eggs from a woman in each cycle, ... 5. Fertilizes more eggs than the ones allowed to be obtained in each cycle. (*Embryo Protection Act*, 1990, section 1)

The declared goal of this provision is to prevent the production of extra corporeal embryos that risk being left aside of a parental project.

In both the Italian and the German Acts, the Legislative aims to protect the interests (even the 'rights') of the embryos. The prohibition to fertilise more than three eggs per cycle also means that if the woman does not get pregnant in the first trial, she will be required to undergo a fresh cycle of ovulation induction again, which entails some risks for her health and reduces the success rates of fertility treatments.[9]

Nevertheless, Reprokult (2002), German feminist movement, has pointed that paradoxical as it may seem, restrictive laws, such as the *German Embryo Protection Act* (1990) have turned out to be the best asset for women's interests, as long as it prevents abuse from IVF doctors who are experimenting on users, and, at the same time, these rules act as a deterrent against scientists and biotech firms that are urgently demanding ova from donors.

It is doubtful, though, that the suggested strategic alliance between 'embryo rights' and women's interests would favour women's rights in the long run. Particularly as in some cases, such as the Italian ruling, the protection of the embryo is clearly at the expense of women's reproductive rights. The message from the Italian Parliament is that the survival of all human embryos is more important than the safety and well-being of the women who undergo assisted reproductive techniques. Predictably, the strengthening of embryo protection will undermine the rights of women who undergo assisted reproduction, and it might also influence other aspects of reproductive rights including the right to abortion.

Extra-commertium nature of eggs

Use of oocytes for reproductive purposes has recently been surpassed by embryonic stem cell research and therapeutic cloning, which have generated an enormous demand for eggs. The combined factors of research, judicial battles and patient outrage about 'rights' to egg donation have led to the development of several networks of egg markets within European borders. Take, for example, the Croatian gynaecologist that stole ova from IVF users to sell to researchers.

Unlike German speaking countries, which directly ban oocyte donation, most European statutes admit this practice by drawing a parallel with organ donation; egg selling is allowed under these regulations as long as there is informed consent and altruistic donation.

The risk of commodification of eggs calls for measures to protect women from possible abuses, and many authors have warned of the inadequacy of gift rules to regulate this matter. Raymond (1990) has argued that reproductive gift relationships must be seen in their totality, not just as helping someone have a child. They cannot be treated as a mere act of altruism: any valorising of altruistic surrogacy and reproductive gift-giving must be assessed within the wider context of women's political inequality. From another perspective, Donna Dickenson (1997) has pinpointed that female and male gametes must be differentiated, as it is women that provide the labour by undergoing super ovulation and egg extraction, as well as the larger labours of pregnancy and childbirth. These features require special provisions to prevent tissue from being appropriated; whereas, the gift model contributes to the process of alienation of women from their reproductive faculties.

Neo-institutionalism: Preserving traditional family structures

The vast majority of European regulations state that reproductive technology treatments are only available for married or cohabiting heterosexual couples of a reproductive age. Therefore, homosexual and single women are not eligible for gamete donation.

The French *Publique Health Code* (2004), for instance, provides that:

> Assisted reproduction aims to fulfil the parental project of a couple [...] The man and woman forming the couple have to be alive, of an age of to procreate, married or living together for more than two years. (*Publique Health Code* 2004, section L, 152–2)

Similar provisions have been issued by other Parliaments in countries, such as Sweden (Act no. 1140/1984, on *Artificial Insemination*, section 1– 7.2), Norway (Act no. 56/1994, on *Medical Use of Biotechnology*, section 2.2), Denmark (Act no. 460/1997, on *Artificial Fertilisation*, section 2) and Italy (Act no. 40/2004, on *Medically Assisted Procreation*, section 5.1); although, Spanish[10] and British[11] laws constitute exceptions to these general ruling.

Most ART laws presume that it is in the child's interest to be born into a home where there is a loving, stable, heterosexual relationship. However, these provisions conflict with mainstream current social politics, as new laws are being enacted in Europe to protect the rights of homosexual couples. European countries are, on the one hand, recognising the right of same-sex couples to set up a family and adopt children, while, on the other, they enforce a pro-traditional family ideology for reproductive technology users, refusing to give single women and same-sex couples access to donor gametes. For this reason biomedical procedures are perceived as having a potentially more profound transforming effect on family structures than any other social movement. As Marilyn Strathern has put it 'the way in which choices that assisted conception offers are formulated, will affect thinking about kinship. And the way people think about kinship will affect other ideas about relatedness between human beings' (Strathern, 1992, p. 15).

It is relevant to note that the discussion about the impact of biotechnology on traditional family structures was preceded by an earlier period of 'biotechnological optimism'. Many sociological reports of the 1980s revealed a positive and optimistic approach to biomedical technologies, and public opinion was confident about the benefits that new biological discoveries would bring to humanity. Shortly after, however, prestigious studies, such as the *Bioulac Report* (1992) alerted authorities to the situation of the family in Europe. Traditional family structures based on the lifelong relationship of the heterosexual couple were beginning to lose grounds, and reproductive technologies began to be seen as an added threat to the preservation of those structures rather than a means of progress. Within this context, some academics started to warn of the dangers of commodifiyng the human embryo. Mary Therese Meuldes Klein and Catherine Labrousse Riou, for instance, insisted on the idea of the inalienability of the human body and made the assumption that the dignity of the human being would be better preserved in the bosom of traditional family structures (Labrousse Riou, 1991; Meulders Klein, 1988).

These studies represented a hallmark in some countries' social politics, as the *pris de concience* of the importance of the family, while lawmakers seized the occasion to reinforce the values of stable heterosexual families. French Act no. 653 on *Human Body, Donation and Medically Assisted Procreation* (1994) is illustrative of this phenomenon. This tendency is framed in what Busnelli refers to as 'neo-institutionalism': a specific political trend which intends to 'save all that can be saved of traditional family structures, opening them partially to the technological developments, in a sort of institutional surviving-adaptation of traditional family' (Busnelli, 1996, p. 574).

However, it is important to remark that the promotion of this idea of 'a good family' is not necessarily in the best interests of women. As a matter of fact, the submission of women to men has taken place in the context of traditional family structures. The impact of patriarchal family models in the condition of women has been openly discussed for a long time in feminist public fora and, for the most part, traditional-patriarchal family is seen as being too restrictive, not comprehensive enough to embrace all the expressions and models of families, including same-sex couples and single parenting.

The business of infertility

IVF has always had a strong commercial flavour, as the fertility treatment professionals themselves acknowledge (Winston, 1999). Unlike other branches of medicine, many fertility clinics in Europe and in other countries have adopted aggressive selling strategies, which in the end put at risk the rights of infertile women to receive secure, efficient, adequate and informed medical treatment. While some European laws have already addressed this issue, too many countries still lack provisions to protect women from possible abuses. Women entering IVF programmes often feel deprived of correct and realistic information about risks and success rates, compounded by the fact that clinics often make up figures about pregnancies and 'take home baby rates'.[12]

Many fertility clinics take advantage of the lack of compulsory criteria for the clinical diagnosis of infertility. For instance, the *World Health Organisation* infertility treatment guidelines of 1992 stated that a couple should not be considered infertile until after 2 years of unprotected intercourse; however, currently, the common opinion among European and American fertility clinics is that a couple may be held infertile after 12 months of intercourse, and when the woman is over 35, after 6 months. Indeed, age is another important factor that influences the diagnosis of infertility. Reproductive Medicine has taken advantage of an increasing demand for ARTs from older women, who wish to become mothers at a late age. In Spain and Italy, for instance, women have their first child when they are around 31 years. There are certainly various factors leading to the increase in the average age of maternity; nevertheless, the Spanish sociologist, Margarita Delgado, suggests that there is a direct link between the lack of social support – female employment policies, provision of crèches for the children of working mothers, etc. – and maternity age (Delgado, 2002). Spanish authorities acknowledge that the most frequent cause of infertility among women who undergo IVF is the age at which they decide to have their first child.[13]

This phenomenon which mainly affects southern European countries is not only causing a serious natality decrease but is also making it less likely that women will choose to have children at a younger age. It might be held that 'social infertility' needs to be addressed with social solutions, for example, would it not be better to create a more child-friendly climate from the outset, enabling women to have children at a younger age, instead of addressing childlessness at an older age with reprogenetic technologies?

Conclusion

Considering European ART laws from a gender perspective leads to the conclusion that women's interests and reproductive rights are not sufficiently protected in these regulations.

Many of these laws consider reproductive technologies as therapeutic treatments given to solve infertility problems. In this framework, users tend to be reduced to mere consumers of fertility technologies. The passive role that women are bound to play in the decision-making process of IVF is coherent with the fact that European laws focus on the protection of the third parties' interests rather than women's. As we have seen European Reproductive Medicine regulation focuses mainly on the protection of the interest of the embryo and the defence of future child's interest – apparently better preserved within traditional family structures –, as well as on the interests of fertility clinics and researchers rather than on the rights of women who undergo these treatments.

Permissive regulations of commercial fertility treatments have failed to protect women's interests in front of unscrupulous researchers and fertility clinics. Even though many women have taken advantage of ART to have offspring in these countries, many others have been victims of inefficient and risky treatments, and a few of them have even been stolen of ova and ovarian tissue. Whilst, prohibitive laws, such as the German and the Swiss acts, have certainly preserved women from being exploited by fertility clinics and researchers, they have, as well, put excessive limits to the reproductive will of many. Prohibitive laws ignore that some 'key technologies', such as donor IVF or embryo cryopreservation, are now widely established in Western societies and that they are used by many European women. In any case, let us bear in mind that the declared aim of these regulations is not the defence of women's rights but the protection of the embryo.

Although it falls beyond the scope of this essay and it has been treated in other chapters of this book, it could be suggested as a matter of further discussion, that a fairer regulation of European Fertility Medicine would require recognising the centrality of women's reproductive rights in the context of reprogenetics technology regulation. Vindicating the centrality of women's interests in this context would entail, first, redefining reproductive rights in the era of reprogenetics technology (for instance, the right to get adequate and proportional treatment for infertility, including social and medical preventative measures and the protection of women against inefficient and experimental techniques; the right to decide whether or not to get *in vitro* embryos implanted, when and how many; the right to decide over our own reproductive resources – auto conservation, use, donation and destruction of gametes and ovarian tissue – etc.). And, probably, it would also entail empowering reproductive rights' legal status at the national and international levels – actually, the sole legal instance that recognises this right, though in a non-binding instrument, is the United Nations – to place them in a better position when confronted with other fundamental rights involved in reprogenetics technologies, as the best interest of the child and freedom of research.

Notes

1 Spain passed a law reform to ban embryo freezing in the year 2003 (Act no. 45/2003 amending Act 35/1988 on Artificial Reproduction Techniques). This reform has stressed the inherent contradictions of Spanish ruling in ART matters, which is extremely tolerant in some aspects and over-constraining in others.
2 The most apparent result of the failure to harmonise European regulation on reproductive medicine is that domestic laws are unable to oppose 'reproductive tourism'. Applicants easily trump their national laws demanding these techniques in other countries: for instance, Germans travel to Spain or Belgium for donated eggs, while Spanish couples go to the United States to contract the services of surrogate mothers, to give but two examples.
3 Germany and the United Kingdom have refused to sign the Convention: the former holding that its provisions are insufficient, and the latter that it is too stringent and incompatible with their domestic law.

4 'Tests which are predictive of genetic diseases or which serve either to identify the subject as a carrier of a gene responsible for a disease or to detect a genetic predisposition or susceptibility to a disease may be performed only for health purposes or for scientific research linked to health purposes, and subject to appropriate genetic counselling.' *Convention on Human Rights and Biomedicine* (1997), section 12.

5 'The use of techniques of medically assisted procreation shall not be allowed for the purpose of choosing a future child's sex, except where serious hereditary sex-related disease is to be avoided.' *Convention on Human Rights and Biomedicine* (1997), section 14.

6 The European Union has not enforced any entailing legal instrument on Reproductive Medicine, but the *Charter of Fundamental Rights* (2000) which constitutes part II of the European Constitution sets up in section 3 the prohibition of reproductive cloning of human beings.

7 These practices have a long history of unethical experimentation on infertile women. Jacques Testart, biologist of the first European team that performed an IVF, described his experience from 1978 to 1982 in the infertility unit of *Béclere* Clermont as follows: 'For five years, more than three hundred volunteer women were treated. All of them suffered from severe pathologies in their reproductive system. They were exposed to dangerous hormonal treatments and had to pay many visits to the Hospital each day' (Testart, 1984, p. 87).

8 'The aim of this Act is to promote the rights of all the subjects involved in assisted reproduction, including the rights of the conceived embryo'. Act no. 40/2004 on *Medically Assisted Procreation*, section 1.

   Section 14 of this Act, under the chapter about 'Embryo Protection', states: 1. 'Embryos shall not be conserved or destroyed, except for the provisions of the abortion act. 2. Not more than three embryos may be created in each cycle, and all of them must be transferred at once'. Intentional contravention of this article is punishable with 3 years imprisonment and penalty of €50,000–150,000.

   Finally, section 6 of the same Act provides that: 'Once the egg has been fertilized users may not withhold their consent to implantation, unless there are serious medical reasons for not transferring them'.

9 There is general agreement on the fact that negative effects of massive embryo transfer must be avoided. The question is whether in order to avoid these effects, there is any need to limit the number of eggs that can be extracted and fertilised. Some countries have issued alternative solutions. The new *Code of Practice* (2003) enforced by the HFEA, for example, aims to reduce the risk of multiple births in women undergoing infertility treatment, ruling that a maximum of two eggs or embryos may be transferred during a single cycle of infertility treatment in women aged under 40 years, with no exception, and no more than three in women over this age. In Belgium and Sweden state funding of IVF is dependent on single embryo transfer. Even in Germany, some fertility clinics try to avoid the severity of the Embryo Protection Act, pretending that section 8 does not ban freezing spare human zygotes – before the fusion of nuclei has taken place. German gynaecologists construe the aforementioned section in connection with section 8 that

defines human embryo as follows: 'the fertilised human egg, able to develop, from the fusion of nuclei on'.

10   Section 6 of Act no. 35/1988 on *Artificial Reproduction Techniques* provides that: 'Every woman may be eligible for artificial reproduction techniques, as long as she is eighteen years old, fully able to exercise her civil rights, and gives written informed consent to the practice of these techniques'. According to unofficial numbers from *El País*, 10 November 2003, in Spain single women get 10 per cent of donor inseminations. Gametes, eggs and semen are provided to single women through private clinics and also through the National Health Service. Neither of them ask the applicant whether she is heterosexual or lesbian, single or married, although some state clinics are making decisions about allocation of scarce resources which involve giving less priority to single women on waiting lists.

11   Section 13(5) of the *Human Fertilisation and Embryology Act* (1990) states that: 'A woman shall not be provided with treatment services unless account has been taken of the welfare of any child who may be born as a result of the treatment (including the need of that child for a father), and of any other child who may be affected by the birth'.

     Following the law, the *Code of Practice* (2003) of the *Human Fertility And Embryology Authority* states that account should be taken of the prospective mother's: (1) ability to provide a stable and supportive environment; (2) health and consequent future ability to look after or provide for a child's needs; (3) age and future ability to look after and provide for child's needs; (4) ability to meet the needs of any child or children who may be born as a result of treatment, including the implications of any possible multiple births; and (5) any possibility known to the centre of a disrepute about legal fatherhood of the child.

12   Lene Koch (1990) points out that even well-informed women do not hesitate to undergo any technique the doctor recommends. Some authors have tried to explain this apparently 'irrational' behaviour from the point of view of women's own experience of infertility. There is no doubt that infertility provokes acute social suffering in many women and this suffering drives them to try any solution that is offered to them, even the most inefficient and insecure. Thus, IVF has become a powerful transformer of women's reproductive consciousness and an irresistible technology that few women can refuse: IVF virtually becomes an imperative, even for those women who might otherwise have been prepared to accept their infertility.

13   One of the proposals to encourage natality in Spain consists of a wider covering of the diagnosis and treatment of infertility. The Spanish Parliament passed a Bill in 2001 (BOCG, Congreso de los Diputados, D, n° 227, de 11 de septiembre de 2001) to make reproductive techniques for infertile people available on the National Health Service. The Bill states that, 'to a great extent, we have to bind the low birth rate with infertility, as well as to a series of socio-economic circumstances that happened in the last two decades and that have prevented this rate to grow in the terms that future society might require'.

7

How is Technology Changing the Meaning of Motherhood for Western Women

Lori B. Andrews

Technology has dramatically changed women's social options and social roles. The advent of contraception allowed women to control the timing of their pregnancies and liberated them to pursue education and a career before motherhood. But because women's fertility declines with age, some women who pursue other social options must later turn to reproductive technologies, such as *in vitro* fertilisation to add a baby to the equation. New genetic technologies even promise women choices over the types of children they bear.

Technology can both liberate and enslave women. The risks to Western women in the use of reproductive and genetic technologies are growing. They include:

- inappropriate experimentation on women;
- deficient laws regarding reproductive and genetic technologies;
- viewing women merely as vessels to produce healthy babies, or in the future, embryos or foetuses for stem cell therapies;
- commodifying reproduction by commercialisation;
- changing societal norms to devalue differences among people and discriminate against people based on their gene types.

Experimentation on women

The history of reproductive and genetic technologies has been a history of unethical experimentation on women. There are numerous examples of women being 'tricked' into certain types of research. In one birth control study, women seeking contraceptives were not told they were part of a research protocol in which some women were given a placebo (Levine, 1981, p. 53). Ten of the 76 women receiving the placebo became pregnant.

In the course of developing reproductive technologies, physicians surreptitiously removed eggs and embryos from women who were undergoing pelvic surgery for other reasons (Corea, 1985, pp. 101–3; p. 135). And apparently Lesley Brown, the first woman to give birth to a child conceived through *in vitro* fertilisation, was not initially told how experimental the procedure actually was (Corea, 1985, p. 167). She was led to believe that many women before her had successfully used the technology. Similar deceptions have occurred with each new reproductive technology – such as embryo freezing, egg donation and egg freezing. Women are led to believe that the experimental technology is well established, even when only a few births have occurred in the world based on these technologies.

Regulatory abyss

There is an astonishing lack of oversight for the technologies used to create children. Experimental procedures are introduced into clinical practice without sufficient protection for women on whom they are tried. This is particularly true in the United States. In other areas of medicine, research is initially funded by the US government, and, by federal regulation, must be reviewed in advance by a neutral committee, an Institutional Review Board (IRB), before it can be tried in humans. Reproductive technologies have been held hostage to the abortion debate, and pro-life lobbyists have prevented federal funding of research on reproductive technology. Researchers can still submit their plans to hospital and university IRB, but they usually do not. In fact, according to *in vitro* fertilisation doctor, Mark Sauer, IRB review of reproductive technology proposals is so rare as to be 'remarkable'.

Even those rare studies that go before IRBs are not assessed for their social impact. The federal regulations covering IRBs specifically state that the reviewing committee should not address the social advisability of the project. The regulation in 45 C.F.R. § 46.111 says 'the IRB should not consider possible long-range effects of applying knowledge gained in the research (e.g. the possible effects of the research on public policy) as among those research risks that fall within the purview of its responsibility'. In one instance, where a fertility doctor sought IRB approval, he had already started advertising the procedure before the IRB met. The IRB chairman said; 'Our feeling was that if we approved his study, at least we could monitor his actions and collect meaningful data about the safety and efficacy of the procedure' (Paganussi, 1998, p. A18).

Some countries, such as the United Kingdom – and, in 2004, Canada – have created national oversight bodies to scrutinise the clinics that perform reproductive technologies. But most have not. In the United States, for example, the national Food and Drug Administration regulates the use of new drugs and new medical equipment. But no similar review of innovative reproductive technologies is required. Reproductive technology clinics are in a fierce competition for wealthy patients. Some clinics report as 'pregnancies' small hormonal shifts in a woman's body which show that an embryo had briefly implanted – and then been reabsorbed by her body. Others implant as many as 10 embryos or use infertility drugs indiscriminately to increase the number of babies the clinic created, even though this increases the risk to the woman and the foetuses.

Additionally, medical malpractice litigation, which serves as a quality control mechanism in other areas of health care, does not work as well in this field. The normal success rates for the procedures (e.g. 25% for *in vitro*) are so low that it makes it difficult to prove that the doctor was negligent. Risks to the children may not be discernable for many years, which may be past the period of time a statute of limitations on a legal suit has run, in some states. In 'wrongful life' cases, courts have been reluctant to impose liability upon medical providers and labs for children born with birth defects where the child would not have been born if the negligent act had been avoided; only three states recognise such a cause of action. See, for example, *Curlender* v. *Bioscience Laboratories*, 165 Cal. Rptr. 477 (Cal. App. Ct. 1980).

Experimental techniques are rapidly introduced in fertility clinics in most Western nations without sufficient prior animal experimentation, randomised clinical trials or the rigorous data collection that would occur in other types of medical experimentation (te Veld *et al.*, 1998). *In vitro* fertilisation itself was applied to women years before it was applied to baboons, chimpanzees or rhesus monkeys, leading embryologist, Don Wolf, to observe that *in vitro* was undertaken on women before it was undertaken on non-human primates (Wolf and Quigley, 1984, p. 3).

Women as vessels

Reproductive and genetic services impact people as individuals, but they also impact people as members of groups. These new medical developments disproportionately affect women as opposed to men. In trying to create contemporary policies to deal with reproductive and genetic services, it is useful to analyse the ways in which past social practices and contemporary health care have treated women differently than men.

For decades, Western nations have regulated women's reproductive behaviour to control their sexuality and to attempt to create more worthy children. In the United States, court cases earlier in this century suggested that women should be forbidden to do certain types of work – including being lawyers – on the grounds that it might make them less fit to reproduce. And when courts upheld sexist employment laws that kept women out of employment that men were allowed to pursue, they used as a rationale women's childbearing role:

> that her physical structure and a proper discharge of her maternal functions – having in view not merely her health, but the well-being of the race – justify legislation to protect her from the greed as well as the passion of man. *Muller* v. *Oregon*, 28 S. Ct. 324, 327 (1908)

The premium put on healthy babies has been seen more recently in cases in which courts have been willing to order Caesarean sections for unconsenting women on a doctor's advice that the operation is necessary for the foetus. *Jefferson* v. *Griffin Spalding City Hospital*, 247 Ga. 86, 274 S.E.2d 457 (Ga. 1987). Psychiatrists have been willing to institutionalise pregnant women who are behaving in a manner considered harmful to the foetus. And legal commentators have proposed statutory systems that would hold a woman guilty of child abuse if she risked harm to the foetus by smoking or drinking during her pregnancy or by refusing to follow doctors' orders (Shaw, 1984). Thankfully, recent court decisions in the United States have held that women should be able to refuse risky interventions during pregnancy, such as forced caesarean sections. *In re A.C.*, 573 A.2d 1235 (D.C. Cir. 1987); *In re Baby Boy Doe*, 260 Ill. App. 3d 392, 399, 632 N.E.2d 326, 330 (Ill. App. Ct. 1994).

Nevertheless, there appears to be a growing social interest in subjecting a woman's pregnancy to public control. This is evident, for example, in the prosecution of women who drink alcohol or use drugs during pregnancy (Dinsmore, 1992). Attorney Carol Beth Barnett observes that '[o]nce a woman becomes pregnant, her life, her lifestyle and her medical options become subject to public control and scrutiny … . From this perspective, a woman's womb is like 'quasi-public territory' and a woman's right to bodily integrity and autonomy receives minimal respect' (Barnett, 1993, pp. 886–7). Such an approach conveys the impression to women and to society that women are mere foetal containers.

There are even laws being debated in the United States to prevent certain women from being mothers at all. An astonishing 97 per cent of US obstetricians favour sterilising unmarried women who are poor enough to receive government financial aid (Hornsburg, 1996, p. 535). Several states have proposed legislation providing incentives for women on welfare not to have additional children. These include offering welfare benefits to women who implant the long-acting contraceptive Norplant (Hand, 1993, p. 718; Megan, 1994; Mitchell, 1994; III *Reproductive_Freedom News*) or offering women on welfare cash bonuses for undergoing sterilisation. The use of Norplant is being urged despite the fact that several thousand women have filed suit against the manufacturer with products liability complaints (Broomfield, 1996, p. 234, n.151). In Washington, women on welfare would receive $10,000 for having a tubal ligation after one child was born (Hand, 1993, p. 718). Such laws have not been enacted, though, because of the strong protection that the US Supreme Court has given to reproductive freedom.

Designer babies and the commodification of children

Developments in infertility treatment now make it possible for a child to have up to five parents – a sperm donor, egg donor, surrogate who carries the pregnancy and the couple who raise the child. As more actors get involved in the drama of reproduction, the law is increasingly called upon to sort out the rights and responsibilities of the participants. But the implications of court cases and statutes in this area go far beyond the one in six couples who are infertile (Kong, 1996). The policy decisions that society makes about alternative reproduction will influence reproductive rights generally and will influence the structure of the family and the role of women in the twenty-first Century.

In the United States, the assisted reproductive technology industry has an annual revenue of $4 billion. Annually, in the United States alone, approximately 60,000 births result from donor insemination; 15,000 from *in vitro* fertilisation (National Summary and Fertility Clinic Reports, 1995); and at least 1000 from surrogacy arrangements. In contrast, only about 30,000 healthy infants are available for adoption (National Council for Adoption, 1997). What is so striking about this comparison is that every state has an elaborate regulatory mechanism in place for adoption while only three of the 50 states have enacted legislation to comprehensively address assisted reproductive technologies. Moreover, these states which have introduced regulation are not the states where the most high-tech reproduction is conducted.

The societal response to alternative reproduction has been mixed. Take, for example, the feminist response. On the one hand, these techniques offer a woman further control over her fertility and provide greater choice in establishing alternative family structures (such as a single-parent family in which a woman undergoes artificial insemination by donor sperm). On the other hand, many of these technologies further medicalise the process of conception, pregnancy and birth, potentially lessening the woman's control over reproductive functions.

The laws are deficient in terms of protecting the women involved in reproductive technologies. Rarely are there adequate requirements for informed consent. There is often even an issue about who the legal mother is when reproductive technologies are used.

In at least 34 of the 50 US states, the husband of a consenting recipient of donor sperm is the father of the resulting child. Currently, only five states specifically address parentage in egg donation. Each of these statutes irrebuttably presumes that a child resulting from egg donation is the child of the couple who consented to receive the donated egg. Yet the egg recipient in many other states would have a strong claim to the resulting child. The law generally recognises the woman who gives birth as the legal mother, so the woman who gestates an embryo created with a donor egg will be presumed to be the mother. In states without an egg donation statute, there is nonetheless a small chance that the donor of an unfertilised or fertilised egg would be able to sue to claim parental rights to the resulting child. This might happen, for example, when a childless college student donated an egg, but the procedure of egg removal was negligent and left her infertile.

About half the states have adopted statutes regulating surrogate parenting, but few adequately address issues of legal parenthood. Washington, for example, in *Wash. Rev. Code Ann.* § 26.26.260, decides issues of custody based on an evaluation of each individual case and a determination of what is in the best interest of the child. Other states differ in whether they presume that the contracting couple are the legal parents, such as *Va. Code Ann.* §§ 20-158, 20-161; that the surrogate and her husband are the legal parents, as in *N.D. Cent. Code* §14-18-05; or that the surrogate and her husband are the legal parents unless the child is the genetic offspring of the contracting couple, such as 750 ILCS 45/6(1).

Genetic services today

Like reproductive technologies, genetic services today have a disproportionate impact on women (Lippman, 1991; Mahowald *et al.*, 1996).

Women are more likely than men to be offered and to undergo genetic testing. Additionally, diagnosis of the foetus more often provides information about the mother rather than the father. In the case of a recessive disease, an X-linked disease, and some instances of dominant diseases, the foetus's genetic status will provide information to the mother about her own genetic status, thus influencing her self-image, her personal relationships and her relationships with third-party institutions. Women are more likely than men to worry about their results and, if they are carriers of a mutation for a recessive disorder, think of themselves more negatively (Marteau *et al.*, 1997, p. 52). In contrast, only in a small minority of cases will the foetus' status exclusively provide information about the father. This is only the case when the disorder is a dominant one and the gene is transmitted by the father. But in other instances of dominant disorders, it is the mother who passes on the gene. In the case of recessive disorders, both parents pass on the gene. In the case of X-linked disorders, the mother passes on the genetic mutation and 50 per cent of her sons inherit it.

Situations in which genetic testing is undertaken without the individual's knowledge or consent (as happens during pregnancy) are particularly appalling since women, more than men, feel that doctors should keep out of reproductive decisions. A Swedish study assessing attitudes of women and men towards prenatal diagnosis found autonomy in the decision-making process was more important to women than to men (Sjogren, 1992, p. 2). In response to the question, 'who should decide about prenatal diagnosis, the couple itself or somebody else?': 82 per cent of women indicated that the couple should make the decision, compared to 20 per cent of the male partners. No woman indicated that the couple should not be the ultimate decision maker and 18 per cent were uncertain. Forty per cent of male partners believed that the couple should not be the decision maker in the use of prenatal diagnosis and 40 per cent were uncertain who the decision maker should be. The question proposed medical specialists or public authorities as alternative decision makers to the couple (Sjogren, 1992, p. 4).

It may be more important for women than men to refuse genetic services since women in general perceive greater risks from technology than men do (Marteau *et al.*, 1997; Slovic, 1992). Interestingly, men of colour are similar to women in that respect. Initially, it was suggested that perhaps the greater fear of risks experienced by women and people of colour was due to lesser scientific understanding, but it was found that even well-informed women and people of colour shared those perceptions (Savage, 1993). Fear of technological hazards is not just the product of short-term reactions to the news of some technological disaster (Pilisuk and Acredolo, 1988, p. 23), but is due to systematic differences in the lives of white men versus others: 'Perhaps white males see less risk in the world because they create, manage, control, and benefit from so much of it' (Flynn *et al.*, 1994, p. 1107), notes one group of researchers. White women and minority men and women may be concerned about risk because they are more likely to bear those risks than white men, they have less power and control and they tend to benefit less from technology (Flynn *et al.*, 1994, p. 1107).

Changing societal norms

Today, the extensive use of prenatal testing (with some obstetricians refusing to treat pregnant women unless they agree to undergo such testing) sends the message that it is the duty of women (rather than both parents) to be guarantors of their children's health. When pregnant women do not undergo available prenatal testing, health care professionals blame them for the resulting genetic conditions of their children (Marteau and Drake, 1995). Further blame is heaped on women when genetic testing reveals a son to have a condition that was passed on from the woman via the X-chromosome – such as Fragile X, Duchenne's muscular dystrophy or even (as some researchers suggest) homosexuality. Rabbi Elliot N. Dorff has advocated that 'women with the defective BRCA1 have a duty to inform their prospective mates of the fact' (Colen, 1996, p. 9) – apparently so that the men could choose to marry someone else with 'better genes'. Women may also be criticised for continuing a pregnancy if the foetus is found to have a genetic abnormality (Mahowald *et al.*, 1996). Such an approach has a negative social impact on women by underscoring the long-standing culture of motherhood that has seen women as the sole caretakers of their offsprings' well-being.

Genetic services impact individual women who choose or refuse to undergo testing, but they also have an effect on social expectations for women. They revitalise and reinforce stereotypes of women as guarantors of their offsprings' health and change society's expectations about reproduction.

Impact on pregnancy

The use of prenatal screening changes pregnant women's relationships with their foetuses. The existence of prenatal testing may be turning women's perception of pregnancy from that of a normal, healthy experience into a pathological condition. Even though only a small fraction of women learn that they are carrying a foetus with a genetic abnormality, women now think of their pregnancies as being at risk. In one study, women overestimated the chances of an abnormal pregnancy, and that concern was not diminished through genetic counseling and education (Pryde *et al.*, 1993). The concept of risk dominates the process of becoming a mother in North America today by attaching a risk label to pregnancy, physicians reconstruct a normal experience making it one that requires their supervision (Lippman, 1991).

Instead of bonding with their foetus early in the pregnancy, women who undergo prenatal testing delay bonding until they learn the results of the testing. They often do not tell friends or family members about the pregnancy until they receive the genetic testing results. Overall, this results in what Baruch College sociologist, Barbara Katz Rothman, has called 'the tentative pregnancy' (Katz Rothman, 1986).

Society may make women feel guilty for continuing the pregnancy of a foetus with even a slight disability. This occurred in the case of Bree Walker-Lampley, a California anchorwoman affected with ectrodactyly, a mild genetic condition which fused the bones in her hand. When she decided to continue a pregnancy of a foetus with the same condition, a radio talk show host and her audience attacked the decision as irresponsible and immoral (Allen, 1992; Seligmann and Foote, 1991). Lampley, along with several disability rights groups, filed a Federal Communications Commission complaint in the United States against the radio station for violating the federal personal attack rule and failing to present both sides of the issue (Andrews, 1997, p. 49). The complaint was denied.

The range of conditions that can be screened for prenatally is growing exponentially each year. Over 500 different conditions can be diagnosed through chorionic villi sampling or amniocentesis (Great Lakes Genetics). The availability of these tests affects even those people who decide not to have them. Some women say that friends and relatives have made them feel irresponsible for not having genetic testing; others have felt guilty and responsible if they had a child with a genetic disorder (either after refusing testing or after deciding to carry through the pregnancy of an affected child). Yet, as more and more prenatal genetic tests become available, parents are increasingly feeling that they are put into the position of playing God. Should they have prenatal screening for a disorder that will not affect their child until much later in life – or should they bank on a cure being developed in the child's lifetime? Should they abort a foetus whose disorder is treatable, albeit with some expense? As testing becomes available to tell whether a foetus is at a higher likelihood of suffering from breast cancer, colon cancer, heart disease, diabetes and Alzheimer's disease, should such tests be utilised? What about for alcoholism, violence and other behavioural traits? In studies with varying degrees of scientific repute, genes have been implicated in shyness, bedwetting, attempted rape, homosexuality, manic depressiveness, arson, tendency to tease, traditionalism, tendency to giggle or to use hurtful words and zest for life. Should testing for such traits be allowed prenatally? Should certain tests be required?

The spread of prenatal screening

Every year, approximately 60 per cent of pregnant women (roughly 2.4 million) in the United States undergo prenatal screening to learn about the health of their baby-to-be (PR Newswire 2001). Seventy per cent of pregnant women view their foetus on ultrasound, checking to see if the foetus is developing normally. A large percentage undergo a simple blood test that analyses whether the baby will suffer from spina bifida or anencephaly. Some undergo chorionic villi sampling or amniocentesis. A few use the cutting edge technology of preimplantation screening (Flinter, 2001). With that procedure, the couple undergo *in vitro* fertilisation to create multiple embryos. Then each embryo is tested genetically and the couple choose to implant in the woman only those embryos that they consider appropriate.

Forty years ago, when prenatal screening was first introduced, bioethicist, Paul Ramsey, observed that the 'concept of "normality" sufficient to make life worth living is bound to be "upgraded" ' (Ramsey, 1973, p. 159). That indeed has been the case. More and more genes have been identified, and parents have begun to screen for less and less serious disorders. Now some parents use prenatal screening and abortion not just for serious, life-threatening disorders, such as Tay-Sachs disease (which is painful for the child and generally fatal by age three), but for less serious traits, diseases that are treatable, and disorders that will not manifest until much later in life.

This trend has been exacerbated by the development of preimplantation screening. It is likely that couples will make different choices with that technology than they did with amniocentesis. When a woman undergoes amniocentesis in the fourth month of pregnancy, she may have already felt the foetus move inside of her. She may have bonded with the foetus. If she aborts based on a characteristic of the baby (such as the fact that it is a girl), she will have no child at all. With preimplantation screening the couple often create multiple embryos and choose only two or three to implant. If she learns the genetic make-up of her ten *in vitro* embryos through preimplantation screening, she cannot safely implant them all. It would be too dangerous for her and for the babies to have a multiple pregnancy. Even if she underwent preimplantation screening to choose embryos that do not carry a particular serious disorder, there might be too many such embryos. So, she might choose to implant only the subset of embryos that have a particular desired trait. She might, for example, implant only the males.

Already, preimplantation screening has gone beyond the application to genetic disorders that are fatal in childhood. In a controversial application described in the *Journal of the American Medical Association*, a couple choose to screen their embryo for a gene mutation related to Alzheimer's disease (Verlinsky *et al.*, 2002). Some considered this use unethical. Even if the child later developed the disease, he or she would have decades of healthy, normal life before the disease manifested. Perhaps a cure would even be developed during that time.

As more and more prenatal monitoring techniques become available, social expectations may increase the likelihood that women will use them. A government agency, the Office of Technology Assessment of the US Congress, exemplified this approach. After describing new genetic tests, an Office of Technology Assessment report stated 'individuals have a para-mount right to be born with a normal, adequate hereditary endowment' (Office of Technology Assessment, 1988). Similarly, the report of an NIH task force on prenatal diagnosis states 'There is something profoundly troubling about allowing the birth of an infant who is known in advance to suffer from some serious disease or defect' (Juengst, 1997, p. 19, citing National Institute of Child Health and Human Development, 1979).

Saxton has pointed out the strange contradiction: just at the political moment when laws, such as the American with Disabilities Act, were enacted to protect people with disabilities, genetic technologies are aimed at preventing their birth. Thus, she states that, 'it is ironic ... that just when disabled citizens have achieved so much, the new reproduc-tive and genetic technologies are promising to eliminate their kind – people with Down Syndrome, spina bifida, muscular dystrophy, sickle cell anaemia and hundreds of other conditions' (Saxton, 1998). Such developments are of concern from a disability rights perspective, as Laura Hershey points out, 'prenatal screening seems to give women more power, ... but is it actually asking women to ratify social prejudice through their reproductive "choice"?' (Hershey, 1994, p. 29).

Along similar lines, some couples have a desire to use technologies to predetermine a baby's sex. In India, China, Taiwan and Bangladesh, technicians with portable ultrasound machines go from village to village scanning pregnant women who are desperate to learn whether they are carrying a boy. Many couples abort when they learn the foetus is a girl. In Bombay alone, 258 clinics offered amniocentesis for sex selection (Jones, 1992, p. 12). In one study of 8000 abortions in India, 7999 were female foetuses, leading human rights activists to protest this clear evidence of 'gyne'cide (Jones, 1992, p. 12). In China, when the one-child policy was strictly enforced, families so preferred males that the sex ratio changed to 153 males for each 100 females (Greenholgh, 1995, p. 627).

Thirty-four per cent of US geneticists said they would perform prenatal diagnosis for a family who want a son and another 28 per cent said they would refer the couple to another doctor who would perform such testing (Obser, 1998). Dorothy Wertz, the social scientist at the Shriver Center for Mental Retardation in Waltham, Massachusetts, who conducted the study, said the percentage of practitioners willing to respond to sex selection request had increased by 10 per cent between 1985 and 1995, she stated that, 'autonomy just runs rampant over any other ethical principle in this country' (Wertz and Fletcher, 1989) and suggests that 'it's only going to increase' (Wertz and Fletcher, 1989).

The overwhelming tilt towards boys is not as pronounced yet in the United States as it is in other countries, but social psychologist, Roberta Steinbacher, of Cleveland State University worries about the effect on society if couples were able to predetermine their baby's sex. Twenty-five per cent of people say they would use a sex selection technique, with 81 per cent of the women and 94 per cent of the men desiring to ensure their firstborn would be a boy. Since certain research reveals firstborns are more successful in their education, income and achievements than latterborns, Steinbacher worries that 'second class citizenship of women would be institutionalized by determining that the firstborn would be a boy' (Andrews, 2000, p. 144).

When amniocentesis first came into use 30 years ago, abortion of an affected foetus was viewed as a temporary approach that would soon give way to treating affected foetuses (Lippman, 1994). Not only have such treatments not materialised, they are not being aggressively pursued. Thus Abby Lippman, McGill University epidemiology professor, argues that 'in the current sociopolitical climate of North America, where individual responsibility to prevent health problems takes precedence over social responsibility to support policies that promote the general well-being of all, developing remedies is probably far less likely than developing ways to prevent the birth of those who may have such problems' (Lippman, 1994, p. 26). The developments in diagnosis have become more elaborate, pushing testing back earlier into the pregnancy, through techniques, such as chorionic villi sampling, or even preimplantation embryo screening.

A new eugenics? The merger of genetic and reproductive technologies

While some couples use sperm or egg donors due to infertility, others use egg donors, sperm donors or, in the future, gene donors to 'upgrade' the traits of their children. The designing of children has started subtly, as a result of individual choices in an open market. One couple offered $100,000 for an egg donor who is a smart, tall student at an elite college. A man seeking to sell his sperm for $4000 a vial established a website with his family tree claiming to trace his genes back to six Catholic saints and several European royal families. Thousands of couples turn to the Internet to find genetic parents for their future children. They view pictures of sperm and egg donors, listen to tapes of their voices and review pages of descriptions of their physical features, their hobbies, their SAT scores, their philosophies of life. At the Ronsangels.com website, couples bid on the eggs of attractive models. Given this consumer model, it is not surprising that the parents of a child conceived with sperm from a high-IQ donor asked a reporter; 'why is it okay for people to choose the best house, the best schools, the best surgeon, the best car, but not try to have the best baby possible?' (Andrews, 2000, p. 136). This consumerist approach to children is leading subtly to designer babies. Reproductive technologies are increasingly being used due to social biases. Already, a black woman in England sought a white egg donor – to create a child who would be less likely to be discriminated against (Nutall and Wilkins, 1994).

As technology evolves, parents-to-be will have even more control over the traits of their offspring. In a variety of animal species, scientists have genetically engineered the offspring by adding an additional gene of interest (Chang *et al.*, 2001; Griffith *et al.*, 1999; Hagmann 1999; Lois *et al.*, 2002; Perry *et al.*, 1999; Rudolph *et al.*, 1999) – such as an extra *NR2B* gene to enhance memory (Tsien, 2000). Now genetic engineering is being proposed for human embryos.

The demand for gene insertion in embryos is likely to be quite high. In a US poll, 42 per cent of potential parents surveyed said they would use genetic engineering on their children to make them smarter; 43 per cent, to upgrade them physically. Another survey found that over a third of people wanted to control their children's genes to make sure they had an appropriate sexual orientation.

Germline genetic intervention on people is likely to increase cancer risks, sterility or other problems in the next generation (Newman, 2000). Proponents of genetic engineering of animals and humans suggest that it is no different than selective breeding. But geneticist, Jon Gordon, points out there are enormous differences when only a single gene is being introduced in a complex organism. Gordon notes that unlike selective breeding, where favourable alleles at *all* loci can be selected at one time, gene transfer selects only *one* locus and tries to improve the trait in isolation (Gordon, 1999). In light of this, he comments that this single-gene approach has, 'despite more than 10 years of effort, failed to yield even one unequivocal success' (Gordon, 1999, p. 2023). Instead it has produced disastrous results. When a gene shown to induce muscle hypertrophy in mice was inserted into a calf, the animal did exhibit the desired trait initially, but later exhibited muscle deterioration. The animal had to be shot.

Where researchers inserted an extra *NR2B* gene linked to long-term memory, it increased cognitive and mental abilities of mouse embryos. The resulting animals seemed to move more quickly through mazes than the mice that had not been altered (Tang *et al.*, 1999). Immediately, the question arose about whether such interventions should be undertaken on humans. Yet, subsequent research, by other scientists, learned that the genetic intervention had a downside. The mice were more susceptible to long-term pain (Wei *et al.*, 2001; Weiss, 2001).

The dark side of designing babies

Society does not yet have an adequate framework to develop ethical and policy guidelines for the technologies of prenatal screening, gamete donation and germline genetic intervention. Yet, there are reasons why we as a society should care more about a couple's decision to pay for a genetic enhancement for intelligence than we would if they spent their money on an expensive car or private tutors for their children.

The major reason for concern is that harm could be caused to the children subjected to these interventions if the predictions of risks from the animal research hold true for humans. Moreover, these are not just 'individual' choices in isolation. If wealthy individuals genetically enhance their children to be smarter or taller, the rest of us may feel pressured to do the same, just to allow our kids to keep up: 'Normality' today may be 'disability' tomorrow. Selecting traits also creates a notion, like previously rejected caste systems or guilds, that people can be born into a particular job or purpose. As an example, researchers have suggested cloning legless individuals on the grounds that they would be better suited for space travel (Pizzulli, 1974, p. 520, n. 235, citing J. B. S. Haldane, 1963, pp. 354–5). Such suggestions introduce determinist concepts which threaten individual autonomy.

Moreover, the fads that will be inherent in choices of favoured clones or favoured genes may narrow diversity in society. At one point, there was a run on a sperm bank that was thought to have sperm from a particular rock star, Mick Jagger. Certain types of people may disappear due to market choices, just as certain plants have. In 2000, Seminis, the world's largest vegetable seed corporation, declared that it planned to eliminate 25 per cent, or 2000, of its varieties as part of its 'global restructuring and optimization plan' (Genotypes: Earmarked for Extinction?). Under this market-driven approach, Seminis prefers plants that are hybrids, because farmers cannot replant them for the next season and must purchase seeds annually (Genotypes: Earmarked for Extinction?). The corporation with power over the seeds can retire certain types without public knowledge or oversight. The same might be done in the future by companies with patents on genes or patents on human embryos with particular genetic traits.

Creating a baby is beginning to resemble buying a car, with consumer choices about which features and extras to request. This may lead to unrealistic expectations of the future child, for example, how will parents feel if they pay for 'smart' sperm, and $E = mc^2$ is not the first thing out of their child's mouth? Already, one couple in the United States sued a sperm bank when the babies were not as handsome as they had expected. *Harnicher* v. *University of Utah Medical Center*, 962 P.2d 67 (Utah, 1998).

Making policy for making babies

The ethical and policy tasks ahead of us are enormous and daunting. We are the generation that will decide whether to embrace or reject these technologies. Will we watch sports played by genetically enhanced athletes? Live among cloned human beings? Mandate prenatal screening as admission standards for birth?

Women's groups have sometimes been reluctant to advocate in favour of regulating reproductive and genetic technologies. They are wary because past regulation of reproduction, such as repressive laws about contraception and legal cases forcing women to undergo certain medical procedures, were based on stereotypes about women and narrow views of women's role in society.

In this regulatory vacuum, though, women and children are being subjected to unnecessary risks. Consequently, Western nations should adopt legislation to

- Assure regulatory oversight of reproductive and genetic technologies.
- Expand protections of human subjects in research so that the federal regulations do not just cover participants in federally funded research, but participants in any research.

Collect more follow-up information about the impacts and risks of genetic and reproductive technologies on women and children.

- Clarify who the legal parents are of children created through assisted reproductive technologies.
- Legally recognise an individual's right to refuse genetic testing in all circumstances (except court-ordered paternity testing or forensic testing).
- Legally recognise an individual's right to control who has access to her genetic information (including a ban on health insurers' and employers' ability to collect genetic information about an individual).
- Ban discrimination based on genetic information about an individual (such as denying a woman insurance because she has a genetic mutation that might indicate a greater likelihood of developing breast cancer).
- Ban doctors' and scientists' commercialisation of individuals' tissue (such as patenting a patient's genes or cell lines).
- Ban species-altering interventions, such as human reproductive cloning and genetic interventions that are inherited by subsequent generations (known as 'genetic germline interventions').

These protections are necessary for the reproductive health of women and the welfare of everyone in Western cultures. And women need to be at the forefront of the societal debate to assure such provisions are enacted.

8
Preimplantation Diagnosis: Problems and Future Perspectives

Aitziber Emaldi Cirión

Introduction

This chapter provides an overview of the practice of preimplantation diagnosis. This practice will be explored in two stages: first, we analyse the ethical–legal problems that might arise as a consequence of the inadequate use of the procedure, such as the potentially eugenic nature of the practice, embryo selection, sex selection and embryo experimentation; and second, we undertake an overview of the existing legislation on preimplantation diagnosis in different European countries.

The practice of preimplantation diagnosis

In this chapter we will focus on *in vitro* fertilisation, rather than other forms of assisted reproduction techniques (ART), as it is this technique which is most often used in conjunction with preimplantation genetic diagnosis. In fact, preimplantation diagnosis is becoming increasingly common and an almost routine aspect of in vitro fertilisation procedures.

In vitro fertilisation is a technique which consists in the fecundation of an oocyte outside the maternal organism. Oocytes are extracted by an ovarian follicular punctation, then inseminated in the laboratory and at this point the preimplantation diagnosis takes place. Preimplantation diagnosis is a form of genetic diagnosis: One or two cells are taken from an embryo produced in the laboratory and genetically tested then, depending on the results, the embryo is destroyed, put into storage or implanted. The aim of preimplantation diagnosis is to ensure that the resulting child does not display a specific genetic deviation. The production of excess embryos, to be either destroyed or used, is necessary element of this technique. In addition, in practice, preimplantation diagnosis has almost always been followed by invasive prenatal diagnosis to confirm the findings.

The technique of preimplantation genetic diagnosis is promoted as increasing women's self-determination. The promise being that using this technology a woman can, and should, plan not only when she wants to have children, but also what kind of children she wants to have. For their part, women often see the techniques as a way of liberating themselves from their 'nature' as their 'destiny' and of taking reproduction into their own hands. The concept of 'female self-determination' has positive associations for most women symbolising the rejection of suppression and external control. However, in the context of genetic engineering and reproductive medicine, self-determination does not imply freedom from external control, but rather, a more thorough-going understanding of the individual as fully independent – independent of physicality, restrictions or needs. As a consequence, 'self-determination' from this perspective equates disability with suffering and dependence, and thus roots the impulse to avoid any form of dependence in the concept of 'self-determination'. Furthermore, in this context of preimplantation diagnosis, such decisions have to be reached individually and on the basis of probabilities.

Problems arising from the use of preimplantation diagnosis

Preimplantation genetic diagnosis has been hailed for its benefits; namely for enabling parents to avoid having children with genetic disorders. However, as well as recognising the positive aspects of this technique we must consider the possible dangers.

Technical problems

Therefore, we will now consider the possible problems arising from the use of preimplantation diagnosis. We will focus on two key issues: first, whether studying just one cell can be considered a good representation of the embryo as a whole, especially given that, embryos may exhibit mutations; and second, whether taking a sample cell for genetic analysis causes lesions to the embryo.

So far, legislation has not considered these problems and has allowed, by omission, preimplantation analysis to proceed with little restriction.

This permissive attitude is probably based on the fact that, so far, babies born after preimplantation diagnosis have been clinically healthy.

Gene Therapy

Preimplantation genetic diagnosis allows us to predict some anomalies or genetic diseases that the embryo could develop. Once a disorder is found – as a future hypothesis – we will be able to determine the correct foetal therapy – genetic or non-genetic – and modify or substitute the detective gene accordingly. There are two types of therapy which can be used affecting either the somatic line or the germinal line.

Therapy performed in the somatic line, only affects the embryo, it does not transmit the modified genetic characteristic to future offspring. Therefore somatic therapy does not affect the genetic diversity of future offspring and more broadly does not impact upon humanity's genetic heritage. Consequently, somatic therapy is acceptable from a juridical point of view, because it is justified as being purely therapeutic.

However, this is not the case when gene therapy is performed in the germinal line, as germ-line gene therapy corrects the cells that transmit genetic data to future generations. Accordingly, germ-line gene therapy raises several issues about evaluation, regulation and responsibility.

Because of these concerns UNESCO's *Universal Declaration of Future Generations* (1994, section 3) stipulated that gene germinal therapy is totally forbidden, as it is not permitted to modify the genome of future generations. Therefore the case of gene germinal therapy provides an exception to the general rule that medical intervention in the genome is allowed for therapeutic purposes, namely, that no, intervention is permitted if it will modify the descendents' genome.

However, this said, there are still exceptions to this exception and in some specific cases the use of germinal therapy would be permitted.

In fact, the *Convention on Human Rights and Biomedicine* (1997, section 13) stipulates that genetic manipulation is only allowed 'when its goal is not to introduce a modification on the offspring' so it permits the germinal therapy with a medical goal. Therefore, if the goal is not to modify the offspring's genome but to avoid a genetic disease in the individual concerned – a therapeutic function – then this therapy is allowed.

Moreover, germinal therapy seems to be permitted if it is done indirectly. For example, somatic line intervention that could have undesired secondary effect on the germinal line is not forbidden by this article.

In conclusion, this article stipulates a general rule: that gene therapy with medical goals is permitted as long as such therapy does not modify the genetic heritage of future generations. However, there are exceptions to this rule, germ-line therapy is allowed in two cases: first, if the goal is not to modify the offspring's genome but to avoid a genetic disease – in other words, for therapeutic reasons – and, second, if modifications to the germ line are secondary effects of genetic intervention in the somatic line. However, despite such exceptions being permitted these exceptions are not always permitted by member states. For example, in Spain, genetic manipulation is a crime in some situations. Indeed, the *Penal Code* (Act no. 15/2003, section 159) considers it illegal to perform a manipulation of the human genes to change the genotype, although only if the author's conduct is guided by a different goal from elimination or reducing disorders or diseases.

Eugenics practices

Preimplantation diagnosis makes it possible to discover not only pathologies and serious genetic disorders, but also sex, as well as less serious disorders and some non-pathological characteristics. Therefore, the information provided by this diagnosis makes it possible to carry out certain selective practices, which could be considered eugenic. Preimplantation genetic diagnosis could be used in two types of potentially eugenic practices: first, for 'negative eugenics' making it possible to discard embryos with a genetic or hereditary disorder; and second, for 'positive eugenics', making it possible to choose those embryos with more desirable characteristics – characteristics which may be based on purely subjective, sociocultural criteria – such as the phenotype characteristics of the child. In order to avoid such uses of this technology there has been a proposal to create a list of diseases or anomalies that justify the use of the preimplantation diagnosis (Jacques Testart, 1994). This would be divided into sections for serious genetic diseases, abnormalities and simple predispositions dependent of various genes.

In Spanish legislation, these diseases are regulated by several articles, particularly the *Act on Assisted Reproduction Techniques* (Act no. 35/1988). This instructed the government to establish, within 6 months after the law was enacted, a list of genetic or hereditary diseases that can be detected by the prenatal diagnosis, and be prevented or treated.

This article makes references to prenatal diagnosis, but after several interpretations of the law, we must define prenatal diagnosis in the wide sense. That is, as diagnosis which takes place during pregnancy and also that takes place prior to the implantation of the embryo in the preimplantation diagnosis. Therefore, the Spanish legislation allows the carrying out of a preimplantation diagnosis, while limiting its use to the diagnosis of certain diseases that appear in a list that will be included in a Royal Decree. Nevertheless, the problem is that the list has not been drafted and the Royal Decree has not been approved. Therefore, preimplantation diagnosis is being carried out always before the transfer of the pre-embryo to the uterus.

Transfering abnormal embryos

When preimplantation diagnosis shows that there are no abnormalities, the embryo will be transferred. However, a dilemma arises when abnormalities are revealed. The question which needs to be addressed is whether or not it is permissible to transfer an embryo with a genetic or chromosome abnormality.

This issue arises when the couple wish to transfer an abnormal embryo. In this case, given that the intention of assisted reproductive techniques is to provide couples with healthy children, it is right to refuse to transfer the embryo. This position is supported from a legal point of view, as the law advises not to transfer abnormal embryos (art. 12.1); even transferring embryos or gametes without minimum biological and viability requirements is sanctioned by the *Law on Assisted Reproductive Techniques* (Act no. 35/1988, section 20.B.i.). To conclude, it is not permitted to transfer an embryo that has serious defects that will prevent normal development to the extent that the embryo is unviable or that it lacks the minimum biological requirements. From a comparative law perspective it is interesting to compare the Spanish law and the German *Embryo Protection Act* (1990). The German law is less permissive and therefore prohibits many actions, for example, it prohibits the transfer of more than three embryos as well as the transfer of foreign ova to the woman, however, it does not address what should be done with abnormal pre-embryos after preimplantation diagnosis.

Sex selection

Preimplantation diagnosis makes it possible to choose the sex of the embryo. From the ethical point of view, there are two main reasons given for why sex selection should not be permitted in general: first, it is claimed that if parents could choose the sex of their offspring the result would be a totally disproportionate distribution of genders in society and second, that sex selection without medical reasons would be positive eugenics – in other words it would be enhancement rather than therapy. Alternatively, there are also reasons to allow sex selection. In particular, it is claimed that allowing sex selection would lead to a decrease in the number of abortions. For sex pre-selection would make abortions for sex-linked disorders unnecessary as well as eradicating the abortions carried out for social reasons; a practice already documented in some countries.

From a juridical point of view, in Spain, the *Act on Assisted Reproduction Techniques* (Act no. 35/1988, sections 13 and 20) stipulates that sex selection is forbidden if it does not have therapeutic goals, or if these goals are not authorised, although, the *Act on the Use of Embryos, Foetus and its Cells* (Act no. 42/1988, section 8), states that the application of genetic technology to sex selection is permitted in diseases related to sex chromosomes.

This position is supported by the *Convention on Human Rights and Biomedicine* (1997) which states that, 'The use of techniques of assisted medicine to procreation for sex selection of the person that is going to be born will not be allowed except in the cases in which it is necessary to avoid a serious hereditary disease related to sex.' Thus, interventions for the purpose of gender selection may only be carried out for therapeutic purposes – to avoid a serious gender-related hereditary disease. However, a few words of clarification are needed as the impression given is that gender selection is not prohibited (Aitziber Emaldi Cirión, 2002) when it is to:

1. Prevent the birth of someone who *will suffer* a serious gender-related disease, for example, those who suffer from dominant chromosome X-related disorders, for instance, hypophosphatemia. In such cases, all the daughters of affected males would suffer the condition, whereas male children would not. Hence, given the possible choice between a healthy male embryo and a sick female one, the former is chosen.

2. Prevent the birth of someone who *will carry* a disease although not actually develop it, for example, those with recessive chromosome X-related diseases characterised mainly by the following specific features: the sons of an affected male will not suffer the condition, but female children will be carriers, for example, Duchenne's Muscular Dystrophy. In this case male and female embryos are healthy, but given that the male will not pass on the disorder, the selection of the male embryo is permissible in order to prevent the birth of a female carrier.

Selection of embryos legislative proposals

At the moment, in Spain, there is a new legislative bill on assisted reproduction that is passing through the stages of parliamentary procedure. The most noteworthy aspect of this text is that it allows the use of the preimplantation diagnosis to select embryos for therapeutical reasons. Thus, when a family has a child with a disease, one will be able to use the techniques of assisted reproduction to assist an existing child. Preimplantation diagnosis will be used to select among the healthy pre-embryos one which is also compatible with the sick child. Thereby, the aforementioned pre-embryo will be transferred to the woman so that a new healthy child is born whose tissue will be used to treat the diseased older child.

Surplus embryos

A further area of contention surrounding *in vitro* fertilisation, is the question of what should be done with surplus embryos.

In Spain, the fate of spare embryos is regulated by the *National Commission on Human Assisted Reproduction* as well as the *Assistance Committee of Science and Technology Ethics*. These bodies have advised the legislator to modify the rules, in order to solve the juridical insecurity and the subsequent problems which have surrounded this issue. This has resulted in a new *Act on Assisted Reproduction Techniques* (Act no. 45/2003). This law addresses the need to reduce the number of spare embryos resulting from *in vitro* fertilisation, as well as the maximum time period allowed for cryoconserving gametes and pre-embryos. As a consequence, the new *Law on Assisted Reproduction Techniques* (Act no. 45/1988) outlines that 'cryoconserved embryo accumulation is not desirable'.

This regulation also established a maximum limit to the number of embryos that can be transferred to a woman in each cycle, in order to reduce the amount of multiple births, and so reduce the risks to both mother and child. Thus, following the recommendations of the *National Commission on Human Assisted Reproduction* and the *Assistance Committee of Science and Technology Ethics*, couples or women will be asked to choose (and give their informed consent) the fate of their cryoconserved pre-embryos. Their choice will be either to keep them cryopreserved until they are transferred, or donate them to other couples with reproductive goals.

Again we can compare the laws of Spain to those of the Federal Republic of Germany. In this instance, we find that these questions regarding surplus embryos do not arise for the simple reason that German *Embryo Protection Act* (1990) does not allow spare embryos to be created.

Research and experimentation with human embryos

The *Convention of Human Rights and Biomedicine* (1997, section 18) is open in this matter and allows national legislators to enact laws about research and experimentation with human embryos in the manner they see fit.

In Spain, the law states in a precise and exact manner the conditions of research in order to protect the embryo and to ensure that arbitrary and inappropriate research is not permitted. The purposes for which experimentation and research on embryos is permitted are expressly stated (Act no. 35/1998, sections 14, 15 and 16), as are the necessary requirements for research projects. The most significant requirements are that: first, the embryos must be non-viable; second, research must occur within 14 days; third, only certain centres and qualified teams are permitted to undertake such research and fourth, it must be scientifically verified that the research is necessary and cannot be carried out using animals.

The use of surplus embryos created before 2003 and the interest in embryo research is increasing, especially given the advances in Stem Cell technologies. The first discoveries in this field are creating great expectations in biomedicine and pharmacological research, as well as in its therapeutic power to treat serious diseases that are now incurable. For this reason the Royal Decree 2132/2004 of 29 October has just been enacted. This decree establishes the prerequisites and procedures for soliciting surplus embryos for Stem Cell research. It is noteworthy that the surplus embryos created after the *Act Amending Act 35/1988 on Artificial Reproduction Techniques* (Act no. 45/2003) cannot be used in research and can only be used in reproduction.

Legitimatising preimplantation diagnosis in comparative law

Our discussion has shown that the abuse, or inadequate use of, preimplantation diagnosis generates serious ethical and juridical problems. Furthermore, as some national legislations do not have laws to ensure embryo protection, preimplantation diagnosis has been used as an excuse to practice other eugenic practices. In some countries the fear of the negative use of preimplantation diagnosis, has led to calls for the prohibition of these techniques. Therefore, we will now consider the conditions and requirements that such countries have enacted in order to regulate preimplantation genetic diagnosis, including those of France, Germany, Italy and the United Kingdom.

First we will consider the situation in France, a country which has decided to permit embryo research after much debate. The *French National Advisory Committee of Ethics*, adopted an unfavourable position towards the use of preimplantation diagnosis arguing that the methods were not reliable, and moreover that the physical and psychological problems caused by the interruption of pregnancy were simply being substituted by physical and psychological problems at the preimplantation stage. Therefore, the Committee recommended that because of these ethical considerations preimplantation diagnosis should not be permitted. During the parliamentary debate the Senate followed this recommendation and voted for the prohibition of preimplantation diagnosis. However, in the final text of the Law, preimplantation genetic diagnosis is permitted under very strict conditions. Therefore, at the moment, in France, the biological diagnosis from extracted cells of the embryo *in vitro* is permitted in exceptional circumstances and according to the following requirements: medical indications; indications by a doctor; the couple's written consent; therapeutic purposes and only in authorised establishments. In other words only in exceptional circumstances are a couple offered this procedure, basically in order to avoid the birth of a child with very serious deficiencies.

Recently a new 'Law on Bioethics', has been introduced (2004). This legislation is similar to the past legislation, in relation to preimplantation diagnosis, only permitting the procedure when all of the requirements have been fulfilled.

Second, if we consider the case of Germany we find that the *Embryo Protection Act* (1990) is similarly strict with regard to preimplantation genetic diagnosis. Preimplantation genetic diagnosis is not (yet) permitted in Germany, yet it does offer the possibility of embryo selection and potentially therapeutic applications going beyond the diagnosis of serious hereditary diseases. Experience in other countries shows that it is already being used to chose the sex of a child for social reasons, to increase the *in vitro* fertilisation success rate and to select a suitable embryo as a future organ donor. These are all applications which, according to the Draft Guidelines of the *German Medical Association* are explicitly ruled out. Such prohibition is based on the fear that the use of preimplantation genetic diagnosis could foster eugenic tendencies and a social climate that is hostile towards the disabled, or that preimplantation diagnosis could be used as a key technology for more far-reaching goals, such as interventions in the germline or the cloning of human beings.

In Germany, many are calling for preimplantation diagnosis to be legal and therefore the social debate about the ethical and social consequences is still in progress. The *German Medical Association* recommends that the procedure be allowed for couples at high genetic risk. However, as international practice has already shown, the method also permits expansion of the user group beyond 'high-risk couples'. For example, by selecting the best embryos, scientists hope to increase the success rates of *in vitro* fertilisation for 'older' women. Furthermore, as a result of preimplantation diagnosis, a child's sex and, in future, even its genetic susceptibility to diseases of civilisation, such as cancer and cardiovascular disease, could also become criteria for a selection process. All of which suggests that once permitted the uses of preimplantation diagnosis are likely to increase.

The third country we will consider is Italy which has recently passed a controversial *Act Amending Act 35/1988 on Artificial Reproduction Techniques* (Act no. 45/2003). The most significant articles in this Law are the following: the use of donor gametes and surrogate motherhood have been forbidden; fertilisation techniques are only avaliable for heterosexual partners and finally, preimplantation diagnosis is only permitted for therapeutic and diagnostic purposes. The law also seems to express more draconian elements of Catholic ideology.

Turning fourth to the United Kingdom, we find in *Human Fertilisation and Embriology Act* (1990) that a licence is required to make use of an embryo. Therefore, as preimplantation genetic diagnosis uses an embryo, it is subject to this regulatory framework 'practices designed to secure that embryos are in a suitable condition to be placed in a woman or to determine whether embryos are suitable for that purpose'. It is clear from Parliamentary proceedings that this provision was intended to allow preimplantation diagnosis to be licensed by the Authority for the detection of abnormality. The Authority's own view is that it actually has the power to licence preimplantation diagnosis use for any purpose.

Final remarks

In conclusion, I would argue that the Spanish law offers the most preferable solution to the regulation of preimplantation diagnosis. Preimplantation genetic diagnosis has several benefits, above all for couples that may transmit to their offspring some abnormality and therefore should be permitted in at least some cases. Forbidding preimplantation diagnosis would mean denying many couples who suffer from genetic disorders the opportunity to have children. Preimplantation diagnosis provides such couples with the best means to have healthy children. For this reason legislators should allow its use, yet, at the same time controls need to be established in order to avoid abusive uses of this technology.

That is, it is necessary to limit the practice and forbid its negative consequences.

Finally, I wish to conclude this chapter with a little reflection from the feminist standpoint. Proponents of preimplantation genetic diagnosis demand its introduction in the name of all women. So why are women, resisting the introduction of preimplantation diagnosis? In the women's movement, reproductive medicine and human genetics have been viewed very critically since the 1980s. Women have always fought against the instrumentalisation of women's needs for the interests of research. The desire to have children has always been viewed in its overall social context and critically analysed. Although preimplantation diagnosis would increase the alternatives available to women in reference to reproduction decisions in some cases, it would also establish social pressure to use the technology, which would force women to face new decisional conflicts. Restricting the argument to the level of personal needs conceals the social consequences of this technology.

9
The Impact of New Reproductive Technologies on Concepts of Genetic Relatedness and Non-relatedness

Heather Widdows

This chapter will consider the impact of New Reproductive Technologies (NRTs) on concepts of genetic relatedness and the significance of such concepts for women's rights. NRTs have been praised for increasing reproductive autonomy – allowing women greater control over the timing of their children as well as the 'type' of children they choose to carry. However, before embracing NRTs and advocating that access to them should be a 'reproductive right' it must be asked whether increased access to NRTs is wholly positive for women. This chapter will explore one aspect of the issue, asking whether NRTs reinforce the importance of genetic relatedness and if they do, what this means for women. In particular, it will ask whether an increased emphasis upon genetic relatedness is compatible with supporting social rather than biological relationships and denying an essentialist view of women – women as biological mother – a central position of the women's movement.

This chapter will explore the hypothesis that NRTs support and promote concepts of genetic relatedness – for both couples considering their reproductive choices and in reinforcing wider societal presumptions. By examining this issue it will speak to the broader debate on how women and relationships are (and can be) conceptualised, and thus, in turn, contribute to the debate on whether access to NRTs should be a reproductive right.[1] In assessing this claim this chapter will explore the hypothesis with relation to a number of NRTs: first, *in vitro* fertilisation (IVF); and second, third-party NRTs, particularly, donor insemination (DI) and embryo donation.[2]

Social versus biological relatedness

The issue of genetic relatedness is of import for the debate on reproductive rights because, if NRTs do promote genetic relatedness then for women to claim access to NRTs as reproductive rights conflicts with other core beliefs of the women's movement. For women's rights movements (and particularly, second wave feminism) have championed the recognition of social relationships as of equal (and at times more) importance to genetic relationships – regarding the social parents who provide for and care for the child as the 'real parents' not the biological parents. A view of relationships which is implied by the rejection of essentialist concepts of women: summed up in the denial of a biological understanding of women as 'baby-maker' and the corresponding implication that women can only be 'complete' and 'fulfilled' if they experience genetic or biological motherhood. Therefore to argue for the 'right' to NRTs, implying (and sometimes overtly on the grounds of) the previously rejected essentialism of the necessity of motherhood – and biological motherhood at that – to the experience of womanhood directly challenges the emphasis on social relationships and the denial of essentialism.

Over the last half century, kinship relationships have been changing across Europe. The so-called 'traditional' model of family life in which there are two heterosexual, married parents genetically related to their offspring is declining. As divorce rates increase and alternative 'non-traditional' relationships become ever more prominent, the model in which children live in a nuclear family with their married genetically related parents is less common. Stepfamilies and single parent families account for a large minority of parenting models and childrearing situations. Such a decline in traditional models of genetically related nuclear families would seem to mitigate against the prominence of genetic relatedness and in favour of more complex social models of parenting; a model in which the social role of parent – those who have the day-to-day responsibility for raising the children – is more important than the genetic fact of parenthood. The argument for increased emphasis on social parenting is said to be supported by the increased openness in the process of adoption. It is now the norm for parents to be open about the child's adoptive status, in comparison to 50 years ago. However, these trends towards openness in adoption and towards the importance of social parenting in general are challenged by the increasing use of NRTs and forms of assisted reproduction (AR).[3]

To assert that these practices support and promote genetic relatedness is not an uncontroversial position. Indeed, the opposite position has been argued, namely, that NRTs do not support the traditional family, but encourage more fluid family models. For example, in the case of DI enabling single and lesbian women to conceive without sexual intercourse with a man and reducing men to the role of 'donor' rather than 'father'.[4] However, across Europe, with some exceptions, NRTs have tended to be limited (in law and even more so in practice) to heterosexual, often married couples (Dooley *et al.*, 2002) – again suggesting support for the traditional family. Yet, even if it is the case that NRTs do produce non-traditional models of the family (and clearly in this regard it is possible that they could), the questions of whether the families created are traditional or whether such technologies affirm and reinforce the importance of genetic relatedness, while connected, can be differentiated. For the purposes of this investigation the key question about the importance of genetic relatedness and the implication of female essentialism (equating full womanhood with mother) remains, and it is this aspect of the debate – about whether NRTs support and promote genetic relatedness – which is the primary concern of this chapter. In order to explore this issue IVF and third-party donor practices will be discussed in turn. Finally, and in light of the preceding discussion about conceptions of women, the conclusion will again return to the question of whether access to NRTs should be claimed as a reproductive right. It will conclude NRTs are double-edged, having the potential to both liberate and enslave, and that both potentialities should be considered in the widest possible context before advocating access to NRTs as a reproductive right.

In vitro fertilisation

First then, is the contention that the practice of IVF undoubtedly supports the claim that NRTs support and promote the importance of genetic relatedness. This is shown by the fact that despite high costs and risks and a low success rate IVF is the first choice of most infertile couples – chosen above adoption and other forms of NRTs – and a choice of which society approves. IVF tends to be perceived (by both users of the technology and the wider public) in a surprisingly benign manner. It is regarded as a relatively commonplace medical treatment for infertility and 'public *expectations* and professional *perceptions* concerning the management of infertility have been transformed since the introduction of IVF' (Price, 1999, p. 32). IVF is generally seen as a positive option for those who are struggling to conceive and the risks and traumas associated with it are largely ignored. This benign picture of IVF, as a technological handmaiden for couples wishing to have 'their own' children, has hidden the risks and burdens of IVF.

The risks of IVF are not insubstantial: there are physical risks to the mother, coupled with psychological difficulties for the mother and the father, as well as ongoing financial pressures. Physically, the process of IVF is traumatic and demanding. Women undergo at best uncomfortable and at worst, potentially dangerous, processes of hormone therapy, follicle stimulation and egg harvesting. Moreover, the psychological stress that both women and partners are subject to in the process of ongoing IVF treatments is considerable; stress that is added to with every failed cycle of treatment (Ryan, 2001). The physical and psychological pressures are compounded by a significant financial burden: A cycle of IVF costs around £3000–4000. For many couples meeting the cost of the treatment means saving every available penny and a severe reduction in quality of life. For example, one couple spent £60,000 on consecutive IVF treatments. They did eventually conceive and have twins; however, for the duration of the treatment they were unable to go on holiday, make repairs and improvements to their home and move house, all of which they report they would have done if they had not had to pay for treatment (MacCallum, 2004).[5] In addition to the risks to the woman there are also risks to the child, risks derived from the likelihood of multiple gestations. The frequency of multiple pregnancies since the introduction of fertility drugs in the 1960s and IVF in the 1970s is marked, and by the 1980s the rate of multiple births had more than tripled as a direct result of fertility treatments (Hammon, 1998). As Mary Mahowald notes 'with each order of multiples, risks to both the fetus and pregnant women escalate' (Mahowald, 2002). The risks for the child include not only increased risks in pregnancy and birth (such as respiratory distress and haemorrhage), but also long-term risks and disadvantages associated with premature births (Olivennes *et al.*, 2002; Vayena and Rowe, 2002). In order to avoid multiple pregnancies the number of embryos that are allowed to be implanted has gradually declined; UK guidelines stipulate that the number of embryos that can be implanted in women under 40 years of age is two. While this reduces the risk to the future child and to women in pregnancy, it also, arguably, reduces the likelihood of a successful implantation and birth.

Given the risks associated with IVF and its relatively low success rate (22% of all cycles, HFEA), the willingness of couples to undergo this procedure and the general acceptance of IVF suggests that for many having a genetically related child is of supreme importance.[6] The possibility of success, however small, is felt to be so valuable that the risks – which would normally mitigate against such medical practices – are outweighed by the benefits to parents and to society of genetic benign perception of IVF held by the public (in contrast to other NRT procedures) and the continuing willingness of couples to undergo this treatment attests to the perceived importance of genetic relatedness and against the importance of social parenting. The couple who reproduce using IVF will be the social parents as well as genetic parents, yet the wish to be genetically related to their offspring seems paramount, especially given the comparative risks and costs of other treatments. Therefore, taken together, it would seem fair to conclude that the not insubstantial risks of IVF, and the disappointments attached to the low success rate, are outweighed by the benefit to parents and to the society of genetic and gestational parenthood. Thus, IVF clearly and unequivocally, supports and reinforces the underlying assumption that genetic relatedness is of supreme importance and value.

Third-party NRTs: DI and embryo donation

Having asserted that IVF does indeed support the importance of genetic relationships the question of the importance of genetic relatedness in the practices of the third-party NRTs of DI and embryo donation will now be considered.

Donor insemination, is rather inaccurately called a NRT, as it reputedly began as a medical practice in 1884 when the doctor responsible was suspected of using his own semen to impregnate his many patients (Daniels and Haimes, 1998). In DI, conception is a product of donor sperm and the woman's own egg; therefore, unlike IVF there is no genetic relationship with the 'father'. The 'father' of the child in DI is the husband or partner of the mother and not the donor. In embryo donation (first reported in 1983 [Buster *et al.*, 1983]) neither parent is genetically related to their future offspring. Both gametes are from donors; either embryos are created for donation using both donor eggs and sperm, or they are 'spare embryos' donated by couples who have undergone IVF (Kingsberg *et al.*, 1996).

At first glance it seems bizarre to suggest that these practices could possibly support the claim that NRTs reinforce the importance of genetic relatedness given that in both procedures at least one parent is not genetically related to the future offspring (in DI only the mother is genetically related and in embryo donation neither parents are genetically related – although in both cases there is a gestational relationship[7]). However, although there is no actual genetic relationship in either case, in both cases there is the 'appearance' of genetic relatedness. In other

words the parents can present the pregnancy, birth and future childrearing *as if* there was a genetic relationship between the parents and the
child. Thus, if it indeed is the case that it is important to couples that
they appear genetically related to their child – rather than supporting an
increasing acceptance of non-genetic relatedness (as one might intuitively
expect as the popularity of third-party NRTs increases) – third-party
NRTs might actually indicate the importance of genetic relatedness; for
both couples using the procedures and reinforcing wider social presumptions. Thus, the appearance of genetic relatedness may support
social expectations and norms of parenthood conceived primarily as a
biological relationship (and again by extension reinforce the view of
women as biological mothers) rather than promote the non-genetic relationships of which these relationships are actual rather than apparent
instances.

Gestational relatedness

Before discussing apparent genetic relatedness the suggestion that it is
gestational relatedness that these couples seek must be addressed.
Certainly, for some gestational relatedness is indeed of fundamental
importance than the genetic link: 'for some, the inability to gestate and
give birth represents a greater loss than the inability to have a child
whose genetic complement comprises 50% of their own genes'
(Mahowald, 2000, p. 129).[8] Those who feel this way argue that the
experience of gestation is emotionally important as it allows the woman
to feel that the child is 'hers', and the experience of gestation appears to
strengthen the mother's perception of self as mother. The gestational
link is purported to enhance the relationship between the parents and
the child, because the child 'benefits from the additional bond of being
gestated in its future mother's womb, with the support of its future
father' (Eisenberg and Schenker, 1998).[9] Given this testimony it would
appear that the gestational relationship is indeed important (and
perhaps even more important) for a significant number of couples and
particularly mothers. Yet, it is not clear that those who prise the gestational relationship do not also prise the genetic (or apparent genetic)
relationship. Moreover, if the gestational relationship was of primary
importance, one would expect more couples to choose – especially given
the substantial difference in cost – third-party NRTs in preference to IVF.
Therefore, while it could be accepted that the gestational relationship is
significant (and for some couples the most significant relationship in
the reproductive process and therefore a reason for choosing NRTs over

adoption), it can still be asserted that for many (indeed perhaps for most) couples genetic relatedness – or apparent genetic relatedness – is of fundamental importance.

Apparent genetic relatedness

The question then is why would one claim that practices which rely on third-party gametes and do not produce genetically related children support and promote concepts of genetic relatedness? In DI, the mother is genetically related to the child and the father is not. This would imply that either the genetic link to one parent is felt to be significant (a genetic link to one parent is better than to none) or that genetic relatedness is less important than was concluded from the discussion of IVF, so disproving the initial hypothesis of this chapter. This would seem to be even more the case in embryo donation where there is no genetic link to either parent. As these forms of NRT do not result in genetically related offspring and in light of the claims for the importance of the gestational link, at this point it would seem that the hypothesis (that genetic relatedness is reinforced by NRTs) is false. However, not only must the actual genetic links which are created using third-party NRTs be taken into account, but the perceived genetic links they make possible. Significantly, DI and embryo donation allow the parents to preserve the illusion of genetic relatedness and it is this mirage of genetic relatedness which supports the argument that genetic rather than social parenting is being endorsed by third-party NRTs.

Both embryo donation and DI make it possible for couples to present themselves as genetically related to the child if they choose to keep the means of conception secret. This appearance of genetic relatedness seems to be significant for at least some couples who prize the gestational relationship not for itself, but rather because it allows them to experience pregnancy, birth and childrearing *as if* they had conceived 'naturally'. The similarity to 'normal' genetically related families is used as a reason by some parents to keep the means of conception secret. The fact that the couple are not genetically related seems to be almost forgotten by the parents in their pretence of genetic relatedness to the child.[10] For example, one husband said that, 'at the end of the day it's us that's gone through it all, M's gone through the pregnancy, M's given birth to them, we've brought them up, you know, so it's not an issue that's important really' (MacCallum, 2004). This position could be read in two ways. On the one hand, the father's assertion that genetically relatedness is unimportant in comparison with the pregnancy, birth and upbringing of the child would seem to suggest that here the genetic link is actually less significant: which, as was noted, would be the logical conclusion in DI and embryo donation as there is no, or only one, genetic link to the child. On the other hand, his claim that the genetic link is unimportant, is used as a reason for not disclosing the means of conception and the lack of actual genetic link between himself and his children. This suggests that, despite his assertion, he does think that genetic relatedness (or the lack of it) is important, as it is information that he wishes to suppress. The conclusion would seem to be that it is important for him not only to be the social father (from conception onwards), but also for his child (and others) to assume that he is the genetic father. Much has been written about secrecy and NRTs, particularly in connection to DI, and this issue must now be considered, however, the focus will remain firmly on the question at hand – whether or not third-party NRTs support the increasing importance of genetic relatedness.

Third-party NRTs and secrecy

The wish to appear genetically related and the corresponding secrecy surrounding the practices of DI and embryo donation mitigate the obvious conclusion that genetic relatedness is less important than the experience of parenting (including the pregnancy). In fact the opposite position could be argued, namely, that genetic relatedness is so important that couples wish to maintain the appearance of genetic relatedness where there is no genetic link, even though this involves secrecy, non-disclosure and arguably lying to the child as well as to other family members and friends (or requiring friends and family members to lie to the child). This tendency towards secrecy in third-party NRTs is in contrast to the increasing openness in adoption, where in the last half century parents have been encouraged to be open, in general, and particularly to the child. This move to openness in adoption is premised on the belief that openness is in the best interest of the child and enhances the quality of family relationships. If this premise is true in adoption the question is why is it not also true in the NRT practices of DI and embryo donation?

Reasons for the continued practices of secrecy in DI and embryo donation in contrast to the openness in adoption have been attributed to the differences between the two practices (Widdows and MacCallum, 2002). While it is not possible to address this issue in detail, it is worth briefly listing the five main differences.

The first reason is a practical one, that, for NRT parents, unlike adoptive parents, it is physically possible to hide the means of conception, as pregnancy and birth is the same for NRT parents as it is for 'normal' parents.[11] Second, the legal status of NRT-created children and adoptive children is different. The NRT mother (and her husband if she is married) is the legal parent of the child, whereas, in adoption, parental rights and responsibilities are transferred after birth. A third reason, is that the two practices have different historical roots. Adoption is a social practice which is regulated socially, whereas NRTs are considered to be medical procedures and regulated accordingly.[12] A fourth difference concerns the 'intentionality' of the parents. The child born using NRTs comes into being because of the wishes of the parents (without this intent the child would not exist), whereas in adoption the parents have a similar intent to parent, but their desire does not cause the specific child to come into existence. A fifth reason, and connected, is that the adoptive child has needs that the NRT child does not, namely, the adopted child has a 'history of rejection' to resolve. The argument here is that adopted children need to understand their history and therefore have a greater need to know their origins, in order to reconcile themselves with their 'rejection'. A parallel argument has also been made about NRT children, that 'children created by embryo adoption may see themselves as "spare" or "surplus" goods and may indeed have the same need for information – for access to their story – as other adoptees, even though they have not been abandoned at birth' (Bernstein *et al.*, 1996). However, such a comparison seems extreme – placing a child for adoption can hardly be said to equate to donating an embryo.

From this brief discussion it is clear that there are significant differences between NRTs and adoption. However, the question is whether these differences are enough to justify the disparity in practice; openness in adoption and secrecy in NRTs. This extreme contrast in practice does not appear to be justified by the evidence. While clearly there are differences between the practices, they are not enough to account for why it is in the best interests of the child and the family to be open in adoption and not in NRTs. Openness in adoption is based on the presumption that the child benefits from understanding his or her past and significantly the family benefits from openness and truth and would suffer from secrecy. Clearly, these assumptions about the best interests of the child and the family have been rejected (or ignored) by NRT families and in fact secrecy has been encouraged. To understand some of the reasons for this the practices of secrecy in NRTs must be explored in a little more detail.

There is much literature on why secrecy has been part of the structure of NRTs (Nachtigall, 1993). Not only has the means of conception been kept secret, but also secrecy has been implied by the use of anonymous donors. The use of anonymous donors was so ingrained in the practice of DI that it was termed the 'self-evident principle of DI' (Bateman Novaes, 1998, p. 119). However, in recent years this assumption has been questioned and in some places overturned. Sweden was the first country to make donors identifiable in 1985, followed by Austria in 1992, in the UK donors who registered after 1 April 2005 are required to provide identifying information which is available to the donor conceived children at the age of 18 on request to the HFEA. In these countries the previous assumption that donors would no longer be willing to donate if they were identified proved unfounded (Edvinsson *et al.*, 1990, and Hagenfeldt, 1990 cited by Daniels and Lalos, 1995). In fact, donor numbers increased, helped by public campaigns and a general removal of DI from the closet of secrecy (Daniels and Lalos, 1995). This gradual and still early move towards identifiable donors suggests a move to openness, since, there is no point having identifiable donors if parents do not tell the child that they were conceived using NRTs. Even in Sweden, where the law changed first, as of 2000 only 11 per cent of parents had actually told their children that they were conceived using donor gametes. An additional related reason which is suggested for parents non-disclosure to the child is that it protects the 'father' from the stigma of male infertility (Klock *et al.*, 1994; Lasker, 1998; Nachtigall *et al.*, 1997). However, although this argument may have some validity for DI – as DI challenges the presumption that infertility rests with women (Lasker, 1998; Spallone, 1989) – it does not explain why rates for openness in egg donation (female infertility) are comparable to rates in DI, nor why in embryo donation (where both or neither party is implicated in the infertility) levels of disclosure (and intended disclosure) are at their lowest. Therefore, although it is clear that there may be other reasons for secrecy, they do not seem to be sufficient to account for why secrecy and not openness is the norm in NRT conception and not in adoption: donor numbers do not decline when donation is not identifiable, and secrecy is not only practiced to protect male infertility as it is practiced in the practices of egg donation and embryo donation also. Thus again one returns to the hidden reason, to the hypothesis of this chapter, that what is important for couples is genetic relatedness and if actual genetic relatedness is unattainable then couples will settle for the appearance of genetic relatedness.[13]

The increasing importance of genetic relatedness

Therefore, having considered both IVF and other third-party forms of NRT it seems at least possible to argue that NRTs do indeed reinforce the importance of genetic relatedness; in the wish of IVF couples to have a genetically related child and in the tendency of third-party NRT couples to pretend to genetic relation. This said, and although genetic relatedness (or its appearance) is clearly important for many, this is not universally the case. Some couples who find that they cannot conceive naturally do still choose to adopt and there are cases where couples do not choose IVF, but DI or other forms of third-party NRT (although often because they are so much cheaper) (MacCallum, 2004). So while it would be wrong to conclude that genetic relatedness is the only factor in parents decisions, it clearly is an important factor and one that is reinforced by the increased use of NRTs making actual genetic relatedness (IVF) and apparent genetic relatedness (third-party NRTs) possible for couples who, in another era, would have been forced to adopt and to overtly endorse social relationships as primary parenting relations.

Having recognised that NRTs do indeed support the importance of genetic relatedness, it must also be considered whether – if the argument of this chapter is correct – that as genetic relatedness becomes increasingly important, practices of secrecy in third-party NRTs will change. As preventative genetic testing becomes more prevalent, as well as genetic susceptibility diagnoses, arguably those who do not have access to their genetic history will be increasingly disadvantaged. Indeed it is this pre-sumption – that knowing one's genetic heritage is fundamental – which lies behind the recent move from anonymous to identifiable donors. However, although apparent genetic relatedness may cease to be accept-able and openness become the norm, such moves will do nothing to reduce the social importance of genetic relatedness. Indeed such reason-ing – shown, for example, in the move to identifiable donors – does not support social parenting (by encouraging openness regarding non-genetic relatedness of third-party NRT parents for the reasons that it is the social and not the genetic relationship that is fundamental – as is the claim in adoption) but actually asserts the importance of true (rather than apparent) genetic relatedness.

This conclusion – that knowledge of true genetic relatedness is ever more important – may be illustrated by the fact that NRT parents report in increasing numbers that they 'intend' to be open with their children (for some reason this is reported only in DI and egg donation parents and not embryo donation parents) (Golombok *et al.*, 2004). As has been discussed, only a small number of DI parents have yet told their offspring about their genetic origins (approximately 10% in the United Kingdom). However, in a recent study, the figures of those intending to tell their children has risen to 46 per cent in the case of DI and 56 per cent in the case of egg donation. Past experience may make us doubt whether or not these parents will eventually tell their children about their genetic origins, as often even those who intend to tell their children do not do so, yet the change in intention may prove significant. Yet, even if parents do tell their reasons for doing so it may be as much as a result of society's increasing respect for genetic relatedness as increased openness to social relatedness. It remains to be seen whether such openness (if it occurs) will support the social model of parenting and the acceptance of non-genetically related families, or will further entrench the view that genetic relatedness is the proper model of parenting.

Implications for women's reproductive rights

In this chapter, the manner in which NRTs impact on concepts of genetic relatedness, has been examined in detail, with mixed results. Certainly, IVF reveals and reinforces the importance of genetic relatedness: couples are willing to go through physically and psychologically traumatic processes and to commit themselves to huge economic burdens (bearing in mind that a IVF cycle costs around ten times the price of a DI cycle) in order to achieve their goal of a genetic-related child. Whether third-party NRTs are also testimony to the importance of genetic relatedness is less clear, as the evidence could be used to support different arguments. However, this said, it does seem that the secrecy surrounding third-party procedures, which has caused so much debate, is at least in part attributable to the wish to appear genetically related: attesting to the hypothesis that NRTs support and promote genetic relatedness. Whether this is going to continue to be the case if identifiable donors become the norm remains open to question, however, as suggested above, increased openness does not necessarily point to a recognition of gestational and social relationships, it could also point to the opposite – to the importance of genetic relatedness in the genetic age.

If it is the case that NRTs are further ingraining the importance of genetic relatedness in the contemporary context, then, whether access to NRTs should be striven for as a reproductive right is something that women's rights activists should question. The trauma involved in undergoing NRT treatment is considerable, and should not be taken lightly. Moreover, the importance of genetic relatedness undermines both the non-traditional social structures that have been important to the feminist cause, and re-emphasises the biological role of women as genetic mother and the essentialist view of women. As Dolores Dooley notes, a feminist concern is that 'techniques such as in-vitro fertilisation coexist with a powerful ideology of motherhood as a biological imperative rather than a social relationship' (Dooley *et al.*, 2002, p. 153). Given this, those who wish to assert and work for women's rights should carefully consider whether access to NRTs is really something that benefits and liberates women, or whether it is further entrenching a view of women as a biological/genetic 'baby maker'. At the very least NRTs should be viewed as having both liberating and enslaving potential before asserting access to NRTs as a reproductive right. In addition, the implications of such a right should be considered in the wider social and political context, not just on an individual case by case basis, but as such practices that affect concepts, assumptions and worldviews and so impact upon all women.

Notes

Thanks must go to those who provided useful comments and criticisms of this paper both at the NEWR workshop and also at the International Congress of Bioethics, Sydney, 2004.

1 Bearing in mind that the aim of this chapter is not to answer this final question of whether NRTs should or should not be claimed as a reproductive right, but rather to suggest that there are considerations which the women's movement should take into account and reflect upon before claiming such a reproductive right.

2 There are questions of whether DI is accurately called an NRT – given that it 'is *not* a cure for infertility ... . The woman on whom donor insemination is practiced is ordinarily in perfect reproductive health' (Wikler, 1995, p. 48). In addition to the questions raised in this chapter these reproductive technologies raise many other ethical issues – not least the issue of secrecy which I have explored elsewhere (Widdows, 2002) – however, here I am not commenting on the ethics of these practices in general or specifically but focusing upon the ideological impact of the increased prominence and use of such practices might have on our conceptions and expectations of women and of family relationships. The issues of secrecy will be touched upon later in this chapter, but not in terms of its rightness or wrongness, but rather in order to discover what secrecy reveals about the importance of genetic relatedness.

3 Currently it is suggested that 1 per cent of births in Western societies are attributable to NRTs. It is estimated that by 2010 there will have been around 45,000 births using DI (Blyth, 1988) and current estimates suggest that there have been around 3000 births from egg donation and that there are around 50 births a year from embryo donation (HFEA, informal).

4 Daniel Wikler discusses this issue and notes that while DI is often seen as supporting the 'traditional family' as it 'puts the marital relationship back on track and permits the husband and wife to form a "complete" family unit' (Wikler, 1995, p. 48) it can also be used by single women and lesbians to create non-traditional families, with or without the assistance of medical profession (Wikler, 1995).

5 As noted in the introduction of this volume the prohibitive costs of NRTs limits access to such technologies to the relatively wealthy and indeed it is the injustice of this that has influenced those who call for access to NRTs to be considered a reproductive right. However, for the purposes of this chapter the economic issues will be left aside.

6 Other forms of NRT are much cheaper, for example, DI costs around £300–400 per cycle, with additional costs for ensuring the same donor in any further treatment.

7 The argument that the gestational relationship is important could be applied to IVF, for example, if it were compared to adoption, but as those couples who undergo IVF reject the far cheaper option of DI, it has been assumed that for these couples having 'their own' child – and thus the genetic relationship – is primary. The potential importance of the gestational relationship will be discussed later in the chapter.

8 Similar findings were also reported by J. G. Thornton *et al.*, in the *Journal of Medical Ethics* in 1994.

9 This view is echoed by the comments of a mother who had had two children conceived using donor gametes (in this case embryo donation): 'that's what is so nice about (embryo donation) because you actually go through the pregnancy and give birth, it's your child. I mean, I'm sure people who adopt children feel the same eventually [...] but when you actually give birth, I'm sure there is a stronger initial bond' (MacCallum, 2004).

10 The issue of whether 'non-disclosure' to the child is significant and thus can be considered 'pretence' I have addressed elsewhere (Widdows, 2002).

11 It is of course true that it is far easier to conceal NRT conception than adoption. However, it is not impossible to hide adoption and historically speaking this was not uncommon; adoptive mothers returning from trips abroad with their 'new baby'.

12 For example, the difference in the selection criteria for potential parents of adoption and embryo donation is stark. One procedure is intense, time-consuming and focusing on the social ability of potential couples to be parents and the other essentially concerned only with medial criteria; how likely is it for the woman to conceive (Widdows and MacCallum, 2002).

13 Other reasons which have been given for secrecy, particularly historically, are the stigmas of masturbation and adultery, which are directly or indirectly implied in DI (Pfeffer, 1993). However, although such reasons continue to carry weight in certain groups they cannot be regarded as major factors in favour of secrecy in contemporary Western societies.

Part III

Into the Future: Projections for Reproductive Rights

10
Reproductive Rights in the Twenty-First Century

Hille Haker

In the twentieth century, women's rights more than ever before emerged as a factor on political agendas. Whereas in the first half of the century they were claimed for the most part by the Women's Rights Movement, since the 1970s, the concept of reproductive rights has become one of the background motives for the development of birth control measures and, later, for artificial reproductive technologies (ART).

In this article, I will first look at the history of reproductive rights from an ethical perspective, and then, in the second part, reflect upon the impact of this history for the present debates and the future tasks of the women's rights movement. I am particularly interested in the connection of individual rights and the analysis of social structures, as they have been presented in so-called post-structural thinking. Furthermore, the turn from a right-based ethics to an ethics of responsibility might reveal the need to develop new concepts of parenthood, which meet the standard of moral autonomy and likewise are sensitive to the newer development of biomedicine. My argument rests on the conviction that biomedical practices can only be liberating for women if social and ethical concepts do not treat them as the objects and clients/consumers of technology but also as subjects who determine the ways in which the social practices entailing certain biomedical techniques are understood and conceptualised.

The legacy of the struggle for reproductive rights in the twentieth century

Access to contraceptives, the abortion issue and the notion of reproductive autonomy

Reproductive rights always have been, and still are, one of the most important issues for different kinds and phases of women's movements.

These movements claim that family planning, with respect to the timing and number of children a woman wants to have, should – at least finally – be the woman's decision and not the decision of her husband alone, nor of other family members, religious authorities or the state. Reproductive autonomy as a political slogan in the context of planned motherhood can be described as a negative right, in this case the right to non-violation of female bodily integrity, and the right to non-interference in a woman's way of living.

Reproductive rights and reproductive freedom, however, are not synonyms for liberty in the sense of mere individual autonomy, as this concept is represented in bioethical reasoning. With the rise of feminist bioethical reflection, these concepts based the freedom to make decisions on relational autonomy, combining experiences and structures of relating to and caring for the other with autonomy (Sherwin, 1998). The reference to experiences of care-relations is certainly not arbitrary: In most societies we know, women have a greater share of practising care; in the majority of cases, women rear their children or the children of others; they look after the elderly and other persons dependent on assistance. Many of them, being paid or not, are working in the social field – they know the efforts, strain, and also the value, of this caring work.[1] Most women involved in the women's movement never had any doubt about the connection of liberty and responsibility. Unquestionably they had accepted the latter for a long time, and now claimed respect, social recognition and political and social rights, respectively. The desire to self-determination, therefore, was never conceptualised as an arbitrary desire; it was not formulated apart from the context of female every day work but rather concerned with women's capacity and power, with the autonomy to decide these affairs for themselves.

Stating that women have moral reproductive rights and calling for them to become recognised as legal rights in all countries, has a political as much as an ethical side: politically, it asserts the right to autonomy; ethically it implies that every woman who claims to have reproductive rights makes a claim to be considered as moral agent – and, as such, be accountable for the reproductive decisions she makes. Following this argument, every woman has a moral right to decide according to her moral convictions, whether she opts to become pregnant or not. When being pregnant, she must decide whether to give birth to a child or to terminate the pregnancy, for whatever reasons she herself finds morally acceptable.[2]

As far as this argument rests upon modern ethical reasoning, arising from both Kantian and Utilitarian traditions, women should not have had a problem gaining support for their position and struggle within the ethical community. Ethical opposition was, however, raised especially by religious leaders, above all by the Catholic and other Christian churches who grounded their objections either in an anti-modern, neo-scholastic foundation of natural law theory interpreting the hierarchy of goods as a matter of 'objective truth', or their reservations stemmed from the faith-based assumption of the sanctity of life. Neglecting the necessity of balancing conflicting rights, a reductive interpretation of the concept of human dignity was applied, resulting in the denial of dilemmatic judgements.[3]

Another criticism of the women's rights approach stems from the critique of using human rights as a foundation of ethics: Regarding human rights as a Western articulation of 'identity politics', concealing their indifference against cultural diversity and moral pluralism. With regard to this criticism of ethics, the notion of women's rights (and children's rights, respectively) faces the same problem of justification as non-feminist approaches.[4]

On the political level, however, opposition to women's rights and especially reproductive rights has another focus. Here, the prejudices of 'mainstream' policies, cultural paternalistic contexts and shortage of money for culture-sensitive educational programs or contraceptives, and a general negligence of women's health issues have proved to be obstacles in the women's movement's struggle for social and political rights.

Assisted reproduction for unintended childless couples

With the introduction and implementation of assisted reproduction, women's rights became an important focus within bioethical reflection. In ethical debates of the 1970s and 1980s on reproductive medicine, the 'natural striving' of women to give birth to children was presupposed in many debates about *in vitro* fertilisation, and the metaphor of 'giving nature a helping hand' became a rhetorical phrase of self-understanding for physicians who conceived of themselves as assisting women (and only secondly men) to fulfill their natural destination, namely, to be a parent (Franklin, 1997). Quite obviously, the women's movement and the physicians or medical ethicists were talking about different matters, although ecofeminism and some feminist approaches to bioethics at the same time emphasized the role of mothering, care and relational autonomy over and against a justice-based, contractual concept of autonomy, which was considered 'male' and not applicable in cases of asymmetrical relations (Gilligan, 1993; Noddings, 2003).[5] The danger of this emphasis became obvious when Carol Gilligan's and other 'care-ethics-approaches' were criticised for endorsing an 'essentialist' understanding of femininity and masculinity, and when what was called the essentialism of many presuppositions of reproductive medicine became more and more apparent. Several feminists criticised ART as being one more means to keep women in their social roles as mothers and, moreover, as an excuse to misuse women's bodies in order to experiment with human reproduction, without considering the potential side effects these experiments could have on women and offspring alike. On the other hand, the early period of the women's rights movement, especially in countries with a strong liberal tradition and with loose legal regulations, strongly endorsed reproductive medicine as a right of women to their autonomy. These feminists saw modern reproductive technologies as a useful tool to achieve the overall goal of women's liberation and autonomy.[6] Nevertheless, there is a striking difference in feminist approaches to reproductive rights and other 'liberal' concepts that presuppose individual autonomy rather than seeing it as a goal to be aimed at by way of technological progress. It still could be argued that to leave the decision-making for IVF/ICSI to women and not to regulate it by criminal law (as, for example, is the case in Germany) was an act of empowering women and thus part of the struggle for political autonomy as a negative right. On the other hand, however, ART is dependent on financial, medical and sometimes psychological support that societies pay for, either directly or indirectly, and therefore the question of the status of the 'right' as negative or positive has to be clarified.[7] If taken as negative right, ART clearly favours well-off couples; however, in cases of public funding and access to ART, just distribution of health care goods becomes an obvious and more and more urgent problem. Liberal approaches tried to respond to the situation with the justice-based claim to 'equal access', but this claim certainly requires putting reproductive technologies in relation to basic health care goods.[8] No exhaustive answer to this question has been found yet, but it seems clear that for the last few years the focus of the debate is shifting from individual ethics, emphasising the principle of autonomy, to social ethics, which concerns issues of political and social justice.

Prenatal diagnosis and preimplantation genetic diagnosis

When genetic diagnosis was implemented on a larger scale in the same period as assisted reproduction in the 1980s and 1990s, the problem of autonomy and reproductive rights shifted from the discussion about the right to procreation to the debate on the right to a healthy child.

Whereas prenatal diagnosis initially was introduced to avoid births of offspring with a high risk of 'serious hereditary diseases', at least in Western societies, it soon became a common component of pregnancy monitoring. In other countries – the most quoted being India and China – the risk of poverty or state policies of birth control resulted in sex selection via prenatal diagnosis, so tolerating the vast majority of couples' 'choice' of male children. The difference between medically indicated interventions and 'private', voluntary selection was thereby blurred.[9]

With the introduction of Preimplantion Genetic Diagnosis (PGD) in the early 1990s, a next step was reached. Intended firstly to raise the success rate of assisted reproduction, it soon became the focus of a new way of family planning, based on the goal to prevent offspring with certain genetic risk, implementing pre-pregnancy and prenatal predictive tests, such as Cystic Fibrosis tests, but including also tests for late onset diseases, as Alzheimer's or Parkinson's.[10] But here, the well-known side effects of *in vitro* fertilisation and its risks for women, especially hyperstimulation with serious health-related consequences, had to be weighed against the interests of couples to exclude the risk for their child. As so often in new technologies, one step forced another, and so PGD could not only be used for a medically indicated 'negative' selection, but also for medical or non-medical measures of 'positive selection'. Many regarded this as decisive step to an enhancement technology, enforcing the concept of conditioned parenthood.[11] Furthermore, sex selection for social reasons or as method of sex balancing is becoming another incidence of family planning and considered by some as part of the right to reproductive autonomy (Ethics Committee of the American Society of Reproductive Medicine, 2004a, 2004b; Tizzard, 2004; Watt, 2004). Others, however, see this as surrender of 'classical' medicine to market-based medical services, aimed to fulfil the desires of 'consumers' instead of meeting the health needs of 'patients' (Watt, 2004).

This development has had the effect of several rifts in women's reproductive rights movements: For example, ethnic and cultural diversity with regard to reproduction, the notion of global health care and its priorities; the prospect in the Western world of an all-embracing monitoring of pregnancy; the proliferation of predictive tests and the threat of no insurance if certain tests are not performed (or, seen from the perspective of physicians: not offered); second and third trimester abortions; health risks for women and children caused by IVF and/or ICSI; sex selection by reason of a gender bias; and family balancing programs. These are only the most mentioned problems, and there is no consensus on any of these issues within the women's movement or feminist (bio-)ethics.

Although it is argued that the political right of autonomy might still be achieved by leaving the choice for the above-mentioned services to the women, this position suppresses the social and medical contexts of the new reproductive technologies on a large scale.[12] Feminist bioethicists, in particular, are now faced with the critique initially levelled at mainstream bioethics: namely, that they ignore social and political constraints of reproductive and genetic technologies and endorse the traditional modern liberal theory of the self, indistinguishable from its 'male' counterpart. The critique of care-ethical approaches against this approach found in early feminist ethics and in the renewal of this critique of unjustified one-sidedness in ethical concepts based on critical theory (Benhabib, 1992), or in feminist philosophy and history of sciences (Haraway, 1991; Kay, 2000) has still not been adequately addressed in feminist liberal bioethics. Nor has the Foucaultian analysis of the new technologies as biopower, that is, as an instrument of disciplining members of societies by making them compliant to bio-political measures, been thoroughly used in bioethics.[13]

Embryonic stem cell research

In the last decade, another major step has taken place with the new possibilities of regenerative medicine. Embryos have become a promising resource for research purposes aside from assisted reproduction; the context in which it was originally permitted in several countries in order to improve this technique. For the time being, embryonic stem cells return us to a conception of women as donors (or sellers) of egg cells, and of couples as donors of surplus embryos. With this shift, not only the commodification of the human body has been taken a step further, but also embryo research has been separated from the context of parenthood.

Ethical analysis and future perspectives

Setting the agenda for the twenty-first century

What can be seen by this historical detour, which I stressed in order to see more clearly where we have come from with respect to reproductive rights, is the tension running right through the different concepts of biomedical, bioethical and feminist reasoning on reproductive technologies and rights. Several ethical concepts are based on women's rights but disagree regarding their liberal foundations and their implications; others are more critical of the whole enterprise of the sovereign agent presupposed in human rights reasoning, and hence question the liberal basis of women's rights. Thus, they accuse the proponents of 'individual autonomy' of naiveté, of underestimating the social construction their concepts are based upon, of uncritically endorsing mainstream biopower policies, which, in fact, should be regarded as much more hostile to women than the liberal image of political autonomy appears. The ambivalence of the political and social rights, and moreover, of negative and positive rights, is to be seen against this background. This becomes even more apparent when the global health needs of women are estimated in comparison with the struggle for political rights for ART and genetic diagnosis in the developed countries.[14]

In the following, I will approach the notion of reproductive rights from the perspective of social ethics, and then suggest a new framework for parental responsibility that should serve as normative perspective for the struggle for reproductive rights and the social practice of reproductive medicine, respectively.

The social–ethical approach

Considered from a social–ethical perspective, the notion of reproductive rights must be seen against the background of several societal developments and changes in love relationships, family structures and parenthood over the last 50 years and more. Furthermore, the differences between societies and cultures are not only relevant in socio-historical analysis but also in ethical reflection. In the following, I will write from my own Western (European) perspective without claiming that my argument will have the same relevance to those of other backgrounds.

In Western societies, technological and biomedical progress over the past 50 years has been accompanied by social changes in family structures, parent–child relations and health-care systems. The two 'revolutions' in reproduction, namely, the development of biochemical measures of birth control and the success of assisted reproduction, are part of – and sometimes the motor of – rather radical changes with respect to the concept of parenthood. As social and historical studies have shown (Ariès, 1996; Beck-Gernsheim, 1995, 2002; Duden, 1991, 1993; Giddens, 1992), kinship and parenthood have shifted from a common naturalistic understanding to private choices; not only have partnership and love-relations become more and more reflective or, as Giddens holds, matters of discourse, but so too has the parent–child relation. Whereas birth control resulted in a considerable drop in the number of births per woman, assisted procreation encompasses the distinction between genetic, biological and social parents and questions the traditional, biological concept of parenthood, while at the same time maintaining the latter by responding to the assumed (female) desire to become pregnant and actually give birth to a child (as against adoption or other options of infertile couples). This inherent tension in the concept of reproductive technology results in an ambiguity of the practices. Hence, on the one hand ART endorses the social understanding of parenthood as chosen partnership in asymmetrical relations; on the other hand, however, physicians were (at least in the first two decades of assisted reproduction) reluctant to acknowledge this social trend they were enforcing, and strongly supported regulations concerning access, mostly similar to national adoption laws and practices. But given the different focus of adoption services (to promote an existing child's well being) and ART (to promote a couple's desire for a future child) reproduction clinics soon began to broaden the scope of their potential addressees. Thus, ART became a promoter of social changes by following a market model of medical services.

By the beginning of the 1990s, the question of 'responsible parenthood' in this area was more and more left to the clients themselves – the medical professionals did not wish to intervene in the 'private' sphere of family planning, the legal support for regulation and restriction gradually weakened throughout Europe, and social and political discourse was mainly left to national ethics committees and to academic ethical reflection. Whereas in Western societies a grim debate began over homosexuals' right to adopt children – often misusing the best-interest-standard of the child as a shield against the changes of social norms, homosexual or single person parenthood was *de facto* established in the (in many countries unregulated) field of assisted reproduction.

Certainly, one of the main issues of the (Western) women's movement was to disturb the social construction of a natural desire for motherhood (de Beauvoir), but one cannot ignore that a traditional understanding of motherhood (only secondly fatherhood) is not only a strong motivating factor for couples who seek assisted reproduction but that it is also supported by physicians. Apart from the essentialist position of declaring motherhood to be a *natural* telos of women, procreation cannot be considered as positive right: To claim this would contradict a non-essentialist understanding of women's lives. Even if taken as strong value, feminist ethics must acknowledge, I hold, that this value cannot be translated into a positive right, but rather must be linked to the functions and general features of the quality of life, even if these features are open to interpretation and will differ from individual to individual, and from culture to culture (Gewirth, 1996; Nussbaum, 2000). Given the scarcity of resources and insufficient services in many areas of health care, and particularly women's health care, assisted reproduction might not be one of the highest priorities of women's struggle for reproductive rights. This is even more the case, once the global health care situation, especially of women, is taken into account.

Genetic Diagnosis changed the concept of parenthood, too, as it has impacted upon social dynamics. As women became more independent of their spouses, became more educated and at least partly gained access to well-paid positions in society, deliberate family planning resulted in either a reluctance to have children at all, or it considerably delayed the decision to set up a family. In this situation it is not surprising that pre-natal diagnosis was welcomed by women who feared to endanger their professional career and the independence they, as the first or second generation of 'liberated' women in Western society, had only just gained: contrary to male liberals, feminist liberals argued from this background of well-known dependence and the experience of liberating themselves from it. The growing societal toleration of terminations of pregnancies made it easy to accept not only the legitimacy of terminations for medical reasons, but also of a certain obligation towards a future child. The additional burden on women who have to go into labour in the second or at the beginning of the third trimester of pregnancy and deliver a (dead) child became obvious only later (Stoller, 1996 forthcoming). These circumstances received little attention in bioethical reflection until PGD was promoted in the 1990s, when physicians and bioethicists began to emphasise the negative side effects of late abortions in contrast to selection before pregnancy.

Artificial Reproductive Technologies and prenatal diagnosis provided the first occasion, as I have suggested, to question the concept of positive reproductive rights: Was the *desire* for a child to be interpreted as a *right*? And, with regard to prenatal diagnosis, was the desire for a healthy child to be interpreted as a right to a healthy child?

Bioethics was soon caught in the pitfalls of a much broader discourse on the concept of family and parental responsibility, and particularly utili-tarians or consequentialists (but also religious authorities supervising marriages) asserted the parental responsibility or duty to prevent the birth of children with genetic risks. Translated into practical terms, couples were to understand their new 'responsibility' in terms of pre-pregnancy tests (enforced, for example, by the Cyprus orthodox Christian church and endorsed by several Jewish communities in order to prevent mar-riages between high risk groups), or in terms of terminating pregnancies with genetic or chromosomal disorders, such as Down Syndrome – a non-lethal chromosomal disorder with wide ranges of phenotype expression and strongly related to the age of the woman at conception.

Pre-implantation Genetic Diagnosis certainly gave one more techno-logical answer to the ongoing social debate on reproductive rights and duties, favouring the preventive model of parental responsibility. The medical context was, however, soon transcended when not only med-ically indicated sex selection but also sex selection for social reasons, such as family balancing, was included in the objectives of PGD. PGD, therefore, served the widespread social understanding of reflective parenthood, based on the notion of individual autonomy or choice and the non-interference of a third party into the private sphere, as it represented the moral obligation to prevent 'disabled' children from coming into existence. Bioethicists, in the name of the well-known con-cept of choice and right to non-intervention, soon started to call for the toleration of social selection (Ethical Perspectives, 2003).

At least two social–ethical factors are suppressed in the notion of individual autonomy, which underpins the bioethical concept of 'choice', as it is promoted the libertarian approach to reproductive and genetic technologies: first, the social pressure on women or couples to actually carry out prenatal diagnosis (PND), assisted reproduction or PGD in order to live up to their own wishes and/or the expectation of others on them to have a 'healthy' child is underestimated, as are the social restraints on women's striving towards independence and/or their claim to combine a professional career and parenthood; Foucault's social analysis of 'biopower' gives vast examples of how social pressure in modern societies is transformed from an external force to internal self-discipline, with the result that social norms function as imperatives not to be questioned. What has been called 'voluntary compulsion' with respect to PND, must be of interest to feminist ethical reflection sensi-tive to the critique of social norms and power relations affecting women both in their bodily integrity and autonomy. It is no accident that while historical studies draw attention to the beginning of the eugenics move-ment in the late nineteenth and early twentieth centuries, bioethicists distance modern practices from eugenics and assume that the criticism is referring to the Nazi escalation of eugenics, especially to Hitler's agita-tion against disabled, poor and socially deprived persons and families between 1920 and the early 1930s, later resulting in the horrific euthanasia program against disabled children and adults (Klee, 1999; Weingart *et al.*, 1986). While it is totally understandable that one would wish to distance oneself from the *Nazi* eugenics, however, the problem for ethics lies in the similarity and continuity of current concepts to the *earlier* European and Northern American understanding of eugenics, unrelated still to 'euthanasia' and relying as much on the concept of moral 'responsibility' of individuals as their present counterparts.[15] Individual choice and social norms are interrelated and for this reason feminist ethics must be critical of unquestioned social practices, while at the same time not diverting from the concept of individual autonomy.

Second, the normative concept of parenthood must indeed be reconsidered if it is to be applicable to the new challenges of social and technological changes, respectively. Reproductive medicine endorses a concept of parenthood that is sufficient for the libertarian autonomy model of individual choice, but insufficient for an autonomy concept based on relationality and moral responsibility, as elaborated by Onora O'Neill on a Kantian basis. The question then is whether this concept is applicable to the new forms of parenthood. I assume that the tension between these two understandings of autonomy will haunt the discussion about reproductive rights in the next few decades.

The moral concept of parenthood

Autonomy not only refers to a self-determined life involving no – violent – interference by another person or institution, but also to the concept of moral responsibility.

This concept is a valuable tool to emphasise the complementary concepts of the 'good life', on the one hand, and normativity, on the other. For moral autonomy connects the responsibility to lead one's own life with the responsibility to take into consideration the goals, needs, interests and rights of others. Thus, responsibility does not contradict freedom, but rather is the moral approach to freedom: Freedom without the concept of responsibility is merely egoism and responsibility without freedom is force.

Considered from the perspective of feminist ethics, reflection upon reproductive technology must include the question of how a person can act not only in a free but also in a responsible way, taking into account those who are affected by the consequences of one's actions. In striving for a 'good life', moral agents will ask which goals and which ways of life will be appropriate to and in correspondence with their own self-identity; with their moral convictions and with the ideals they subscribe to. In subscribing to moral agency, however, they will *at the same time* seek to act according to the mutual respect morality is based upon.

The desire for a child is one of the goals, which can be – but is not necessarily – part of a person's identity. Many of the aspects which have been discussed in the feminist discussion of motherhood and female identity, *can* be interpreted as the search for a pluralistic and tolerant model to empower women to live a life they choose for themselves. This liberal presupposition of feminist ethics, based on the concept of negative freedom and the right to autonomy, must not be undermined. The *value* of procreation can be regarded as a negative moral right: Nobody may interfere with the desire for a child, because interference would only be possible by means of violence or coercion. However, when transferred to the area of assisted procreation and genetic diagnosis, this respect for the other's choices cannot be interpreted as a positive right to be supported in procreation, because, as I argued previously, it cannot be upheld, unless one takes an 'essentialist' perspective that sees childlessness as derivative form of life or even as a illness.[16]

With respect to the new preventive approach to parenthood, the notion of a right to a healthy child is based both on the 'choice' model of family planning and on a general judgement about humans' 'quality of life'. Some ethicists have argued that a certain borderline of the future child's life quality and life expectancy must not be crossed lest the concept of responsibility and (societal) solidarity is ridiculed. Others have gone further and claimed future children's right not to live in cases of (severe) disorders. The quality of life-argument can be seen either from the parents' perspective or from the child's perspective, and it is certainly true that at least viability should play a central role in questions of embryo transfer.[17] Here, I am only concerned with the notion of parenthood. The future child's right to health becomes a problematic claim, I hold, if the right to life is undermined by judgements about the health status usually only based on probabilistic genetic data; but this will not be my focus in this article.[18]

Responsibility in asymmetrical relations

The concept of rights and obligations is usually spelled out with view on symmetrical constellations, with asymmetrical relations considered to be morally derivative from these. However, Hans Jonas, in his ethics of responsibility, contested this view, arguing that parenthood is the preliminary model of responsibility (Jonas, 1984). In the same line of argument, Emmanuel Levinas strongly promoted an understanding of moral agency and responsibility different from that usually claimed in the discipline of ethics, stressing the moral asymmetry in the relation between the self and the other. Both philosophers agree that the other (to use Levinas' phenomenological language) puts a certain strain on the (moral) self in demanding a response to his or her quest. In assisted reproduction, the embryo is, however, rarely considered to be an 'other' in the sense of another person, for this would require a parent-like perspective that biomedicine more and more has given up.[19] Instead, the embryo is defined in biological terms, with little reference to the social and philosophical concepts of personhood and parenthood. What impact would it have, however, to situate the question of the right or responsibility towards the embryo within the concept of parenthood, rather than in the concept of personhood?

First, it is quite evident that parental responsibility in the era of ART and genetic diagnosis starts earlier than with pregnancy. In the case of assisted procreation, it starts with medical treatment of the woman's body. Already in this phase, the 'future child' is envisioned – as is also the case in the imagination of any planned pregnancy. Following this line of prospective parental perception, which is strongly entangled with aesthetic and ethical imagination, regarding an embryo as a (possible) future child, would replace (or at least complement) the biomedical perspective, and construct the treatment of different types of intervention within the framework of parental responsibility rather than freedom of research or medical progress.

Traditionally, parenthood is indeed defined with reference to the concept of responsibility, and consideration of *actual* parenthood is indeed constructive for either pre-pregnancy or prenatal *prospective* parenthood: The specific asymmetry of the parent–child constellation places the child in a situation of exorbitant dependency on his or her parents. Parents have an almost unlimited power over the lives of their children, no matter how much they love them. Psychoanalysis and post-structural reasoning have shed light on the process of subjectivation, a process that cannot only be described as the psychic development of a self to autonomy and sovereignty, but that must also be seen in light of the subjectivation to the other and social norms mediated by the other, preliminary to the parents (Haker, 2005 forthcoming; Butler, 1997, 2003). The analysis of power is transformed into an ethical understanding, however, if not only the sovereign agent is reflected upon, but moreover, the agent who is – and remains – exposed to the other, and is urged to respond to the other *responsibly*: As Levinas has shown so eloquently, in this responsible response, which constitutes the self as moral self, the power relation between the self and the other is turned upside down, and the asymmetry caused by power is transformed into a specific moral asymmetry that cannot be described in terms of contractualism or mere reciprocity (Haker, 2005 forthcoming). Similarly, one may hold that in addressing the parents and showing the need to be cared for, the child is indeed urging the parents to respond responsibly; in their moral perspective, parents are indeed *free* to respond or refrain from it, but at the same time this freedom is entangled with the (moral) necessity to respond. The self's negative freedom is surely limited by the encounter with the other, though in the case of a newborn child this is far from being an encounter with a person in the strict sense.

Parents – perhaps more than any other persons in different relations and constellations – are irreplaceable in their role, though replaceable as individuals, and there is vast historical evidence that biological kinship-relation is not a necessary condition for the child's well being, but yet, the concept of parenthood is indispensable in its function for the child, changing only over the years, with the child's physical and psychic development.[20] The moral claim to feed the child, to teach it whatever it needs to barely or socially survive, to care for its well being – this is not articulated sufficiently in the language of mutual rights and justice demanding to give the other his or her 'share' of life. In this respect, care ethics was and is correct that much more, namely love, time and reliability is needed, and Onora O'Neill is right in claiming that parenthood in this respect is unconditioned (O'Neill, 2000). The empirical question whether individual parents actually meet these demands to be responsible, is not so much of theoretical but all the more of practical relevance; and societies have developed means to ensure that the rights of children are met (e.g. the UN declaration of children's rights). What has to be clarified in the coming decades is whether the new technologies do not force us to extend this concept, rather than constricting it to the traditional borderline of birth. To me, this appears either misogynic (the child must be perceivable by the public eye (Habermas, 2003)) or obsolete in view of the new visualisation of the foetus *in vivo*. In the new era of biomedicine and biotechnology, women (and men) must redefine their roles with respect to reproduction and parenthood, not only in assisted reproduction or genetic diagnosis but also with respect to their potential donation of egg-cells or (frozen) embryos, either for other couples or research projects.

The normative question today, then, is whether the recognition of an embryo on the condition of his or her assumed health, his or her sex or other features that couples might seek, affects the concept of responsibility in parenthood. I am not questioning the love parents feel towards their daughters and sons, no matter how they came into existence. I am more concerned about the effects on the concept of parenthood itself. Regarding these effects, there is some evidence in the decline of social tolerance towards children with genetic health risks or disabilities. On the reflective level, there is a growing influence of the prevention model in biomedical ethics, opposite to a model of individual and societal care and solidarity for those children (and families) who in fact have a positive right to different kinds of medical, educational and professional services (Kittay, 1999). The liberal model of non-interference, well intended to broaden the couples' choices, might in fact rather reduce their options, if it becomes more and more unacceptable to give birth to a child that does not meet the health conditions couples, physicians and the society behind them consider necessary in order to 'deserve' respect. Here again, the social ethical perspective emphasising the interdependence of individual and social norms should prevent feminist ethics from being naïve and uncritical.

When medically assisted abortion became a political issue once again in the 1970s, it clearly was part of the social movement of women's liberation. For several decades, the debate has been construed polemically as conflict of the women's right to autonomy and the embryo's/foetus' right to life. Feminist ethicists became trapped in this discussion, since it seemed that they could not uphold the right to abortion without questioning the right to life of an embryo. This position conflicted with and over against those who claimed the hierarchy of rights must be consistent as it contradicted the hierarchy, placing autonomy over life. Accordingly some simply did not acknowledge a right to life on the side of embryos or foetuses, while others argued for the acknowledgement of a moral dilemma (and not just a conflict), with two equal rights and obligations, respectively.

Following this line of argumentation, it seems already misogynic to state the conflict in the narrow terms of 'autonomy' versus 'life'; since it ignores and undermines the fact that women act as *moral* agents, seeking to act responsible towards themselves *and* their future child. Furthermore, it condemns the moral specificity of pregnancy, which can be described as the woman's *absolute* irreplaceable responsibility for the embryo/foetus. In comparison to decisions about pregnancy, which only women can make, in case of the *in vitro* embryo, the situation is less clear and the absolute irreplaceability of the woman is not yet established. Regarding the massive biomedical intervention, it is evident that an individual or couple, the physicians and biologists, and societies behind them *share* the responsibility for the human being they are 'creating'. Even though the debate on the status of the embryo has endorsed a reductive perspective isolating the embryo from the specific context of agency, especially biologists' or physicians' detached analysis of embryos *in vitro* should not too easily be compared with pregnancy. Scientists – especially those who are endorsing embryo research and embryonic stem cell research – have argued that it is exactly for the reason that pregnancy has not started the concept of parenthood is inappropriate and should be replaced by the biologist concept of 'living material'. Embryos, they claim, do not show any relevant feature of personhood, and therefore should not be considered as persons. But this construction again is a pitfall that must and can be avoided. For it leaves the parental perspective behind, rests upon the embryo only, regardless of the relation prospective parents might have towards him or her (embryos are engendered, as sex selection should make clear). Even those parents who permit using their surplus embryos for research purposes, once considered them as their possible children and not *only* as cells that could also originate from other animals than the human being. Are they wrong?

Seen in this light, the precedence of the scientific construction of the embryo in the ethical discussion is rather an expropriation of prospective parents than an enforcement of their autonomy. ART, if not handled very sensitively, can become one more instrument of reducing the concept of humanness and humanity to an inappropriate biologistic concept. Feminist ethics, being aware of the new challenges for the concept of parenthood, but also being aware of the ongoing history of violations of women's rights in different contexts, should be on the watch for disempowering tendencies arising from the new reproductive and genetic technologies, and embryo research, such as stem cell research (Haker, 2005 forthcoming; Schneider, 2003).

But what would it mean to (re-)claim the relational understanding of embryos *in vitro* and prospective parents? First, it would (re-)connect the embryo to the concept of parenthood, and second, it would encourage further reflection on this concept under the new conditions of ART and genetic diagnosis, questioning what was merely presupposed in the hitherto discussions, namely that the preventive model of parenthood equals the concept of responsibility.

With reference to the notion of responsibility, it might be instructive, furthermore, to stress the connection between the (dominantly Western) perspective on reproductive and predictive technologies and the international agenda of women's rights: *all* parents are responsible for their (present and future) children, and all societies must ensure that they are capable of living up to these responsibilities. As we know well, in many contexts societies do not fulfil their obligations to support parents in being able to take care of children, be it in providing health services, education, or even food or clean water. Millions of parents, but in particular mothers, are left alone in their struggle to provide children with their most basic needs, and lack a basic life quality of their own.

The future of feminist reproductive ethics and reproduction rights

The desire for a child makes women vulnerable, since it may be (and socially still is) tightly connected to their identity as women. In the context of clinical biomedicine, infertility is viewed as technical problem, which can be repaired by a highly sophisticated medical procedure. Even if women are asked for their consent to all kinds of biomedical procedures, it is obvious that there is a technological 'slippery slope', especially when alternatives are rarely discussed. *In vitro* research on embryos changes the traditionally necessary connection of an embryo and a woman (and a man or a biological or social prospective parent, respectively) into a contingent relation. With the new developments of non-reproductive cloning, therapeutic cloning and the development of embryonic stem cells, women are made to play a specific role as 'donors'/ 'sellers' of ova that are 'harvested' from their body after hormone stimulation, or as 'donors'/ 'sellers' of foetal cells. The rhetoric of encouraging, particularly, the altruistic collaboration of *women* with research and science is complemented by the rhetoric of property rights and commercialisation, when women (and couples) are considered the 'owners' of surplus embryos after *in vitro* fertilisation procedures (Dickenson, 2002). What we can see today, is another shift within the reflective concept of parenthood, dividing the child's existence between being the object of property in the prenatal phase, and being a person with own rights after birth.[21] Moral respect towards children is only a recent normative claim, resulting in the political UN *Declaration of Children's Rights* only in the 1990s. Claiming that children should not be deprived of their basic rights, namely to live, to be fed, to be subject of health-care services, to be educated and more, among other things means that the debate on the adequate protection of the embryo must be put in perspective.

Concluding my socio-historical remarks and situating the social—ethical and normative reflection within the tradition of feminist ethical thinking, I would like to enumerate what I sense are the tasks of the coming years and perhaps decades.

1. Gender as a (socially constructed but yet effective) category of and within technology must be acknowledged and reflected upon; this is partly the disciplinary task of philosophy and history of science, but it is also a task of ethics in the sciences, aimed at overcoming unquestioned mythologies of technology and developing tools to improve the situation of those who need improvement most.

2. Reproductive ethics will and must be refocused on the global struggle for basic health care, especially with view on the outraging lapses in genomic research relating to the most common infectious diseases causing the death of innumerable men, women and children in developing countries (World Health Organisation, 1992). This struggle will and must emphasise the need to de-marginalise minority groups (ethnic minorities, low income families, and also persons with genetic risks).

3. Feminist ethics must criticise the ongoing and increasing commercialisation of the (female) body and the subjection of women's 'autonomous' compliance to the rules of the biomedical market.

4. The perception of pregnancy monitoring as means of preventive measures and the misogynic and discriminative concept of responsible parenthood as obligation to prevent the birth of children with health risks must be rejected.

5. The struggle for women's reproductive autonomy must continue and put in a global perspective but distinguished from non-moral concepts of mere self-determination: Women are moral agents who claim all political and social rights, basic health care, information and education on birth control and health-related practices, and generally equal rights to their well-being and freedom.

6. Within Europe, the role of the different religions and churches will and must be more thoroughly analysed with regard to their attitude towards women's (reproductive) rights. In the coming years, the relation of state policies and religion will be an important issue concerning the cultural side of the unification process. Feminist theory as well as feminist ethics should strive to take part in this assumedly explosive discourse.

7. The concept of reproduction and the moral concept of parenthood in the era of assisted reproduction, genetic diagnosis and regenerative medicine must be further reflected upon. Social constraints, however, must not be forgotten in this discussion that is mainly taken up by bioethics: The changes in family structures call for a new understanding, including the organisation of family work and professional careers for both sexes; new models of fatherhood must be developed and encouraged; changes of social images of sex and gender must be acknowledged and endorsed. Finally, the conflict between the prevention model and the non-discrimination model has not been adequately discussed within feminist ethics itself. Against the scientific, economic and bioethical isolation and abstraction of the human embryo from the context of parenthood, the moral understanding of

parenthood as responsibility in an asymmetrical constellation and parenthood must be (re-)applied and further developed.

Notes

1   In the context of globalisation, this has become a problem in itself, as women migrate from underdeveloped countries leaving their families and even children to work in developed countries. This kind of trafficking has become a serious concern for the international social order and has been labelled 'care-drain'; with allusion to the often stated 'brain-drain' of highly educated professionals from developing countries to developed countries.

2   Without reference to the moral autonomy of the moral agent, no deontological moral theory is acceptable. The normativity of a moral claim must be integrated with the practical identity of the agent to be more than an extrinsic imperative. The tension between the normative claim and the desire of the agent is constitutive for moral identity itself. A deep insight into the ethical violence as part of the tension of 'norm' and 'desire' is found in Butler (2003).

3   The Catholic position on reproductive interventions is a mixture of the natural law tradition, as referred to in the two principles of justice and charity, and the doctrine of the sanctity of life. However, the scholastic tradition is only partially received in contemporary Magisterial writings: while the normative approach is open to different medium principles in the application of the principles of morality, especially represented in the medium principle of equity (epikeia), that is, the recognition and acknowledgement of contextual circumstances as necessary part of moral judgements, the value for life is rather an evaluative perspective orientating the application of the principles. As such, it is an expression of faith, too. What many critics, for example, P. Singer, R. Dworkin or John Harris, do not acknowledge, however, is that there was and is much discussion and critique of the hierarchical ethical assumptions *within* theological/religious ethics. Theological or religious ethics, especially stemming from the Catholic tradition, thus often is identified with the Magisterial position, and its writings taken as scientific argumentations which are not their paramount intention. Although religious *feminist* ethicists share the frustration the women's movement experienced especially in discussions with Vatican leaders over the last decades, their scholarly contributions are as much ignored within the church as well as within the ethical community.

4   For a response to the critique of human rights see Nussbaum (2000).

5   See R. Tong for an overview of feminist approaches to bioethics (Tong, 1997).

6   For a comparison of the Anglo-American and the German discussion see Hoffmann (1999); see also, out of the many collections, Purdy (1996).

7   Some might argue that the same reasoning applies in the case of right to terminate pregnancy. To some extent, this is true, since feminists fought especially for the medical service. Medical support can be argued for, if conceived of as a service in a severe situation of conflict. Again, the blurring of the concept of autonomy as the individual's freedom and the moral autonomy concept might explain many of the ethical problems accompanying the problem of abortion.

8   ART may become part of the public health-care system in some countries, while other health-care services are not sufficiently funded or implemented as, for example, is the case in Cameroon. I am grateful to a student in a recently held bioethics class quoting the case of his country.

9   Even in cases of medical selection, it can be argued that the difference between medical intervention and a new kind of privatised, voluntary eugenics is blurred.

10 The shift from using genetics for infertile couples to fertile couples was not difficult, since several genetic dispositions are accompanied with subfertility.

11 This term reflects the initial attitude towards the features of the selected embryos. It is not meant as contempt of parents who certainly will (or will not) love their child as 'unconditioned' as much as any other parents do (or do not). However, selection and choice between different embryos before implantation is to be interpreted as part of a development in reproductive technology, which functions more and more according to the rules of perfection or 'matching' with external purposes, such as the desire to give birth to a child as donor for an elder sibling.

12 For example, see the different works of I. de Beaufort who strongly endorses the notion of individual autonomy.

13 An exception in this regard is a recent issue of the *Journal of Medical Humanities* (2003).

14 However, it would be erroneous to assume there are no major concerns in developed countries, too. The example of the United States of America may suffice: here, more than 40 million people have no health insurance. Given that poverty hits women and children more often and usually harder than men, this grievance is as important as the consideration of developing countries having introduced ART and genetic technologies in the private health sector.

15 Again, the problem I am concerned with here is not the individual decision of couples but the theoretical framework of reasoning within which their decision-making is taking place. The prevention model is such a framework that is only rarely been contested in 'mainstream' bioethics.

16 Certainly, it has been argued that infertility is not just childlessness but undesired childlessness, and can be interpreted as illness. This is true to a certain point, but I would still argue that societal and public health-care support for assisted procreation can only be subjected to societal priorities of public health-care services.

17 Preimplantation genetic diagnosis selecting embryos with chromosomal disorders, for example, has raised the success rate of IVF/ICSI considerably.

18 This argument can only be valid if viability itself is at stake, as in most chromosomal disorders; in these cases the 'right to life' looses its object, and a transfer cannot be justified for both the child's and the woman's interest. This also holds true for termination of a pregnancy, if the woman requests it. Apart from these rare and tragic 'cases', one enters borderline cases, which I would hold should be handled on a case by case basis rather than regulating them by laws.

19 By definition, the 'embryo' is expelled from being subject to respect. The question, however, remains whether the re-definition of respect due to human beings as persons in the strict sense only, is appropriate in the first

place. If the embryo *in vitro* is perceived as 'future child' prospective parents are responsible for, this question cannot be so quickly set aside.

20 The development from the asymmetrical to a symmetrical relationship between parents and children enabling them to become 'autonomous' selves, is a continuous process; hence Jonas's emphasis on this 'telos' of parenthood. J. Habermas similarly stresses reciprocity as part of the concept of parenthood. (Habermas, 2003)

21 I borrow the term 'being the object of property' from Patricia Williams who has related this to the history of slavery. The analogy is not as simple as identifying slavery with embryo research – this would indeed ridicule the former; rather it is the neutralisation of human beings what is at stake here – this, I would hold is based on an ethically unjustifiable claim, namely, the merely arbitrary beginning of moral respect. The history of denial of rights should teach us to be critical of moral judgements, which are merely based on biological 'facts'.

11
Ownership, Property and Women's Bodies

Donna Dickenson

Introduction

Does advocating women's reproductive rights require us to believe that women own a property in their bodies? In this chapter I will argue that it does not. Although the concept of owning our own bodies – 'whose body is it anyway?' – has polemical and political utility, it is incoherent in philosophy and law. Rather than conflate the entirely plausible concept of women's reproductive rights and the implausible notion of property in the body, we should keep them separate, so that the weakness of the second concept does not contaminate the purity of the first.

It is perfectly true the notion of women owning property in their own bodies appears to represent an important step forward from the position that women can have no other relation to property than as its objects: that others have a property in women's bodies but they themselves do not. Women are indeed treated as objects, as sexual property, in the new forms of chattel slavery, which many commentators have identified as being on the increase. However, a woman's body is not literally sold in prostitution, so long as she is not a slave. Prostitution, still less trafficking, does not necessarily equate with the literal sale of women's bodies. If women's bodies are not being literally sold, then no property in women's bodies is being assumed to exist. There is an enormous injustice, yes, but that is not the cause of it.

Trafficking does provide a contemporary and urgent instance of how the language of property in women's bodies can be put to good political purposes by opponents of gender injustice, just as it was in the earlier stages of second-wave feminism in relation to campaigns for the right to abortion, for example. The problem is not whether these campaigns are justified and necessary; in my view, they certainly are. Indeed, if anything the need to defend abortion rights is more vivid and pressing today than in the 1970s. The question is whether the language of property in the body is the best language to use for these good political ends. This doubt is not just an academic irrelevance: If we use confused concepts, we risk allowing our opponents to dismiss our otherwise valid claims. Relying on weak arguments merely gives aid and comfort to the enemy.

There are other, better arguments on which we can rely to provide a firm foundation for women's reproductive rights. I will conclude that in relation to abortion, IVF and egg extraction, women do possess a *right in the labour of their bodies*, although not in their bodies themselves. This right is unique to women's labour in childbirth and pregnancy, not found in any other instances in medical ethics, and not capable of providing a similar foundation for men – because men simply do not labour to the same extent in the process of human reproduction. It means, in my view, that women possess an absolute and inviolable right to determine whether or not they will undergo pregnancy, submit to hormone stimulation in IVF, retain the children they bear in contract motherhood or allow their ova to be used for other people's ends. So the right to control one's reproductive labour is in fact a very strong right, and, in my view, one which is more coherent philosophically than property in the body.

Why is property in the body a weak concept?

In this section, I want to examine the weaknesses of property in the body as a philosophical concept. It is equally unsatisfactory from a legal point of view: we do not own our bodies, at least not in the Anglo-American legal tradition. Rather, the common law views tissue taken from the living body either as abandoned or as *res nullius*, no one's thing; in relation to the dead body, the law of England only recently began to permit people to direct the disposal of their own bodies and still circumscribes the rights of relatives to control the uses to which the body may be put. Although the legal status of property in the body is an important topic in itself, however, for the purposes of this chapter I want to concentrate on the universally applicable philosophical aspects of the concept, not on legal peculiarities of the common law tradition.

There are several ways to approach the question of why property in the body is philosophically incoherent. One route is through feminist theory's insistence on the embodied self (Butler, 1987), a notion also found elsewhere in philosophy, for example, in Kant and Hegel

(Dickenson, 1997, pp. 92–103). Kant is often cited as the locus of the assertion that we are barred from using our bodies as mere tools, since that would entail treating ourselves as mere means – although to our own ends rather than those of another subject. In modern Kantians, this prohibition is frequently expressed as an affront to our human dignity, our intrinsic value as members of the kingdom of ends, in contrast to the relative values that prevail in the commodified marketplace. While Kant clearly states that we are not authorised to sell any parts of our bodies, he seems to make exceptions for non-vital elements, such as hair, although he is uneasy even about that. However, in other situations, for example, in the permissible amputation of a diseased foot, Kant does appear to draw the dualistic distinction between body as object and moral person as subject, so that we are entitled to 'use' the body in such a way as to preserve the person.

In more complete contradistinction to Cartesian mind–body dualism, Hegel denied that there was any such thing as a pure, transcendent self, existing apart from its embodied form. We only exist as embodied selves. If this is true, then our selves cannot be separated from our bodies, and we cannot be said to own our bodies (Dickenson, 1997, pp. 100–1). There is literally nothing or no one there to do the owning.

This has extremely important consequences for both marriage, as Hegel recognises, and prostitution, as he does not. Neither is a proper subject of contract: in other words, there can be no contracts of marriage or prostitution, because 'the object about which a contract is made is a single *external* thing' (Hegel, 1967, p. 75, emphasis added). Since we are embodied beings, a woman's body cannot be that external thing to her. It is therefore incoherent to allow that a woman can be party to either a marriage contract or a trafficking contract, if the subject of the contract is conceived of as her body. If, however, the subject is seen as sexual services using the body, rather than the body itself, that may be another matter – although I have examined that argument elsewhere and also found it wanting (Dickenson, 2005).

The idea of the embodied self has been attractive to feminists, Hegelian and otherwise, who want to 'reclaim the body'. Because the body has traditionally been associated in Christian interpretations with uncleanness, and likewise with women, reclaiming the body is a feminist project. For example, the feminist theorist, Karen Green, has argued for an embodied notion of reason, avoiding the dualistic division into mind and body, which often translates into men being associated with mind and reason, but women with body and emotion (Green, 1995).

That, then, is one reason why the notion of owning the body is philosophically dubious: it relies on a dualistic split between self and body, but we are actually embodied selves. The second reason why we should distrust the notion that we own our bodies requires us to look more closely at the assumptions and history behind the commonly held belief that we *do* own our bodies. As John Maynard Keynes said, 'Practical men, who believe themselves to be quite exempt from any intellectual influence, are usually the slaves of some defunct economist' (Keynes, 1936, ch. 24, p. v). Had Keynes been a philosopher rather than an economist, he might equally well have maintained that common sense ideas usually come from dead philosophers.

The ultimate source of the conventional belief that we own our bodies is usually thought to be John Locke, but in fact, Locke never says we own our bodies; he is careful to distinguish between the labour of our bodies and our bodies themselves (Waldron, 1988). Thus on Lockean grounds there is indeed no general property in the physical body; but there is instead a property in the *person*, construed as agency and intention. We can only own that which we have laboured to create; we do not create our bodies in Lockean terms – God does: 'Humans, then, do not have creators' rights over their bodies. But they can be regarded in [a] strong sense as the creators of their own actions (and *a fortiori* of their work and labour)' (Waldron, 1988, p. 179). If there is anything special about my work, it is not that it is the labour of my body, but that it represents my agency, a part of myself, my moral personhood. It is intimately linked to my personhood, because a person can be seen as a being conscious of free and responsible action. People own their actions, including their labour; they do not own their bodies.

Even though some feminists have wrongly claimed that women *do* own their bodies (Hirschon, 1984; Pateman, 1988), the distinction between owning the body and owning the labour of the body is actually good news rather than a disaster, as far as women's reproductive rights are concerned. I have argued elsewhere (Dickenson, 1997, ch. 3, 2001, 2002) that women's reproductive labour, although not singled out by Locke, is a particularly strong instance of the right to the labour of our bodies. In Locke we have a property right in that with which we have mixed our labour, in what we have laboured to create. That right in turn derives from the link between our labour and our agency, our individuality, our personhood – not literally between our labour and our bodies, but between our labour and the uses to which we put our bodies for the sake of our aims, goals and projects.

In human reproduction, I argue, women labour to create other bodies, rather than their own. Therefore the products of women's reproductive labour constitute the unique exception to the general principle that we cannot own our bodies, because God creates them, not we ourselves. Women do not create their own bodies, but they do create bodies for others. In fact this is not an exception to the principle found in Locke at all, but rather entirely consistent with the Lockean logic. Women *do* labour to create the bodies of their foetuses in pregnancy and childbirth. The labour which women put into superovulation, egg extraction and early pregnancy also qualifies as labour which confers a property right in a Lockean model, I think, and which can be a valuable protection against the commodification of reproductive tissue.

However, one need not take a liberal, Lockean line to believe that women have a property right in their own reproductive labour. A feminist Marxist analysis would likewise support women's property rights in the forms of embryonic tissue which they have laboured to create – e.g. in the stem cell technologies – because they have added surplus value. The point is that the notion of women's rights in their own *reproductive labour* is an important but underused weapon for women activists, one that can be justified philosophically, based on stronger arguments than the dubious concept of property in the body. It also gives women an innate strategic advantage, because only women can possess such a right, and only in relation to reproductive rights. Indeed, to accept the notion of property in the body is to privilege patriarchy, according to the feminist writer, Moira Gatens, because male bodies are privileged above female in a phallocentric culture (Gatens, 1992, p. 135).

The notion of property in reproductive labour, on the other hand, gives women an advantage in very concrete examples of conflict with patriarchal norms, for example, in relation to genetic parentage and 'surrogate' motherhood, as I shall try to show later. I shall also clarify the position in regard to which kinds of property rights in foetal tissue this right entails. For now, I simply want to make it clear that women do not own the bodies of their babies as they might own a car which they have bought with wages from salaried labour. They have certain kinds of property rights in their reproductive labour, but not all rights, and certainly not where another human being is concerned, once the baby has been born. Property is not an all-or-nothing concept, but it is something, and that something has been recognised too little in regard to women's reproductive labour.

In the rest of this chapter, I want to use some concrete examples from reproductive rights and the New Reproductive Technologies to show

how a Lockean labour theory of rights can more firmly ground women's rights to reproductive entitlements and tissue than can the philosophically confused notion of property in the body. The three cases to which I shall apply the labour theory of women's reproductive rights are abortion, contract motherhood and the use of enucleated ova in the stem cell technologies.

Abortion

Women's property in the labour of pregnancy and childbirth is typically ignored by *both* sides in the abortion debate. Instead, the controversy normally centres on whether or not the foetus is a person. Even Judith Jarvis Thomson's famous defence of abortion uses a metaphor about *housing* the baby – the violinist hypothetical – and ignores the labour women put into labour itself, into childbirth (Thomson, 1971). Opponents of abortion, similarly, give no weight to the pain and suffering entailed by childbirth, at best allowing an exception only if the women's life is in danger – in contrast to all other patients, who are presumed to have a right to refuse pain and suffering. No competent adult other than a pregnant woman can be forced to submit to pain and suffering on behalf of another person: for example, even a tissue-matched relative cannot be forced to donate bone marrow. This inadequacy in the ethical debate is peculiar, not least because the foetus is not even a person in the common law.

Only through women's willingness to continue pregnancy and endure the labour of childbirth does the foetus become a person. If women are unwilling to put their reproductive labour to this purpose, whose countervailing rights can stop them? No one's, I would argue, because the foetus is in fact no one – until the woman's reproductive labour makes it someone. This is not just a matter of the law; it is a matter of physiology. Why is this palpable fact so easily ignored? Is it because women's rights to control their labour in childbirth are the last great taboo?

A proper evaluation of women's labour in childbirth leads to radical consequences in the abortion debate: to the absolute right of the woman to request abortion at any stage, even in the third trimester; to the absence of rights vested in the putative father; and to the absolute right of the woman to request abortion for any cause. Some may not be willing to follow this logic to its extreme, and may therefore question whether women's property in their own reproductive labour is too dangerous a concept. To my way of thinking, it is not dangerous enough: it has been far too insufficiently recognised. The countervailing arguments, I think, are merely scaremongering. In fact the numbers of third-trimester terminations are very small; the common law already recognises that the father has no right to force the putative mother to undergo childbirth; and we should trust women not to undergo abortions for frivolous reasons, since the procedure itself is far from frivolous.

A more serious objection might be this: the pregnant woman's property right in her own labour seems to extend to a property right in the baby. If we own that with which we mix our labour, on a Lockean argument, then the mother might be thought to own the baby. In fact the argument for property rights in and through labour does not go so far as to entail slavery, ownership of persons; it only extends to ownership of things. Something may be either a person or a thing in law; I think it is abundantly clear that the baby is a person, not a thing, and therefore cannot be owned by the mother or anyone else. But what about contract motherhood and 'surrogacy'? What are the implications for these areas of a woman's property right in her own reproductive labour?

Contract motherhood

Because a woman has a sort of property right in her own reproductive labour does not necessarily mean that she can do whatever she likes with the foetus. Property is seen in jurisprudence as a 'bundle' or collection of rights, as several sets of interlocking relationships. In the case of abortion, we are mainly concerned with the *right to exclude others* from deciding on the abortion. This sort of property right might also be conceived of as a *privilege*, that is, a legal liberty or freedom, 'unlike a *claim-right*, which generates a corresponding duty in others to do something, a privilege involves not a correlative duty but the absence of a right on someone else's part to interfere' (Munzer, 1990, p. 18). There is also a case for calling the type of property right in labour enjoyed by a pregnant woman an *immunity*, from having her control challenged by anyone else. The right of ownership of real estate, for example, is an immunity against being forced to sell against one's will.

In the case of 'surrogacy', or contract motherhood – the term I prefer because it does not prejudge that the birth mother is merely a 'surrogate' and not the 'real' mother – we are looking at a different sort of property right, a different stick in the bundle. The right in question is the power to transfer custody of a baby, once born, to another party for payment. Is this baby-selling? Does a woman's reproductive property right in her labour extend this far? If babies are not objects but people, it might well be argued that this is indeed baby-selling, and that women's reproductive rights should not extend to contract motherhood.

I think this is correct: the 'surrogacy' contract is clearly in the baby, and contracts in human beings are null and void in a non-slave society. This is indeed the position in English law, although not in American public policy. (In this sense contract motherhood is also a less than ideal term, since the contract is not binding.) However, there remain issues about the period *before* the birth of the baby, when the putative mother's reproductive rights are insufficiently protected by the current position. That is, if a 'surrogate' mother miscarries, gives birth to a stillborn child or suffers adverse consequences of pregnancy, she has no legal protections. So it seems to me that there is an argument for recognising women's reproductive rights to undergo impregnation for the purposes of 'surrogacy', and to be compensated for any adverse events, but not to be compelled to hand over the baby after delivery, on the grounds that this is indeed baby-selling.

'Surrogate' motherhood illustrates how the concept of property in the body can be a two-edged sword for women's rights. If we think in terms of property in the body, which men can possess as well, we may well be led down the path of accepting genetic parenthood as 'real' parenthood and gestational motherhood as less genuine. This is indeed what the term 'surrogate' implies, particularly in the case where the 'surrogate' is not also the genetic mother. That can have disastrous consequences for women, as was illustrated in the US case of *Baby M*, where the court, finding for the genetic father, William Stern, forced the gestational mother, Mary Beth Whitehead, to surrender the child at birth on the grounds that her only function had been 'to be impregnated and to carry *his* child to term' (*In the Matter of Baby M*, cited in, Dickenson, 1997, p. 160, emphasis added). Clearly the judge believed that the baby was already the 'property' of the father, and indeed the court added that Stern had never made a valid contract for the surrender of the child – not because such a contract would constitute baby-selling, but because 'he cannot purchase what is already his' (*In the Matter of Baby M*, cited in, Dickenson, 1997, p. 160).

On the other hand, 'surrogate' motherhood has at least forced society and the courts to take women's reproductive labour seriously. In another US case, that of *Anna J* (1991), the court did recognise that what the woman was selling was not the baby, but her pain and suffering in pregnancy and childbirth: not far off the idea of her property right in her own reproductive labour. To make that position consistent, however, the only part of the 'surrogacy' contract that should be enforceable would have to be the part up till the child's birth. Although 'surrogacy' contracts may be seen as exploitative because they typically involve working-class women and middle-class commissioning couples, economic imbalance is not the real source of exploitation. The core difficulty is the failure to recognise women's property rights in pregnancy and labour, particularly when 'surrogates' are seen as merely 'renting out their wombs'. That is to radically downplay what women undergo in the labour of childbirth.

Ova donation, cloning and stem cell technologies

How can women's reproductive rights in their own labour be protected in relation to ova donation, cloning and the stem cell technologies? I want to conclude with the example of stem cell technologies, and the related issues of therapeutic cloning and the need for enucleated ova, because these issues illustrate the failure to count women's reproductive labour into the equation. Just as the debate over abortion has centred on the status of the foetus, rather than the woman's right to control her own labour in pregnancy and childbirth, so too has the controversy over reproductive cloning inevitably gravitated to the identity of the clone. In relation to therapeutic cloning and the stem cell technologies, interest has been solely focused on the status of the embryo or foetus as a source of the genetic material used. Only very occasionally (e.g. Dickenson, 2001; Holm, 2002) has the need for enucleated ova in these technologies been mentioned as an ethical issue, and as a source of potential exploitation of women.

There are two methods of producing stem cells which rely on embryonic or foetal material for the genetic content, each relying on women's reproductive labour, but to a different degree. The first method uses embryos grown *in vitro*, developed through fertilisation of the mother's ova with the father's sperm: primarily 'spare' embryos which are not to be implanted. (It would also be possible to create embryos from gametes 'harvested' expressly for this purpose.) In this first method, stem cells are derived from the inner cell mass of the blastocysts; the outer cellular layer, which would normally develop into the placenta, is dissolved. Since the blastocysts are used before implantation, the woman's 'sweat equity' is reduced, but she has still undergone the labour of stimulation with fertility drugs (super-ovulation) and extraction of ova – painful and moderately risky procedures. The second method relies on derived stem cells from primordial germ (gonadal) cells in aborted foetal tissue; here the woman has put in the labour and discomfort endurance of early pregnancy, along with enduring the pain of abortion – arguably also form of 'sweat equity'.

In addition to these two methods of producing the genetic content of the stem cell's nucleus, there is a third, less reliable method using adult somatic cells. This method is often said to be ethically neutral, because it does not raise issues about the moral status of the embryo or foetus. Thus, in attempting to find a compromise position in the highly polarised ethical debate around stem cell research – between nearly complete prohibition in Germany versus the more liberal position in the United Kingdom – it has generally been assumed that somatic stem cell technologies, which do not use embryonic or foetal tissue, raise few or no ethical problems. However, the need for enucleated ova in the stem cell technologies is just as great whether or not one uses embryonic, somatic or foetal tissue; indeed, somatic stem cell techniques are probably more wasteful of ova because they have a higher failure rate, adult cells being less totipotent.

A genuine public policy debate must take into account possible pressures for illicit sale and import of enucleated ova, particularly since ova are also in short supply at IVF clinics. Particularly since enucleated ova have no genetic content (apart from small quantities of mitochondrial DNA) some researchers have also raised the spectre of exploitation of Third World women in supplying ova (Dickenson, 2002). Certainly there is already evidence of large quantities of ova being extracted (legally or illegally) and sold commercially in other countries, for example, the United States (Jacobs *et al.*, 2001), Croatia and Iran.

A feminist model sensitive to women's alienation from their reproductive labour might want to take a more radical tack in countering commercial interests in the new stem cell technologies. This need not be a full-fledged property claim, and given the legal and philosophical incoherence of the concept of property in the body, it probably should not be. It need only be as great as to protect the tissue from being appropriated by others, under penalty of the Theft Act in the United Kingdom, for example, which has been ruled in one case (R. v. Kelly, cited in Grubb, 1998) to extend to body parts on which labour has been expended. In his influential model, A Theory of Property, Stephen Munzer argues that 'persons do not own their bodies, but they do have limited property rights in them' (Munzer, 1990, p. 41). These he views as primarily powers (to transfer, waive and exclude others from the use of one's body parts) rather than as claim-rights (to possess, use, manage and receive income) (Munzer, 1990, p. 22, following Honore, 1961). As with contract motherhood, we would want to distinguish different sticks in the property bundle. The primary concern in this example would be to protect women from actual theft of their ova for use in the stem cell technologies, without their consent, or even from undue pressure to consent to dangerously high regimes of ovarian stimulation so that the extra ova can be used for commercial purposes.

Stem cell technologies highlight the 'use-value' which women produce in the reproductive labours of super-ovulation, egg extraction, and the work of early pregnancy and abortion. It is abundantly clear that these pregnancy-derived tissues have value, and enormous value. What is shown by the commodification of bodily products, such as stem cells, is that there is no firm divide, as Marx thought there was, between the use-values produced through social means of production and the absence of use-values in reproduction.

Normally, however, we simply do not notice that women are putting in labour through undergoing super-ovulation or egg extraction, just as we do not fully recognise women's property rights in the larger labours of pregnancy and childbirth. Consider the cloning debate, where again, the great bulk of writings turn on the personal identity of the clone. There is never any mention of the possible exploitation of the contract mothers who would be required to produce clones – remember that it took 267 sheep to produce Dolly. We can remain smugly unaware that these 'surrogate' mothers will be needed, because we just do not notice the labour of pregnancy and childbirth. I have argued throughout that we should do so, by recognising that women have a property right in their reproductive labour. These three examples illustrate in different ways exactly how that right could be applied, and how important it is to do so.

12
Beyond Europe: Rhetoric of Reproductive Rights in Global Population Policies

Sirkku K. Hellsten

The world is still witnessing a fast population expansion. The United Nations' *State of World Population Report 2004* from UNFPA, the United Nations Population Fund, estimates that the population will grow from the current 6.5 billion to 9.1 billion by 2050. The increase of 2.6 billion is equivalent to the combined populations of China and India today (UNFPA, 2004). However, while population grows fast in poor countries, which are already struggling to feed their people, the numbers are stagnating in rich nations. In many of the developing countries growth rates tend to be between 2.1–2.5 per cent (from the average of 1.5–1.7) – and sometimes they are even higher than this. In fact, populations in the poor regions have more than quadrupled in less than 50 years, while in many affluent European countries the population is further declining.

The UN report points out that many countries are making real progress in carrying out a bold global action plan that links poverty alleviation to women's rights and universal access to reproductive health. According to the report ten years into the new era opened by the 1994 *International Conference on Population and Development* (ICPD) in Cairo, the quality and reach of family planning programs have improved, safe motherhood and HIV prevention efforts are being scaled up and governments embrace the ICPD Programme of Action as an essential blueprint for realizing the Millennium Development Goals across the world (UNFPA, 2004).

However, inadequate resources, gender bias and gaps in the local and global distribution of the resources and services to the poor and adolescent are undermining further progress. Yet, while the threat of population expansion in the developing world is of international concern, the

decline of population in many European countries appears to be considered as a serious problem. Consequently, while worldwide population
control and family-planning programs are implimented, women in
Europe are encouraged to 'make more babies'. Various public and private
services offering the latest reproductive technology, as well as many
social entitlements, are made available for European women to produce
more offspring. Both concerns are set in a framework, which considers
procreation to be one of the most fundamental human needs, and
which regards individuals' reproductive choices as basic rights.

In order to discuss consistency of regional and international policies,
this article analyses the relations between reproductive rights, international population policies and the ethical principles and values these
policies are based upon. My purpose is to discuss how these values and
principles, which are in general considered as universal, tend to be contextualised and their policy requirements are interpreted accordingly.
Such disparity enforces inequality not only between men and women
but also among women across the globe. On the one hand, these differences can be seen already in Europe in the treatment of minority
women. On the other hand, in the global context, they are even more
evident. In order to get to the heart of the problem of inequality of
women in relation to reproductive policies this chapter needs to take a
global rather than a merely European focus. It also uses a philosophical,
rather than a strictly empirical, approach to show that regional and
international rhetoric, politics and ethics do not always go hand in
hand. In fact, the premises and arguments, which lie behind various
policies are problematic as are the understandings of the central, supposedly shared concepts. There are also inconsistencies between principles
and practices.

This chapter does not deny the concern we should have about
population growth, but rather is concerned with the international community's tendency to accept different interpretations of the contents of
the global, universal human rights in different economic and social
contexts. I shall not focus upon whether flexibility in the interpretations
of human rights is unjustified in all cases, but rather, I want to point out
the kinds of contradictions such an approach causes in local and global
discussions on reproductive rights and debates on population policies.

The main purpose of this chapter therefore is to show that despite the
recent rhetorical shift from the utilitarian promotion of the overall good
to that of reproductive rights, the changes in actual policy implementa-
tions are less evident. I suggest that the language of rights is often used as
semantic gloss to conceal the structural global injustices in population

issues that are used to further justify global inequality. Thus, I shall argue that the current liberal, rights-based approach to social justice, which draws its normative force from universalisation of values, such as the individual's moral autonomy, can be truly plausible and internationally acceptable if, and only if, it can be internationally consistently implemented. In order for this to happen a re-evaluation is needed to assess what equal and universal protection of human rights actually means within and without Europe; particularly, when it comes to the rights of women in developing countries in relation to their reproductive choices.

Change in ethics and politics or change in rhetoric?

While we may agree that every one should have a right to reproduce, if they so choose – during our history various measures have been used to curb this right in order to control population growth. The moral justification has usually been that population control and population policies are central to human well-being. However, when looked at more closely, the ethical basis for these policies has often been, at best, ambiguous and, at worst, contradictory or plain unjust. While overall well-being, in the utilitarian sense, might be the explicit goal, sometimes the action taken has been (directly or indirectly) suppressive towards either individuals or particular social collectives (such as people living in particular geographical areas) or genetic entities (collectives of individuals who are considered in some way or another genetically 'inferior' or 'defective').

Eugenic tendencies can easily be justified using utilitarian arguments that claim that our choices and actions are right if they promote the greatest happiness of the greatest number; even if this may, in some cases, require us to sacrifice individual rights or well-being. During recent decades, however, there seems to have been a shift from this utilitarian justification towards the protection of the rights of individuals. This is illustrated in policy statements and international agreements, where particular attention has been paid to the protection of the rights of women and especially to the promotion of (what is called) 'reproductive rights'.

The logical assumption is that since the protection of individual rights presumes respect for autonomy, population policies based on the language of rights, must then also be autonomy-respecting and anti-paternalist. However, when it comes to the population policies implemented in Third World countries, and particularly, among women living in the poorest environments, this may not always be the case.

Thus, while this 'rights-based' approach is no doubt, in today's world, politically more correct and ethically more desirable than utility-based approaches (which justify even coercive population control programs), we still need to consider whether this linguistic shift, from collective good to individual rights, has really encouraged radical change in actual policies worldwide.

For and against population control

In order to tackle these issues of paternalism and autonomy in more depth, we need to first take a brief look at the main ethical arguments that are generally presented for and against population control: the right-based approach is, in general, thought to correct the persistent injustice built into the utilitarian promotion of collective good: that focuses on the well-being of the future generations and/or the protection of the well-being of present generations as a whole, and thus, can be used to defend paternalistic or coercive population control policies. Recently the liberal ideology has taken a dominant place in the issues of global justice, and it has become the main ethical basis for the promotion and protection of human rights. The liberal 'human rights' approach has vigorously opposed, and argued against, the violations of individual's rights in the name of the utilitarian collective good in population issues.

The defenders of individual rights do not argue against population control *per se*, only against practices, which are autonomy-restricting. The liberal, right-based defense for population policy issues claims that in these programs individual rights should be given priority over the collective good. If we are serious about protecting the well-being of individual members of society we need to start by protecting their rights and allowing them the opportunities to make rational and autonomous decisions for themselves in reproductive issues. While this undoubtedly appears to be a plausible ethical conclusion, an important question of ethics still remains: how much autonomy is actually allowed (rather than how autonomous the choices really are) in Third World countries by the liberal right-based approach? Or, in other words, has the change in language really contributed to the change in global politics and power relations – and has it made women worldwide more equal, if not to men, at least to each other.

Reproductive rights as population wrongs

It emerges that the debate is (particularly, when theological and other spiritual rather than philosophical issues are set aside) between two opposite ethical positions: on the one hand, those who are against paternalistic and coercive population regulation are those who wish to protect individual rights and people's autonomous choices (there is still, of course, the problem of who is accepted as a right-bearer). On the other hand, those who would allow such paternalistic and coercive policies are those who wish to maximise the collective good of a society.

From global perspective, however, the situation is not a clear choice between the ethical traditions of utilitarian maximisation of the collective good and the promotion of individual rights. After all, both types of ethical argumentation can be used in any given circumstance to promote any desired goal. Whether we argue according to the utilitarian or the liberal ethical reasoning, in general, the solutions tend to favour autonomy of the Western donor powers and give less choice to the people of the Third World – whether we talk about men or women. However, with regard to reproductive issues, third world women tend to suffer from 'double paternalism': first, from the patriarchal social hierarchy; and second, from the paternalistic policies of international donor representatives. Difficult dilemmas arise when both of these authorities set contradictory demands on women and, particularly, when external policies conflict with local values.

Let us now return to *the collective good argument*. When utilitarian argument is set in a different environment, namely that of the industrialised countries, it is logically plausible to argue that the maximisation of overall happiness might actually require us to increase the number of people: the greater the number of happier people the greater the overall happiness. In poor parts of the world this argument would be absurd, because it would lead to a situation in which population increase was suggested as a solution to the over-population problem. But in rich countries, this argument could help to solve the problem of declining population. The overall happiness of society requires that we reproduce more taxpayers, more professionals, more educated people to run our societies and contribute to its resources. The fact, that there is over-population in the world does not play any role in this argument. Depending on the intentions and aims we have, it is always possible to define the collective good as whatever community we consider appropriate for any given situation. The rich countries are not willing to radically increase their immigration quotas from the poorer regions of the world in order to balance their population needs. Instead, it is considered moral to encourage increased procreation within the original or prevailing population of these areas.

In a similar way the restriction of population growth, particularly in the Third World, can be justified by appealing to individual rights.

Examples of such rights are the individuals' rights to well-being now and here, and not the rights of the future generations. Or they are women's rights to have control over their own bodies based on individual autonomy and not women's 'communal' desire for large families. In other words women should be able to make decisions concerning the size of the family they want to have – as long as this family remains small enough: usually the choice that is considered autonomous is the one that coincides with the preferences of the donor community.

Thus, the real question for ethics is not whether the arguments from collective good or individual rights *per se* are ethically more desirable in population policies. Instead, and before we get too contented with the new language of rights, we should reconsider the issues of the global inequality in population policies.

Right to reproduce as duty not to reproduce?

This brings us to the ambiguous use of the term of *reproductive rights*. Reproductive rights are considered to embrace certain human rights recognised in national and international legal and human rights documents (such as the ones produced by the *Fourth World Conference on Women, Beijing Declaration and Platform for Action*, Beijing, China, 17 October 1995, principles 94, 95, 97, 216, 223; *International Conference on Population and Development* (ICDP), *Programme of Action*, Cairo, Egypt, 18 October 1994, principles 8, 7.3; *World Conference on Human Rights, Vienna Declaration and Programme of Action*, 14–25 June 1993). These include the basic right of all couples and individuals 'to decide freely and responsibly the number and spacing of their children and to have the information and education and means to do so, the right to attain the highest standard of sexual and reproductive health and the right to make decision concerning reproduction free of discrimination, coercion and violence' and the right to reproductive health, which is defined by the World Health Organization as 'a state of complete physical, mental and social well-being in all matters related to the reproductive system and its functions and processes' (see the *Fourth World Conference on Women, Beijing Declaration and Platform for Action*, Beijing).

One feature of these two interrelated definitions is their broadness and their ambiguous use. Although most people would agree that reproductive rights have to protect women's reproductive health, and that this has to do with women's physical and psychological health in relation to their reproductive roles, these interconnected definitions have not necessarily led to a comprehensive agreement on how to deal with these issues of reproduction nor in providing – if not the same, at least equal in relative terms – reproductive health services in the global context. In fact, the broad definitions allow for a selective approach, which stresses one or more components of reproductive health and rights to the neglect of others, depending on the social, cultural, political and economic circumstances. Thus, it has been possible for institutions and individuals with quite divergent agendas to espouse reproductive health and rights and yet to mean quite different things by them depending on their other interests and goals as well as resources available. This selective understanding of reproductive rights is usually paid for by those who are the politically, economically and socially most deprived.

Thus, the normative status of 'reproductive rights' is at its best unclear and relative to the circumstances, especially when it comes to their global application. Usually reproductive rights are used primarily to refer to a woman's right to decide whether or not she wants to produce offspring. While this right clearly includes rights to contraception and abortion, it also covers rights to use medical technology to assist in childbearing; such as infertility treatments, artificial insemination and other reproductive aids. With the help of modern bio- and gene technology this also provides women with a choice regarding what kind of offspring they want, by eliminating serious diseases, birth defects and in general undesired genetic conditions (providing, of course, that she has the financial means to do so). Thus, it also gives women a chance to decide if they want to improve the 'quality of children' that they are to produce.

In the Third World countries the same rights have a lot more limited scope – they tend to refer to women's 'rights not to reproduce'. A woman's right to decide the size of her family is not the right to have as many children as she and her spouse may want to, but to control the size of her family by not having (many or any) children. However, this may not to be a locally desirable choice in cultures in which children are valued as the wealth of the family. Claiming such a right would seem irrational in a community in which women and families without children are seen as 'defective'; indeed, their communities may even shun such families. While this is a social fact in many developing countries, especially in those with collectivist rather than individualist cultural traditions, many liberals could claim that if the members of these communities were fully rational and autonomous they would not hold such attitudes. However, these attitudes are not based merely on cultural differences, but also on the economic and social resources available. While not having (many) children is in general (particularly as taught by Western population policy programs) thought to be the economical, rational choice in the developing world, in traditional, patriarchal communities women without children may end up in an economically weaker position, since, without family to take care of them in their old age women may have no means of survival. In a society in which children are practically the only social insurance for the couple's old age, the decision to have many children is not only clearly the rational economic choice but also an investment on the part of both parents. Since in poor countries, due to the lack of basic health care services many children do not survive past their early years, parents may have to have many children in order to guarantee that they will have surviving offspring to take care of them in their old age (Cassen *et al.*, 1994; Erlich, 1968).

Some may counter-argue that the balance is there if we compare the number of children reproduced in particular parts of the world. It is only that people who reproduce less have better access to infertility treatment, other procreation supporting measures as well as child benefits. Those who already reproduce plenty offspring should be guided to family planning and allowed to have access to safe terminations of pregnancy. However, this claim has some flaws when it comes to the universalisation of the liberal, rights-based concept of justice.

First, the rights-based approach considers choices to be context-dependent in the first world while it denies the importance of this context in the Third World countries. This means that if we claim that the reproductive choices of people living in poor countries are irrational, we could as well argue that it is irrational for the residents of developed countries to reproduce only little or no offspring: because the high standards of living and social services that makes it unnecessary to have many children are not going to be maintained in the long run without an increased birth rate to provide the labour force and taxpayers of the future.

Second, if there is universal rationality, and choices should not be considered to be context-dependent then, if we take the liberal demand for autonomy seriously, we should be free to decide on the content of our choice. In other words, we either have to promote universal rationality or respect individual autonomy in relation to its rationality within local social settings. If we take rationality as our context of autonomous choice, then we have to be willing to make sure that women all over the world have the same choices and the same scope, that is, they all have equal resources, access to education and social power. These choices cannot then be directly dependent on the number of children people have, or rather should have, otherwise they are no real choices at all.

All in all, the question of reproductive rights in relation to population policies is not merely a question of local cultures and/or irrational choices, but it is a question of global and local distribution of wealth. As noted earlier, in many poor countries in Africa and Asia, for example, the fact that all women should have the right to make choices regarding their own bodies, reproduction and health and the right of access to a broad range of integrated services tied to primary health care remains a far-off ideal. While, at the same time, in the rich societies the promotion of reproductive rights includes access to the latest and most expensive medical technology used, for instance, for infertility treatments and genetic therapy or engineering.

Original position and global reproduction policies

From the point of view of the modern liberal concept of justice, as presented by the famous American political philosopher, John Ralws, we need to start thinking about justice from the point of view of 'original position' in which all the concerned are in equal position to choose rationally the universalisable principles of justice (Rawls, 1971, 1993). If this 'original position' is not the same for every one, then a rational choice will not produce the same results. Thus, in a society in which there are no social services available and no public resources to take care of those without social and family networks, it is undoubtedly a rational choice to invest in family. Thus, in affluent countries with various public resources and services not having (many) children is thought to be an economically more rational choice. Whereas, in traditionally patriarchal communities women without children may actually end up in an economically weaker position, as they may be left with no one to care for them during their old age. These choices are all rational, their autonomy, however, is related to the social context they are made in.

Thus, our personal reproductive choices depend often on the context and on the resources available. The population policies, for their part, tend to be relative not only to the resources but also to the prevalent number of indigenous and local populations of a particular country. All in all, in the talk about reproductive rights, the actual rights promoted do not seem to have the same normative scope in the poor countries as they have in the rich ones. Thus, in the West and the North, as part of the population policies, the use of all the latest medical treatments for infertility as well as other gene and biotechnological means for artificial or alternative reproduction techniques are justified in the name of individuals' reproductive rights. In poorer global East and South, the population policies tend, almost exclusively, to focus on decreasing birth rates and hence on issues of effective birth control, legalising abortions and sterilisation programs. This approach is justified in the name of individuals' reproductive rights (or in general women's right to make decisions concerning their own bodies).

In addition to the imbalance and injustice that is created by the various, context-related interpretations of the content and scope of reproductive rights, there are other conceptual problems involved in the use of the term 'reproductive rights'. These conceptual ambiguities lead to informal fallacies that can cover up, or lead us away from, other serious ethical problems.

Reproductive rights as human rights

One of the problematic conceptual issues is the relation between 'reproductive rights' and 'human rights' in general. After all, if reproductive rights are to be considered as human rights, they clearly cannot be merely the rights of women, but men have to have them also (Cassen *et al.*, 1994; Erlich, 1968; Hellsten, 2002).

However, since in general from the feminist point of view, the main problem with the human rights approach is that women always have to fight for their humanity, the issues of men's rights are not the focus of reproductive rights because they are more enforced and protected than women's rights. And it is clear, that in societies with a patriarchal rule women's rights do not have an equal status as individual human rights in general – if they exist at all they always remain as 'women's rights' that are either an addition to, or a deviation from, other universal human rights. Whether we talk about the not so distant past – and even present – of the Western societies or whether we focus on traditional societies in the Third World countries, women as individuals are easily left outside the scope of the human rights discourse. As long as women's rights are discussed in terms of collective rights of women, women themselves can be seen as a deviation from the rest of humanity (that is, mankind). In other words, if women's rights are special gender-based rights, women's rights issues remain aside from the protection of universal rights of individual human beings. Instead of being universal rights, they are left to compete with other collective group rights and minority rights, including the cultural rights with patriarchal tendencies (Hellsten, 2002; Heyd, 1992).[1]

Thus, in order to gain true gender equality, reproductive rights have to include the rights of men also. This, however, makes the situation complex: men's reproductive rights are indirect – they cannot be fulfilled without the help of women as the final 'reproducers' of the offspring (since at least for time being, until cloning and other new medical and biotechnologies are fully developed and taken into every-day use, men cannot reproduce on their own) (Hellsten, 2002; Heyd, 1992). And it is precisely this situation that demands that we extend the concept of reproductive rights and consider what rights do, or should, men have in women's reproductive decisions. Once again we get tangled with cultural traditions and the values we give to family and to each other, and the role of autonomy in all of our decisions.

Set in this wider gender-inclusive rather than merely gender-sensitive framework of human rights discourse the protection of 'reproductive rights' becomes a many-sided issue. Women have to either argue why their reproductive rights as women's rights *per se* are to be given a special status among other human rights and why reproductive rights, for instance, should have priority over other rights, such as the (man's) cultural rights to maintain patriarchal social structures. Or women have to come up with an answer why their reproductive rights should be taken more seriously than those same reproductive rights of men. Otherwise, other things being equal, there is a real danger that women are doomed to remain as means for men to claim their procreative rights.

Altogether the main problem with the protection of 'reproductive rights' is to decide whose rights are we really talking about. We need to consider what do these rights really entail in various contexts. If human rights, in general, are rights that can be claimed from the state and maybe, in some cases, from other public institutions, then they appear to be very relative to what each state or institution has to offer – in policies, in cultural traditions and in resources. 'Reproductive right' appears to be too vague, too ambiguous and too relative a concept and one which can be rhetorically used to support any goal in any given cir-cumstance and situation. Rather than bringing equality between men and women – they may actually create and justify further inequality among women globally.

Paternalism on maternal choices

From the problems of reproductive rights we can move to the issue of paternalism in population policies in the Third World countries. Our starting point was that with the shift from utility-based programs to rights-based programs, we seem to have solved some of the problems of paternalism and reduced the violations of autonomy. The new family-centered population programs themselves should now promote rather than violate individuals' autonomy and rights.

In general, the Western concept of paternalism, which is based on the core values of liberal traditions and which defines paternalism as a restriction and suppression of 'a rational agent's autonomy', does allow – and sometimes actually appears to require – the Western donor community to interfere in order to guide development in the 'right' direction. However, there is a curious in-built feature of the Western liberal and inherently anti-paternalistic ethical approach in that it actually justifies extensive interference in the matters of those who are not considered as fully autonomous and fully rational moral agents. Particularly, when we analyse the problem of paternalistic, external interventions in the population programs, the Millian and later Feinbergian distinction between 'harm to others' and 'harm to self' principles disappear when it comes to the realisation of these programs in the Third World countries. Many international development projects on population issues tend to belittle the point of view and prevailing values of the aid recipients, despite the fact that, autonomy and independence are rhetorically promoted as the final goal of these very same programs. Thus, when crossing international borders the donor agencies appear to be readier to interfere with the choices of individuals on the basis of 'harm to self'-principle, than they would consider appropriate within merely Western social and cultural context: when interference to autonomous choices is only justified on the 'harm to others'-principle.

The international, though mainly Western, donor and 'expert' community seems to be certain that their choices are right and regard 'primitive' people in 'alien' cultures as having 'irrational' traditions and being less autonomous. But, if we are truly to avoid paternalism, how can we interfere with people's choices in lifestyles and values? If an individual insists that holding certain cultural traditions is important for her life, could we deny this by convincing her that she would be better off if she rejected these old customs of her culture? If her culture values children, then should we not allow her to make up her own mind regarding the size of her family? How can we persuade her to have a better life with less or no children without being paternalists?

This would not be such a central problem for the Western ethical thinking if it did not so clearly contradict the very basis of liberal anti-paternalism as first was presented by John Stuart Mill in his classic anti-paternalist statement in *On liberty* (1859) Mill notes for instance that:

> the only purpose for which power can be rightfully exercised over any member of a civilized community, against his will, is to prevent

harm to others. His own good, either physical or moral, is not a sufficient warrant. He cannot rightfully be compelled to do or forbear, because it will be better for him, because it will make him happier, because in the opinion of others, to do so would be wise, or even right. These are good reasons for demonstrating with him, or reasoning with him, or persuading him, but not compelling him, or visiting him with any evil in case he do otherwise. To justify that, the conduct from which it is desired to deter him, must be calculated not to produce evil to someone else. The only part of the conduct of any one, for which he is amenable to society, is that which concerns others. In the part, which merely concerns himself, his independence is, of right absolute. Over Himself, over his body and mind, the individual is sovereign. (Mill, 1986, orig. 1859, p. 16)[2]

If we accept that, a global human rights protection and liberal anti-paternalism should be universalised in all societies, we then would have to agree on its two main principles: first, that harm to others is a relevant ground for retracting individual or collective freedom; and second, that harm to self is not. As Feinberg notes, we should regard (legal) paternalism 'as a liberty limiting principle that justified (state) coercion to protect individuals from self-inflicted harm, or in its extreme version, to guide them, whether they like it or not, towards their own good' (Feinberg, 1973, p. 45). In general then, paternalism is defined as coercing people primarily for what is believed to be their own good.

In many third world communities big families are values and women's role as mother emphasised. Thus, in many cases family planning and birth control can be considered as 'undesirable' or even 'unnatural' intervention to the values and lifestyles of these communities. If we follow the Millian request that we should not attempt to show people what is their own good, such intervention can only be done if we assume that it prevents harm to others. Yet, if we wish to claim harm to others, then we have to identify those who are harmed. We may try to prevent harm to unborn children, however, to do this we would have to move away from the rights agenda and towards utilitarian maximisation of the collective good or overall happiness.

The international donor community is likely to claim that intervention is allowed in the name of realisation of one's 'true autonomy'. Values, beliefs and traditions that encourage or require women to have many children are to be eradicated as irrational and as choices that no 'truly autonomous' people would make. Looking at ourselves, it is seldom that we would admit that we are not able to make 'fully rational' choices. This way what is considered to be 'fully rational' by the majority becomes a criteria for a choice, and we end up with 'only one right choice policies'. In any case, if it is only the fully rational and autonomous agents who have the right to choose the 'only rational way available', how far have we really come from the utilitarian policies that maximise the overall utility of the greatest number?

However, as Feinberg points out, one can be constrained without being frustrated, and then intervention is questionable. As an example, Feinberg gives the following: A man can be having the time of his life while in a room, either because he does not know that the door is locked or because he does not care; or an armed guard with a gun at one's head can 'force' one to vote for the candidate one had intended to vote for all along for one's own reasons (Feinberg, 1973, p. 5). In comparison, if people in Third World countries do not feel coerced to have a big family and are not frustrated by the threatening population problem, why should we interfere and, if we do, how can we justify our paternalistic agendas?

Thus, a curious feature of Western liberal and rights-based ethical approach is, that it can in itself restrict one's autonomy in order to promote 'real autonomy'. It gives a theoretical framework for benevolent paternalism: Either you are autonomous and make the 'right choices', that is, the same choices as other rational and autonomous beings; or you are not fully autonomous and you can be emancipated from false belief with the help of paternalistic guidance so that in the end you will learn to make the 'right choices'. While this paternalism might be benevolent, it still denies what it claims to promote – individual choice. Instead, it claims that there is a particular direction for rational development that all women in the poor countries should aim for (following the model of their 'sister' in affluent countries). These are the policies of Plato's philosopher king, who in his wisdom knows better than others what is best for all – these are also the policies of R. M. Hare's omniscient Arch Angel who can calculate the objective, overall utility of the society on behalf of us, context-dependent individuals.[3]

Conclusion

In conclusion, I shall note that in population policies, there has been a semantic shift from society or 'earth/environment'-centered agendas of population control towards family-centered population policies which focus on the empowerment of women and help them to claim their reproductive rights (McMahan, 1998; Qadeer, 1998). The 'new' population policies *sound* more politically correct in the present international dialogue and political situation. They comply with the promotion of human rights and they even appear to give more space for cultural diversity. However, being politically correct does not necessarily mean that they are just or that they bring about global equality in distribution of power, resources and well-being, or replace people's actual choices. While in many parts of the world more voluntary family planning and modern birth control is needed, the global policies tend to plan for the families rather than leave the family planning to the individuals' choices.

While it might still be left open whether paternalistic practices can sometimes be justified in particular contexts, the pretense that paternalism no longer exists at the global level even among women themselves, does not promote social justice and gender equality. All in all, it can be questioned how 'the semantic cosmetics' of politically correct language can be – and sometimes are – used to cover up policies that in other terms would not be accepted. The practical ethical question is the following: would the 'individual interests and rights' of women in the developing world be taken seriously if they were not seen as means of serving utilitarian 'global' interest, whether demographic or eugenic?

Notes

1 Another relevant discussion here would be the relationship between reproductive rights and rights of future generations. Whether future generations can be considered to have rights, see, for example, Heyd, 1992; Parfit, 1982.

2 Of course, it can be noted here, that even Mill – though in general considered as one of the first serious promoters of women's rights – is talking about 'he' and limits his anti-paternalism to civilised societies.

3 The ethical question is whether paternalism in itself is answer to the population issues or should the social circumstances be changed first. Our moral intuition tends to say that these must go hand in hand, we can change the behaviour of people with education, but in order to educate people they have to have the basic material standards of living. If we merely try to enforce birth control and family planning in cultures which consider children as rewards and signs of wealth, the results can be disastrous. If we merely increase the standards of living without education, this results in waste of resources.

Bibliography

Adams, M. (ed.) (1990) *The Wellborn Science: Eugenics in Germany, France, Brazil, and Russia*, London: Oxford University Press.

Adsera, A. (2004) 'Changing fertility rates in developed countries, the impact of labor market institutions', *Journal of Population Economics*, 17, 17–43.

Agence France Presse (2005) 'Polish opposition blocks abortion debate in parliament'. Available at: http://web.lexis-nexis.com/professional/ [Accessed 15 February 2005].

Ahn, N. and Mira, P. (1999) 'A Note on the charging relationship between fertility and female employment rates in developed countries', Madrid: Fundación de Estudios de Economía Aplicada.

Allen, C. (1992) 'Boys only: Pennsylvania's Anti-Abortion Law', *The New Republic*, 206, 16.

American Bar Association (2003) 'Christian Democrats threaten to leave ruling coalition over abortion issue'. Available at: http://www.abanet.org/ceeli/countries/slovakia/may2003.html [Accessed 3 May 2005].

Amnesty International (1997) *Female Genital Mutilation: A Human Rights Information Pack*, AI Index: ACT 77/05/97, London: Amnesty International.

Andorka, R. and Balázs-Kovács, S. (1986) 'The social demography of Hungarian villages in the eighteenth and nineteenth centuries (with special attention to Sarpilis, 1792–1804)', *Journal of Family History*, 11, 169–92.

Andrews, L. (1997) 'Body science', *American Bar Association Journal*, 83, 44–9.

—— (2000) *The Clone Age*, New York: Henry Holt and Company.

ANSA English Media Service (2005) 'Fertility Law Referendum mostly allowed'. Available at: http://web.lexis-nexis.com/professional/ [Accessed 13 January 2005].

Arie, S. (2004) 'Proposal to curb free abortion angers Italy', *The Guardian*, 9 August. Available at: http://www.guardian.co.uk/international/story/0,,1278955,00.html [Accessed 3 May 2005].

Ariès, P. (1996) *Centuries of Childhood*, London: Pimlico.

Barnett, C. B. (1993) 'The forgotten and the neglected', *Golden Gate University Law Review*, 23, 863–98.

Bateman Novaes, S. (1998) 'The medical management of donor insemination', in K. Daniels and E. Haimes (eds), *Donor Insemination: International Social Science Perspectives*, Cambridge: Cambridge University Press, pp. 105–30.

Beck-Gernsheim, E. (1995) *The Social Implications of Bioengineering*, Atlantic Highlands, NJ: Humanities Press.

—— (2002) *Reinventing the Family: In Search of New Lifestyles*, Malden, MA: Polity Press.

Belew, K. L. (2004) 'Stem cell division: abortion law and its influence on the adoption of radically different embryonic stem cell legislation in the United States, the United Kingdom, and Germany', *Texas International Law Journal*, 39, 479–519.

Benhabib, S. (1992) *Situating the Self: Gender, Community, and Postmodernism in Contemporary Ethics*, New York: Routledge.

Bernstein, J., Berson, A., Brill, M., Cooper, S., Ferber, G., Glazer, E., Kaufman, A., Levin, S., Lynn, S., Silverstein, D., Springer, J. and Steinberg, S. (1996) 'Safeguards in embryo donation', *Fertility and Sterility*, 65 (6), 1262–3.

Blyth, E. (1988) 'What do donor offspring want to know about their genetic origins?' *Journal of Fertility Counselling*, 5, 15–17.

Bohman, M. and Sigvardsson, S. (1990) 'Outcome in adoption: lessons from longitudinal studies' in D. Brodzinsky and M. Schechter (eds), *The Psychology of Adoption*, New York: Oxford University Press, pp. 93–106.

Bonino, E. (2004) 'Join forces to banish the mutilation of women', *International Herald Tribune*, Wednesday, 15 September, p. 8.

Bouclin, S. (2002) 'Abortion in post X Ireland', *Windsor Review of Legal and Social Issues*, 13, 133–71.

Bowlby, J. (1969) *Attachment and Loss, Vol. 1. Attachment*, London: Hogarth Press.

Brand, A. E. and Brinich, P. M. (1999) 'Behavior problems and mental health contacts in adopted, foster, and nonadopted children', *Journal of Child Psychology and Psychiatry*, 40, 1221–9.

Brennan, T. (2004) 'Edward Said and comparative literature', speech delivered at conference 'Edward Said: A Continuing Legacy' at SUAS – University of London, 3 October 2004.

Bridge, C. and Swindells, H. (2003) *Adoption: The Modern Law*, Bristol: Jordan Publishing Ltd.

British Association for Adoption and Fostering (1991) *Form F*.

—— (2003) 'Statistics'. Available at: http://www.baaf.org.uk/info/stats/all_lac_stats.pdf [Accessed 3 May 2005].

Broberg, G. and Roll-Hansen, N. (eds) (1996) *Eugenics and the Welfare State: Sterilization Policy in Denmark, Sweden, Norway and Finland*, East Lansing, MI: Michigan State University Press, pp. 77–149.

Brodzinsky, D. (1990) 'A stress and coping model of adoption adjustment' in D. Brodzinsky and M. Schechter (eds), *The Psychology of Adoption*, New York: Oxford University Press, pp. 3–24.

—— (1997) 'Infertility and adoption adjustment: considerations and clinical issues' in S. Leiblum (ed.), *Infertility: Psychological Issues and Counselling Strategies*, New York: Wiley, pp. 246–62.

Brodzinsky, D. and Huffman, L. (1988) 'Transition to adoptive parenthood', *Marriage and Family Review*, 12, 267–86.

Brodzinsky, D. and Pinderhughes, E. (2002) 'Parenting and child development in adoptive families' in M. Bornstein (ed.), *Handbook of Parenting*, Vol. 1, Mahwah, NJ: Lawrence Erlbaum Associates, pp. 279–311.

Brodzinsky, D., Schechter, D., Braff, A. M. and Singer, L. (1984) 'Psychological and academic adjustment in adopted children', *Journal of Consulting and Clinical Psychology*, 52, 582–90.

Brodzinsky, D., Smith, D. W. and Brodzinsky, A. B. (1998) *Children's Adjustment to Adoption. Developmental and Clinical Issues*, Vol. 38, London: Sage Publications.

Broomfield, M. G. (1996) 'Controlling the reproductive rights of impoverished women: is this the way to "reform" welfare?', *Boston College Third World Law Journal*, 16, 217–44.

Bucur, M. (2002) *Eugenics and Modernization in Interwar Romania*, Pittsburgh: University of Pittsburgh Press.

Burns, L. H. (1990) 'An exploratory study of perceptions of parenting after infertility', *Family Systems Medicine*, 8, 177–89.

Busnellid (1996) 'Quali regole per la procreazione assistita?', *Rivista di Diritto Civile*, 5, 574–5.

Buster, J. E., Bustillo, M., Thorneycroft, I. Simon, J. A., Boyers S. P., Marshall J. R., Seed R. G., and Louw J. A. (1983) 'Nonsurgical transfer in in-vivo fertilized donated ova to five infertile women: report of two pregnancies', *Lancet*, 2, 223–4.

Butler, J. (1987) *Subjects of Desire: Hegelian Reflections on Twentieth-Century France*, New York: Columbia University Press.

—— (1997) *The Psychic Life of Power: Theories In Subjection*, Stanford, CA: Stanford University Press.

—— (2003) *Kritik der ethischen Gewalt*, Frankfurt am Main.: Suhrkamp.

Cadoret, R. J. (1990) 'Biologic perspectives of adoptee adjustment' in D. Brodzinsky and M. Schechter (eds), *The Psychology of Adoption*, New York: Oxford University Press, pp. 25–41.

Campion, M. J. (1995) *Who's Fit to Be a Parent?*, London: Routledge.

Carey, W. B., Lipton, W. L. and Myers, R. A. (1974) 'Temperament in adopted and foster babies', *Child Welfare*, 53: 352–9.

Cassen, R. (ed.) (1994) *Populations and Development: Old Debates, New Conclusions*, New Brunswick: Transaction Publishers.

Centre for Reproductive Law and Policy and NANE (2002) *Supplementary Information on Hungary: Scheduled for Review By the UN Human Rights Committee during its Seventy-Fourth Session*. Available at: http://www.nane.hu/egyesulet/mediafigyelem/crlp_eng.html [Accessed 10 May 2005].

Centre for Reproductive Rights (2001) *Trends in Reproductive Rights: East Central Europe*. Available at: http://www.crlp.org/pdf/pub_bp_trendsinrr_ece.pdf [Accessed 10 May 2005].

Center for Reproductive Rights and *Poradna pre obcianske a ludske prava – Centre for Human and Civil Rights (2003) Body and Soul: Forced Sterilisation and Other Assaults on Roma Reproductive Freedom in Slovakia*, In consultation with Ina Zoon: New York and Bratislava (http://www.poradna-prava.sk/dok/bodyandsoul.pdf) [Accessed 10 May 2005].

Chang, A. W. S., Chong, K. Y., Martinovich, C., Simerly, C. and Schatten, G. (2001) 'Transgenic monkeys produced by retroviral gene transfer into mature oocytes', *Science*, 291: 309–12.

Charles, H. (1992) 'Whiteness – politically colouring the "non" ' in H. Hinds, A. Phoenix and J. Stacey (eds), *Working Out – New Directions in Women's Studies*, London: Palmer, pp. 29–35.

Charlesworth, H., Chinkin, C. and Wright, S. (1991) 'Feminist approaches to international law', *American Journal of International Law*, 85: 613–45.

Cholewinski, R. (1998) 'The protection of human rights in the new Polish Constitution', *Fordham International Law Journal*, 22: 236–91.

Chubb, B. (1992) *The Government and Politics of Ireland*, London: Longman.

Cohn, D. A. (1990) 'Child-mother attachment of six-year-olds and social competence at school', *Child Development*, 61: 152–62.

Cole, E. S. and Donley, K. S. (1990) 'History, values, and placement policy issues in adoption' in D. Brodzinsky and M. Schechter (eds), *The Psychology of Adoption*, New York: Oxford University Press, pp. 273–94.

Colen, B. D. (1996) 'Proceedings of the workshop on inherited breast cancer in Jewish women: ethical, legal, and social implications', *CenterViews*, 10: 7–10.

Collishaw, S., Maughan, B. and Pickles, A. (1998) 'Infant adoption: psychosocial outcomes in adulthood', *Social Psychiatry and Psychiatric Epidemiology*, 33: 57–65.

Congregation for the Doctrine of the Faith (31 July 2004) 'Letter to the Bishops of the Catholic Church on the Collaboration of Men and Women in the Church and in the World' by Cardinal Joseph Ratzinger, approved by Pope John Paul II. Available at: www.vatican.va/roman_curia/congregations/cfaith/doc_doc_ index.htm [Accessed 10 May 2005].

Cook, R., Parsons, J., Mason, B. and Golombok, S. (1989) 'Emotional, marital and sexual functioning in patients embarking upon IVF and AID treatment for infertility', *Journal of Reproductive and Infant Psychology*, 7: 83–93.

Corea, G. (1985) *The Mother Machine*, New York: Harper and Row.

Cornia, G. A. and Paniccia, R. (1996) 'The transition's population crisis: an econometric investigation of nuptiality, fertility and mortality in severly distressed economies', *Moct-Most*, 6: 95–129.

Council of Europe Parliamentary Assembly (2003) *Impact of the 'Mexico City Policy' on the Free Choice of Contraception in Europe.* Available at: http://assembly. coe.int/Documents/WorkingDocs/doc03/EDOC9901.htm [Accessed 10 May 2005].

—— (2004) *The Situation of Women In the Countries of Post-Communism Transition.* Available at: http://assembly.coe.int/Documents/WorkingDocs/Doc04/ EDOC9997.htm [Accessed 10 May 2005].

Czerwinski, A. (2004) 'Sex, politics, and religion: the clash between Poland and the European Union over abortion', *Denver Journal of International Law and Policy*, 32: 653–74.

Daly, K. (1988) 'Reshaped parenthood identity: The transition to adoptive parenthood', *Journal of Contemporary Ethnography*, 17: 40–66.

—— (1990) 'Infertility resolution and adoption readiness. *Families in Society', The Journal of Contemporary Human Services*, 71: 483–92.

Danchin, P. D. (2002) 'U.S. unilateralism and the international protection of religious freedom: The multilateral alternative', *Columbia Journal of Transnational Law*, 41: 33–135.

Daniels, K. and Haimes, E. (eds) (1998) *Donor Insemination: International Social Science Perspectives*, Cambridge: Cambridge University Press.

Daniels, K. and Lalos, O. (1995) 'The Swedish Insemination Act and the availability of donors', *Human Reproduction*, 10: 1871–4.

Dányi, D. (2001) 'Demográfiai átmenetek (Valóság, tudomány, politika)' (Demographic transitions. Reality, science and politics) in L. Cseh-Szombathy and P. P. Tóth (eds), *Népesedés és nésedéspolitika (Population and population policy)* Budapest: századvég Kiadó, pp. 429–51.

Davis, A. (1982) *Women, Race and Class*, London: The Women's Press.

Deane, S. and Lodge, M. (2000) 'Divided loyalties: The Catholic Church and abortion policy in Ireland, a comparative perspective', paper for the Political Studies Association-UK 50th Annual Conference 10–13 April 2000, London. Available at: http://www.psa.ac.uk/cps/2000/DeaneShelley&LodgeMartin.pdf [Accessed 10 May 2005].

Delgado, M. (2002) *Estudio sobre la evolución de la maternidad en España entre 1975 y 2000*, Madrid: CSIC.

Demographic statistics, Data 1960–99 (1999) European Commission.

Department for Education and Skills (2005) *Intercountry Adoption*. Available at: http://www.dfes.gov.uk/adoption/intercountry/ [Accessed 10 May 2005].

Department of Health (1998) *Adoption – Achieving the Right Balance*, London: Department of Health.

Dickenson, D. (1997) *Property, Women and Politics: Subjects or Objects?*, Cambridge: Polity Press.

—— (2001) 'Property and women's alienation from their own reproductive labour', *Bioethics*, 3 (15): 205–17.

—— (2002) 'Commodification of human tissue: Implications for feminist and development ethics', *Developing World Bioethics*, 1 (2): 55–63.

—— (2005) 'Philosophical assumptions and presumptions about trafficking for prostitution.' in C. van den Anker and J. Doomernik (eds), *Trafficking and Women's Rights*, Basingstoke: Palgrave Macmillan.

Dinsmore, J. (1992) *Pregnant Drug Users: The Debate Over Prosecution*, National Center for Prosecution of Child Abuse: American Prosecutors Research Institute.

Dooley, D., McCarthy, J., Garanis-Papadatos, T. and Dalla Vorgia, P. (eds) (2002) *The Ethics of New Reproductive Technologies*, Oxford: Berghman Books.

Dorkenoo, E. and Elworthy, S. (1996) *Female Genital Mutilation: Proposals for Change*, London: Minority Rights Group.

Duden, B. (1991) *The Woman Beneath the Skin: A Doctor's Patients in Eighteenth-Century Germany*, Cambridge, MA: Harvard University Press.

Duden, B. (1993) *Disembodying Women: Perspectives On Pregnancy and the Unborn*, Cambridge, MA: Harvard University Press.

The Economist (2005) 'Right turn ahead: as the ex-communists fade away, their rivals jostle for the spoils, 17 February 2005. Available at: http://economist.com/displaystory.cfm?story_id=3672846 [Accessed 10 May 2005].

Eisenberg, V. H. and Schenker, J. G. (1998) 'Pre-embryo donation: ethical and legal aspects', *International Journal of Gynaecology and Obstetrics* 60 (1): 51–7.

Emaldi Cirión, A. (2002) *Las intervenciones sobre el genoma humano y la selección de sexo, El Convenio de Derechos humanos y biomedicina. Su entrada en vigor en el ordenamiento jurídico español*, Bilbao-Granada (ed.) Cátedra Interuniversitaria Fundación BBVA-Diputación Foral de Bizkaia, de Derecho y Genoma Humano, Ed-Comares.

Emaldi Cirión, A. (2001) *Ep Consejo genético y Sus implicaciones jurídices*, Bilbao-Granada (ed.) Cátedra Interuniversitaria Fundación BBVA-Diputación Foral de Bizkaia, de Derecho y Genoma Homano, Ed-Comares.

Erikson, E. H. (1968) *Identity: Youth and Crisis*, New York: Norton.

Erlich, P. R. (1968) *The Population Bomb*, New York: Ballantine Books.

Ernst, J. L., Katzive, L. and Smock, E. (2004) 'The legacy of Roe: the constitution, reproductive rights, and feminism: the global pattern of U.S. initiatives curtailing women's reproductive rights: A perspective on the increasingly anti-choice mosaic', *University of Pennsylvania, Journal of Constitutional Law*, 6: 752–95.

Essen and Johnsdotter (2004) 'Female genital mutilation in the West: traditional circumcision versus genital cosmetic surgery' *Acta Obstetricia et Gynecologica Scandinavica*, 83: 611–13.

Ethical Perspectives (2003) *Special Issue: Reproductive Rights*, 10: 3–4.

Ethics Committee of the American Society of Reproductive Medicine (2004a) *Preconception Gender Selection for Nonmedical Reasons*1, Fertility and Sterility*, 82: 232–5.

—— (2004b) *Sex Selection and Preimplantation Genetic Diagnosis*1, Fertility and Sterility*, 82: 245–8.

Evolution démographique récente en Europe 2000 (2000) Strasbourg: Council of Europe Publishing.

EU Business (2005) 'Portugal sets 2006 as year for EU Constitution, abortion referendums', 10 March. Available at: http://www.eubusiness.com/afp/050310170932.r2blbqgn [Accessed 10 May 2005].

European Commission (1998a) *Care in Europe* (Medium-term Community Action Programme on Equal Opportunities for Women and Men. Joint Report of the 'Gender and Employment' and 'Gender and Law' Groups of Experts) *Employment and Social Affairs*, Brussels: European Commission.

—— (1998b) *Equal Opportunities for Women and Men in Europe? Eurobarometer 44.3*, Brussels: European Commission.

—— (1999) *Employment Rates Report 1998: Employment Performance in the Member States*, Brussels: European Commission.

European Commission [Comission Européenne] (2000) *MISSOC. La protection sociale dans les États membres de l'Union européenne en 1999*, Brussels: European Commission.

European Commission Network on Childcare and other Measures to Reconcile Employment and Family Responsibilities (1995) *A Review of Services for Young Children In the European Union, Employment*, Industrial Relations and Social Affairs, Brussels: European Commission.

European Monitoring Centre on Racism and Xenophobia (EUMC), Council of Europe (2003) *Breaking the Barriers – Romani Women and Access to Public Health Care*, Luxembourg: Office for Official Publications of the European Communities.

European Social Statistics. Demography (2002), European Commission.

European Roma Rights Center (2004) *Breakthrough: Challenging Coercive Sterilisations of Romani Women in the Czech Republic*. Available at: http://www.errc.org/cikk.php?cikk=2071&archiv=1 [Accessed 10 May 2005].

European Women's Lobby (2005) *EWL Position Paper: Women's Sexual Rights in Europe*. Available at: http://www.womenlobby.org/Document.asp?DocID=864&tod=212619 [Accessed 10 May 2005].

EUROSTAT (several years) *Social Protection Expenditure and Receipts*, Luxembourg.

Feingberg, J. (1973) *Social Philosophy*, Englewood Cliffs, NJ: Prentice Hall.

Feminist Majority Foundation Feminist Daily News Wire (2004a) 'Spain's new prime minister makes women's equality a top priority', 11 May. Available at: http://www.feminist.org/news/newsbyte/uswirestory.asp?id=8433 [Accessed 10 May 2005].

—— (2004b) 'Three women stand trial for abortion in Portugal', 8 July. Available at: http://www.feminist.org/news/newsbyte/uswirestory.asp?id=8534 [Accessed 10 May 2005].

Fergusson, D. M., Lynskey, M. and Horwood, L. J. (1995) 'The adolescent outcomes of adoption: a 16-year longitudinal study', *Journal of Child Psychology and Psychiatry*, 36: 597–615.

Fleishman, L. (2000) 'The battle against reproductive rights: the impact of the Catholic Church on abortion law in both international and domestic arenas', *Emory International Law Review*, 14: 277–314.

Flinter, F. A. (2001) 'Preimplantation genetic diagnosis: needs to be tightly regulated', *British Medical Journal*, 322: 1008.

Flynn, J., Slovic, P. and Mertz, C. K. (1994) 'Gender, race, and perceptions of environmental health risks', *Risk Analysis*, 14: 1101–08.

Franklin, S. (1997) *Embodied Progress. A Cultural Account of Assisted Conception*, New York: Routledge.

Fränznick, M. W. and Wieners, K. (1996) *Ungewollte Kinderlosigkeit. Psychosoziale Folgen, Bewältigungsversuche und die Dominanz der Medizin*, Weinheim: München.

Freeman, E. W., Boxer, A. S., Rickels, K., Tureck, R. and Mastroianni, L. (1985) 'Psychological evaluation and support in a program of *in vitro* fertilization and embryo transfer', *Fertility and Sterility*, 43: 48–53.

Friedlander, H. (1995) *The Original of Nazi Genocide: From Euthanasia to the Final Solution*, Chapel Hill: University of North Carolina Press.

Futris, T. G. and Pasley K. (2003) 'Adolescent parenthood' in J. J. Ponzetti, Jr. (ed.), *International Encyclopedia of Marriage and Family*, New York: Thomson Gale, pp. 25–31.

Gatens, M. (1992) 'Power, bodies and difference,' in M. Barrett and A. Phillips (eds), *Destabilizing Theory*, Cambridge: Polity Press, pp. 120–37.

'Genotypes: Earmarked for Extinction?' (2000). Available at: http://www.gene.ch/gentech/2000/Jul/msg00066.html [Accessed 10 May 2005].

Gewirth, A. (1996) *The Community of Rights*, Chicago: University of Chicago Press.

Giami, A. (1998) 'Sterilisation and sexuality in the mentally handicapped', *European Psychiatry*, 13 (Suppl. 3): 113–19.

Giddens, A. (1992) *The Transformation of Intimacy: Sexuality, Love, and Eroticism in Modern Societies*, Stanford, CA: Stanford University Press.

Gilligan, C. (1993) *In a Different Voice: Psychological Theory and Women's Development*, Cambridge, MA: Harvard University Press [1982].

Glasse, A. (1998) 'US and Norway "used insane for Nazi-style tests" ', *The Times*, Wednesday, 29 April.

Golombok, S. (1992) 'Psychological functioning in infertility patients – Review', *Human Reproduction*, 7: 208–12.

Golombok, S., Cook, R., Bish, A. and Murray, C. (1995) 'Families created by the New Reproductive Technologies: quality of parenting and social and emotional development of the children', *Child Development*, 66: 285–98.

Golombok, S., Lycett, E., MacCallum, F., Jadva, V., Murray, C., Abdalla, H., Jenkins, J., Margara, R. and Rust, J. (2004) 'Parenting infants conceived by gamete donation', *Journal of Family Psychology*, 3 (18): 443–52.

Gordon, J. W. (1999) 'Genetic Enhancement in Humans', *Science*, 283: 2023–24.

Graumann, S. and Mildenberger, E. H. (2002) 'Ethics or politics?', *Reprokult (Women's Forum for Reproductive Medicine): Reproductive medicine and genetic engineering. Procedings of the Conference held in Berlin from 15 to 17 November 2001*, Federal Centre for Health Education, 110–15.

Great Lakes Genetics. Available at: http://www.genetest.com [Accessed 10 May 2005].

Green, K. (1995) *The Woman of Reason: Feminism, Humanism and Political Thought*, Cambridge: Polity Press.

Greenberg, M. (1999) 'Attachment and psychopathology in childhood' in J. Cassidy and P. Shaver (eds), *Handbook of Attachment*, London: Guilford Press, pp. 469–96.

Greenholgh, S. (1995) 'Engendering reproductive policy and practice in peasant China: for a feminist demography of reproduction', *Signs*, 20: 601–27.

Griffith, A. J., Ji, W., Prince, M. E., Altschuler, R. A. and Meisler, M. H. (1999) 'Optic, Olfactory, and Vestibular Dysmorphogenesis in the Homozygous Mouse Insertional Mutant Tg9257', *Journal of Craniofacial Genetics and Developmental Biology*, 19:157–63.

Grubb, Andrew (1998) ' "I, me, mine": bodies, parts and property', *Medical Law International*, 3: 299–313.

Gruenbaum, E. (2001) *The Female Circumcision Controversy: An Anthropological Perspective*, Philadelphia, PA: University of Pennsylvania Press.

The Guardian (2002) 'The legal challenge to abortion rights', 17 June 2002. Available online from: http://web.lexis-nexis.com/professional/ [Accessed 11 May 2005].

The Guardian (2005) 'US retreats in women's rights row', 5 March 2005. Available online at: http://www.guardian.co.uk/international/story/0,,1430947,00.html [Accessed 11 May 2005].

Guillod, O. (2002) 'Pays germaniques et Russie', in M-T. Meulders-Klein, R. Deech and P. Vlaadingerbroek (eds), *Biomedicine, the Family and Human Rights*, New York: Aspen Publishers, Inc, pp. 437–58.

Habermas, J. (2003) *The Future of Human Nature*, Cambridge, UK and Malden, MA: Polity press.

Hagmann, M. (1999) 'Fertility therapy may aid gene transfer', *Science*, 284: 1097–8.

Hajnal, J. (1965) 'European marriage patterns in perspective' in D. V. Glass and D. E. C. Eversley (eds), *Population in History*, London: Arnold, pp. 101–43.

Haker, H. (forthcoming 2005a) 'Narrative bioethics' in C. Rehmann-Sutter and D. Mieth (eds), *Biomedicine and the Future of the Human Condition*, Dordrecht: Kluwer.

—— (forthcoming 2005b) 'The fragility of the moral self', *Harvard Theological Review*, 98.

—— (forthcoming 2005c) 'Ethical aspects of embryonic stem cell research', in C. B. W. Hauskeller (ed.), *Stem Cell Research*, Muenster: Agenda Verlag.

Haldane, J. B. S. (1963) 'Biological possibilities for the human species in the next thousand years', in G. Wolstenholme (ed.), *Man and His Future*, London: J and A Churchill.

Halliday, F. (1988) 'Hidden from international relations: women in the international arena', *Millenium*, 17: 419–28

Hammon, K. R. (1998) 'Multifetal pregnancy reduction', *Journal of Obstetric, Gynaecological and Neonatal Nursing*, 27: 338.

Hancock, I. (2000) 'Downplaying the *Porrajmos*: the trend to minimize the Romani Holocaust', Review of G. Lewy's *The Nazi Persecution of the Gypsies* (2000). Available at: http://www.geocities.com/Paris/5121/lewy.htm [Accessed 11 May 2005].

Hand, J. R. (1993) 'Buying fertility: the constitutionality of welfare bonuses for welfare moms who submit to norplant insertion', *Vanderbilt Law Review*, 46: 715–54.

Haraway, D. J. (1991) *Simians, Cyborgs, and Women: The Reinvention of Nature*, New York: Routledge.

Hartmann, B. (1995) *Reproductive Rights and Wrongs: The Global Politics of Population Control*, Boston, MA: South End.

Hegel, G. W. F. (1967) *Philosophy of Right*, Translation by T. M. Knox Oxford: Oxford University Press.

Hellsten, S. K. (2002) 'Multicultural issues and human rights in maternal-fetal medicine' in D. Dickenson (ed.), *Ethical Issues in Maternal-Fetal Medicine*, Cambridge: Cambridge University Press, pp. 39–60.

Helsinki, Watch (1992) *Struggling For Ethnic Identity: Czechoslovakia's Endangered Gypsies*, London: Human Rights Watch.

Hershey, L. (1994) 'Choosing disability', *Ms*, July/August, 26–32.

Hershov, L. (1990) 'The seventh annual Jack Tizard memorial lecture: aspects of adoption', *Journal of Child Psychology and Psychiatry*, 31: 493–510.

Heyd, D. (1992) *Genethics: Moral Issues in the Creation of People*, Berkeley: University of California Press.

HFEA (1990) *The Human Fertilisation and Embryology Act*, London: HMSO.

—— (2004) *Code of Practice*, 6th edition, London: HFEA.

Hinsliff, G. (2005) 'I want to wake up this nation's conscience', *The Guardian*, 27 February 2005. Available at: http://observer.guardian.co.uk/uk_news/story/0,,1426378,00.html [Accessed 11 May 2005].

Hirschon, R. (ed.) (1984) *Women and Property – Women as Property*, London: Croom Helm.

HMSO (2002) *Adoption and Children Act 2002*, London: HMSO.

Holm, S. (2002) 'Going to the roots of the stem cell controversy', *Bioethics*, 16: 493–507.

Home Office (2004) *Home Office Circular 010/2004 about The Female Genital Mutilation Act 2003*. Available at: http://www.homeoffice.gov.uk/docs3/hoc1004.html [Accessed 11 May 2005].

Honore, A. M. (1961) 'Ownership', in A. G. Guest (ed.), *Oxford Essays in Jurisprudence*, Oxford: Oxford University Press.

Hooper, J. (2003) 'New Fertility Law divides Italy', *The Guardian*, 12 December 2003. Available at: http://www.guardian.co.uk/italy/story/0,,1105906,00.html [Accessed 11 May 2005].

Hoopes, J. L. (1982) *Prediction In Child Development: A Longitudinal Study of Adoptive and Nonadoptive Families*, New York: Child Welfare League of America.

Horsburgh, B. (1996) 'Schrodinger's cat, eugenics, and the compulsory sterilization of welfare mothers: deconstructing the old/new rhetoric and constructing the reproductive rights of Natality for Low-Income Women of Color', *Cardozo Law Review*, 17: 531–82.

Humphrey, M. (1975) 'The effect of children upon the marriage relationship', *British Journal of Medical Psychology*, 48: 273–9.

Irish Human Rights Commission (2005) *Submission of the Irish Human Rights Commission to the UN Committee on the Elimination of Discrimination Against Women*. Available at: http://www.ihrc.ie/_fileupload/banners/CEDAW_Final1.pdf [Accessed 11 May 2005].

Jacobs, A., Dwyer, J. and Lee, P. (2001) 'Seventy ova', *Hastings Center Report*, 31 (4): 12–14.

James, S. and C. Robertson (2002) *Genital Cutting and Transnational Sisterhood: Disputing U.S. Polemics*, Urbana: University of Illinois Press.

Jonas, H. (1984) *The Imperative of Responsibility: In Search of An Ethics for the Technological Age*, Chicago, IL: University of Chicago Press.

Jones, G. (2005) 'Blair on defensive as Cardinal puts abortion at heart of general election', *The Telegraph*, 16 March 2005.

Jones, O. D. (1992) 'Sex selection: regulating technology enabling the predetermination of a child's gender', *Harvard and Journal of Law and Technology*, 6: 1–62.

Jones, H., Diop, N., Askew, I. and Kaboré, I. (1999) 'Female genital cutting practices in Burkina Faso and Mali and their negative health outcomes', *Studies in Family Planning*, 30 (3): 219–30.

Jones, H. W. and Cohen, J. (2001) 'IFFS surveillance 01', *Fertility and Sterility*, 76, (Suppl. 1).

Jourdan, L. (1999) 'Gypsy hunt in Switzerland: long pursuit of racial purity', Translation by B. Smerin, *Le Monde diplomatique* October 1999. Available at: http://mondediplo.com/1999/10/11gypsy [Accessed 11 May 2005].

Juengst, E. (1997) 'Prenatal diagnosis and the ethics of uncertainty', in J. Monagle and D. Thomasma (eds), *Health Care Ethics: Cultural Issues for the 21st Century*, Rockville, MD: Aspen Publishers, Inc., pp. 15–29.

Juffer, F. and Rosenboom, L. G. (1997) 'Infant-mother attachment of internationally adopted children in the Netherlands', *International Journal of Behavioral Development*, 20: 93–107.

Katz Rothman, B. (1986) *The Tentative Pregnancy*, New York: Viking Penguin, Inc.

Kay, L. E. (2000) *Who wrote the book of life? A History of the Genetic Code*, Stanford, CA: Stanford University Press.

Kenrick, D. and G. Puxon (1995) *Gypsies under the Swastika*, Hertfordshire: University of Hertfordshire Press.

Kevles, D. (1985) *In the Name of Eugenics: Genetics and the Uses of Human Heredity*, Harmondsworth, UK: Penguin.

Keynes, J. M. (1973 [1936]) 'The general theory of employment, interest and money' in Donald Maggridge (ed.) *The Collected Writings of John Maynard Keynes*, London: Macmillan.

Kingsberg, S. A., Applegarth, L. D. and Janata, J. W. (1996) 'Embryo donation programmes and policies in North America: survey results and implications for health and mental health professionals', *Fertility and Sterility*, 73 (2): 215–20.

Kissling, F. (1998) 'Catholicism', *Reader's Companion to U.S. Women's History*. Available at: http://college.hmco.com/history/readerscomp/women/html/wh_004700_catholicism.htm [Accessed 11 May 2005].

Kittay, E. F. (1999) *Love's Labor: Essays on Women, Equality, and Dependency*, New York: Routledge.

Klaus, M. H. and Kennell, J. H. (1976) *Maternal-Infant Bonding*, St Louis: Mosby.

Klee, E. (1999) *'Euthanasie' im NS-Staat. Die Vernichtung lebensunwerten Lebens*, Frankfurt: Fischer.

Klock, S. C., Jacob, M. C. and Maier, D. (1994) 'A prospective study of donor insemination recipients: secrecy, privacy and disclosure', *Fertility and Sterility*, 62: 477–84.

Koch, L. (1990) 'IVF, a rational choice?', *Reproductive and Genetic Engineering: International Journal of Feminist Analysis*, 3: 235–42.

Kohn, M. (1995) *The Race Gallery: The Return of Racial Science*, London: Jonathan Cape.

Kong, D. (1996) 'Statistics are fertile grounds for debate', *The Boston Globe*, 4 August, p. A35.

Konnertz, U. and Haker, H. (forthcoming 2005) *Ethik Geschlecht Wissenschaft*, Paderborn: Mentis.

Labrousse Riou, C. (1991) 'La maîtrise du vivant: matière à procès', *Pouvoirs*, 56: 85.

Lambert, L. and Streather, J. (1980) *Children in Changing Families: A Study of Adoption and Illegitimacy*, London: MacMillan.

Larson, E. (1995) *Sex, Race and Science: Eugenics in the Deep South*, London: Johns Hopkins University Press.

Lasker, J. N. (1998) 'The users of donor insemination' in Daniels, K. and Haimes, E. (eds.) *Donor Insemination: International Social Science Perspectives*, Cambridge: Cambridge University Press, pp. 7–32.

Laxton-Kane, M. and Slade, P. (2002) 'The role of maternal prenatal attachment in a woman's experience of pregnancy and implications for the process of care', *Journal of Reproductive and Infant Psychology*, 20: 253–66.

Levinas, E. (1998) *Otherwise than Being, or, Beyond Essence*, Pittsburgh, PA: Duquesne University Press.

Levine, R. (1981) *Ethics and Regulations of Clinical Research*, Baltimore, MD: Urban and Schwarzenberg.

Levy-Shiff, R., Bar, O. and Har-Even, D. (1990) 'Psychological adjustment of adoptive parents-to-be', *American Journal of Orthopsychiatry*, 60: 258–67.

Lippman, A. (1991) 'Prenatal genetic testing and screening: constructing needs and reinforcing inequalities', *American Journal of Law and Medicine*, 17: 15–50.

—— (1994) 'The genetic construction of prenatal testing: choice, consent, or conformity for women?' in K. H. Rothenberg and E. Thomson (eds), *Women and Prenatal Testing: Facing the Challenges of Genetic Technology*, Columbus: Ohio University Press, pp. 9–34.

Lois, C., Hong, E. J., Pease, S., Brown, E. J. and Baltimore, D. (2002) 'Germline transmission and tissue-specific expression of transgenes delivered by lentiviral vectors', *Science*, 295: 868–71.

MacCallum, F. (2004) 'Families with a child conceived by embryo donation: parenting and child development', Unpublished Ph.D. thesis, London: City University.

Mahowald, M. B. (2000) *Genes Women and Equality*, Oxford: Oxford University Press.

—— (2002) 'The fewer the better? Ethical issues in multiple gestation' in D. Dickenson (ed.) *Ethical Issues in Maternal-Fetal Medicine*, Cambridge: Cambridge University Press, pp. 247–60.

Mahowald, M., Levinson, D. and Cassell, C. (1996) 'The new genetics and women', *The Milbank Quarterly*, 74: 239.

Malta Today (2004), 'Waiting for Europe – the long march to emancipation …', 9 May 2004. Available at: http://www.maltatoday.com.mt/2004/05/09/e4.html [Accessed 11 May 2005].

Margalit, G. (2002) *Germany and its Gypsies: A Post-Auschwitz Ordeal*, Madison: University of Wisconsin Press.

Marie Stopes International website (2005) Available at: http://www.mariestopes.org.uk/ [Accessed 11 May 2005].

Marteau, T. M. and Drake, H. (1995) 'Attributions for disability: the influence of genetic screening', *Social Science Medicine*, 40: 1127–32.

Marteau, T. M., Dundas, R. and Axworthy, D. (1997) 'Long term cognitive and emotional impact of genetic testing for carriers of cystic fibrosis: the effects of test results and gender', *Health Psychology*, 16: 51–62.

Mason, M. C. (1993) *Male Infertility – Men Talking*, London: Routledge.

Maughan, B. and Pickles, A. (1990) 'Adopted and illegitimate children growing up' in L. N. Robins and M. Rutter (eds), *Straight and Devious Pathways from Childhood to Adulthood*, Cambridge: Cambridge University Press, pp. 36–61.

McClintock, A. (1995) *Imperial Leather: Race, Gender, and Sexuality in the Colonial Contest*, New York: Routledge.

McMahan, J. (1998) 'Problems of population theory', *Ethics*, 92: 96–127.

Megan, K. (1994) 'Proposal offers money for contraceptive use ...', *The Hartford Courant*, 17 February, editorial, p. A1.

Mercurio, B. (2003) 'Abortion in Ireland: an analysis of the legal transformation resulting from membership in the European Union', *Tulane Journal of International and Comparative Law*, 11: 141–80.

Mertus, J. (1998) 'Human rights of women in central and Eastern Europe', *American University Journal of Gender, Social Policy and the Law*, 6: 369–484.

Meulders-Klein, T. (1988) 'Le droit de l'enfant face au droit a l'enfant', *Revue Trimestriere du Droit Civil*, 2: 664.

Miall, C. (1987) 'The stigma of adoptive parent status: perceptions of community attitudes toward adoption and the experience of informal social sanctioning', *Journal of Applied Family and Child Studies*, 36: 34–9.

Mill, J. S. (1986 [1859]) *On Liberty*, New York: Prometheus Books.

——— (1987[1859]) *On Liberty*, New York: Prometheus Books.

Miller, B. C., Fan, X., Christensen, M., Grotevant, H. D. and van Dulmen, M. (2000) 'Comparisons of adopted and nonadopted adolescents in a large, nationally representative sample', *Child Development*, 71: 1458–73.

Miller, P-G. (1999) 'Member state sovereignty and women's reproductive rights: The European Union's response', *Boston College International and Comparative Law Review*, 22: 195–212.

Ministry of Local Government and Regional Development, Kingdom of Norway (2001) Initial report submitted by Norway pursuant to Article 25, Paragraph 1 of The Framework Convention for the Protection of National Minorities. Available at: http://odin.dep.no/krd/engelsk/publ/rapporter/016071-220003/dok-bn.html [Accessed 11 May 2005].

Mitchell, P. (1994) 'Lawmaker puts money on birth control idea', *The Orlando Sentinel*, 16 February, editorial, p. D5.

Mohanty, C. T., Russo, A. and Torres, L. (eds) (1991) *Third World Women and the Politics of Feminism*, Bloomington: Indiana University Press.

Morning Star (2005) 'Polish MP's reject abortion law reform', 16 February 2005. Available at: http://web.lexis-nexis.com/professional/ [Accessed 11 May 2005].

Muheres en Red (2004) *El Congreso cambiará la ley para poder perseguir fuera de España las mutilaciones genitales*. Available at: http://www.mujeresenred.net/news/printbrev.php3?id_breve=73 [Accessed 11 May 2005].

Mullally, S. (2005) 'Gendered citizenship: debating reproductive rights in Ireland', *Human Rights Quarterly*, 27 (1): 78–104.

Muller, M. E. (1996) 'Prenatal and postnatal attachment: a modest correlation', *Journal of Obstetric, Gynaecologic and Neonatal Nursing*, 25: 161–6.

Muller-Hill, B. (1988) *Murderous Science: Elimination by Scientific Selection of Jews, Gypsies, and Others in Germany 1933–1945*, Translation by G. R. Fraser, Oxford: Oxford University Press.

Munzer, S. R. (1990) *A Theory of Property*, Cambridge: Cambridge University Press.

Nachtigall, R. D. (1993) 'Secrecy and unresolved issue in the practice of donor insemination', *American Journal of Obstetrics and Gynaecology*, 168: 1846–51.

Nachtigall, R. D., Tschann, J. M., Quiroga, S. S., Pitcher, L. and Becker, G. (1997) 'Stigma, disclosure and family functioning among parents and children conceived through donor insemination', *Fertility and Sterility*, 68: 83–9.

Namkee, A. and Mira, P. (eds) (1999) *A Note on the Changing Relationship Between Fertility and Female Employment Rates in Developed Countries*, Madrid: Fundación de Estudios de Economía Aplicada.

National Council for Adoption (1997) *Hotline Information Packet*, Washington: National Council for Adoption.

National Institute of Child Health and Human Development (1979) *Antenatal Diagnosis: Report of a Consensus Development Conference*, Bethesda, MD: NIH.

National Population Policies 2001 (2002), New York: UN Department of Economic and Social Affairs Population Division.

National Summary and Fertility Clinic Reports (1995) 'Assisted reproductive technology success rates'. Available at: http://www.cdc.gov/reproductivehealth/ART/ARTReports.htm#1995 [Accessed 11 May 2005].

Neue Zurcher Zeitung-NZZ (2003) 'Forced sterilisation allowed in exceptional cases', 5 September. Available at: http://www.nzz.ch/eng/index.html [Accessed 5 September 2003].

Neue Zurcher Zeitung-NZZ (2004). 'Victims of forced sterilisation win compensation in Switzerland', 31 March 2004. Available at: http://www.nzz.ch/eng/index.html [Accessed 31 March 2004].

Newman, S. A. (2000) 'Don't try to engineer human embryos', *St. Louis Post-Dispatch*, 25 July editorial, p. B15.

Noddings, N. (2003[1984]) *Caring: A Feminine Approach to Ethics and Moral Education*, Berkeley, CA: University of California Press.

Nussbaum, M. C. (2000) *Women and Human Development: The Capabilities Approach*, Cambridge: Cambridge University Press.

Nuttall, N. and Wilkins, E. (1994) 'Watchdog to report on designer baby', *The Times (London)*, 1 January, editorial.

Obser, J. (1998) 'Drawing the line', *Newsday*, 16 June, editorial, p. C08.

OECD (1999) *A Caring World: The New Social Policy Agenda*, Paris: OECD.

—— (2002) *OECD Employment Outlook*, Paris: OECD.

Office of Technology Assessment, U.S. Congress (1988) *Mapping Our Genes – Genome Projects: How Big, How Fast?*, Washington, DC: U.S. Government Printing Office.

Olivennes, F., Fanchin, R., Ledee, N., Righini, C., Kadoch, I. and Frydman, R. (2002) 'Perinatal outcome and development studies on children born after IVF', *Human Reproduction Update*, 8: 117–28.

O'Neill, O. (2000) 'The "good enough parent" in the age of the new reproductive technologies', in H. B. Haker and D. Beyleveld (eds), *The Ethics of Genetics in Human Procreation*, Aldershot: Ashgate, 33–48.

Oosterveld, V. (1993) 'Refugee status for female circumcision fugitives: building a Canadian precedent', *University of Toronto Faculty of Law Review*, 51 (2): 277–87.

Ordover, N. (2003) *American Eugenics: Race, Queer Anatomy, and the Science of Nationalism*, Minneapolis, MN: University of Minnesota Press.

PR Newswire (2001) 'Dynacare, Intema Join Forces to Offer Advanced Prenatal Testing', 16 April, Available at: http://www.dynagene.com/about/press/4162001.html [Accessed 11 May 2005].

Paganussi, P. J. (1998) 'Fertility Frontier', *Washington Post*, 23 February editorial, p. A18.

Parfit, D. (1982) Future generations, further problems, *Philosophy and Public Affairs*, 11: 113–72.

Pasquinelli, C. (ed.) (2000) *Antropologia delle mutilazioni genitali femminili: una ricerca in Italia*, Rome: AIDOS.

Pateman, C. (1988) *The Sexual Contract*, Cambridge: Polity Press.

Perry, A. C., Wakayama, T., Kishikawa, H., Kasai, T., Okabe, M., Toyoda, Y. and Yanagimachi, R. (1999) 'Mammalian transgenesis by intracytoplasmic sperm Injection', *Science*, 284: 1180–3.

Pfeffer, N. (1993) *The Stork and the Syringe*, Cambridge: Polity Press.

Pilisuk, M. and Acredolo, C. (1988) 'Fear of technological hazards: one concern or many?', *Social Behaviour*, 3: 17–24.

Pizzulli, F. C. (1974) 'Asexual reproduction and genetic engineering: a constitutional assessment of the technology of cloning', *Southern California Law Review*, 47: 476–584.

Plomin, R. and DeFries, J. (1985) *Origins of Individual Differences in Infancy: The Colorado Adoption Project*, Orlando, FL: Academic Press.

Population Council (1997) *Female Genital Mutilation: Common, Controversial, and Bad for Women's Health*. Available at: http://www.popcouncil.org/publications/popbriefs/pb3(2)_1.html [Accessed 11 May 2005].

Price, F. (1999) 'Solutions for life and growth?' Collaborative conceptions in reproductive medicine' in J. Edwards, S. Franklin, E. Hirsch and F. Price (eds), *Technologies of Procreation: Kinship in the Age of Assisted Conception*, London: Routledge, pp. 53–9.

Pryde, P. G., Drugan, A., Johnson, M. P., Isada, N. B. and Evans, M. I. (1993) 'Prenatal diagnosis: choices women make about pursuing testing and acting on abnormal results', *Clinical Obstetrics and Gynecology*, 36: 469–509.

Purdy, L. (1996) *Reproducing Persons: Feminist Issues in Bioethics, Ithaca*: Cornell University Press.

Qadeer, I. (1998) 'Reproductive health – a public health perspective', *Newsletter of Women's Global Network for Reproductive Rights*, 4.

Rahman, A. and Toubia, N. (2000) *Female Genital Mutilation: A Guide to Laws and Policies Worldwide*, London: Zed in association with CRLP and RAINBO.

Ramphal, S. (1988) 'Where is the time-bomb ticking?' in N. Polunin (ed.), *Population and Global Security*, Cambridge: Cambridge University Press.

Ramsey, P. (1973) 'Screening: an ethicists' view,' in B. Hilton, D. Callahan, M. Harris, P. Condliffe and B. Berkley (eds), *Ethical Issues in Human Genetics: Genetic Counseling and the Use of Genetic Knowledge* (Fogarty International Proceedings No. 13) New York: Plenum Publishing Corporation, 147–59.

Raval, H., Slade, P., Buck, P. and Lieberman, B. (1987) 'The impact of infertility on emotions and the marital and sexual relationship', *Journal of Reproductive and Infant Psychology*, 5: 221–34.

Rawls, J. (1971) *A Theory of Justice*, Cambridge: Cambridge University Press.

Rawls, J. (1993) *Political Liberalism*, New York: Columbia University Press.

Raymond, J. (1990) 'Reproductive gifts and gift giving: the altruistic woman', *Hastings Center Report Gesetz zum Schutz von Embryonen*, 20 (6): 7–11.

Read, D. (1998) *Out of sight, out of mind: the report of a survey into inter-agency policies and procedures relating to female genital mutilation (FGM) in England and Wales*, London: FORWARD.

III (1994) *Reproductive Freedom News*, March 11, p. 5.

Reprokult (Women's Forum for Reproductive medicine) (2002) *Reproductive medicine and genetic engineering. Proceedings of the Conference held in Berlin from 15th to 17th November 2001*, Cologne: Federal Centre for Health Education.

Robila, M. (ed.) (2004) *Families in Eastern Europe*, London: Elsevier.

Robinson, G. E. and Stewart, D. E. (1996) 'The psychological impact of infertility and new reproductive technologies', *Harvard Review of Psychiatry*, 4: 168–72.

Romeo Casabona, C. (2003), 'El derecho a la vida: aspectos constitucionales de las nuevas biotechologías', *El derecho a la vida. Actus de las VIII Jornadas de la Asociación de Letrados del Tribunal Constitucional*, Madrid: Tribunal Constitucional y Centro de Estudios Políticas y Constitucionales, pp. 11–54.

Rudolph, K. L. Chang S. Lee, H. W., Blasco, M., Gottlieb, G. J., Greider, C., and Depinho, R. A. (1999) 'Longevity, stress response, and cancer in aging telomerase-deficient mice', *Cell*, 96: 701–12.

Runcis, M. (1998) *Steriliseringar i folkhemmet*. [Sterilization in the Swedish Welfare State], Stockholm: Ordfront.

Russell, A., Sobo, E. and Thompson, M. (2000) *Contraception Across Cultures: Technologies, Choices and Constraints*, Oxford: Berg.

Rutter, M., O'Connor, T. G., Beckett, C., Castle, J., Croft, C. M., Dunn, J. *et al.* (2000) 'Recovery and deficit following profound early deprivation' in P. Selman (ed.), *Intercountry Adoption. Development, Trends and Perspectives*, London: BAAF, pp. 107–25

Ruxton, S. (1996) *Children in Europe*, London: NCH Action for Children.

Ryan, M. A. (2001) *The Ethics and Economics of Assisted Reproduction: The Cost of Longing*, Washington: Georgetown University Press.

Saclier, C. (2000) 'In the best interests of the child?' in P. Selman (ed.), *Intercountry adoption – Developments, Trends and Perspectives*, London: BAAF, pp. 53–65.

Sangeeta, F. (1999) 'From family planning to reproductive health', *Newsletter of Women's Global Network for Reproductive Rights 1*.

Savage, I. (1993) 'Demographic influences on risk perceptions', *Risk Analysis*, 13: 413–20.

Saxton, M. (1998) 'Disability rights and selective abortion', in R. Solinger (ed.), *Abortion Wars: A Half Century of Struggle, 1950–2000*, Berkley, CA: University of California Press, pp. 374–93.

Schneider, I. (2003) 'Within and beyond the limits of human nature', Unpublished paper from the conference *'Pro-Life' and 'Pro-choice': Overcoming the Misleading Controversy* at the Center for Genetics and Society and Heinrich Böll-Stiftung, 12 October, Berlin.

Schneider, I. (2003) 'Gesellschaftliche Umgangsweisen mit Keimzellen: Regulation zwischen Gabe, Verkauf und Ververäußerlichkeit', in S. Graumann and I. Schneider (eds), *Verkörperte Technik – Entkörperte Frau Biopolitik und Geschlecht*, Frankfurt and New York: Campus, pp. 41–65.

Seidelman, W. (1996) 'Nuremberg lamentation: for the forgotten victims of medical science', *British Medical Journal*, 313 (1): 1463–7.

Seligmann, J. and Foote, D. (1991) 'Whose baby is it anyway?', *Newsweek*, 28 October editorial, p. 73.

Selman, P. (2000) 'The demographic history of intercountry adoption' in P. Selman (ed.), *Intercountry Adoption. Developments, Trends and Perspectives*, London: BAAF, pp. 15–39.

Sen, G. (1994) 'Reproduction: the feminist challenge to social policy,' in G. Sen and R. C. Snow (eds), *Power and Decision: The Social Control of Reproduction*, Boston: Harvard School of Public Health, pp. 5–18.

Shaw, M. (1984) 'Conditional prospective rights of the fetus', *Journal of Legal Medicine*, 5: 63.

Shell-Duncan, B. and Hernlund, Y. (2000) *Female 'Circumcision' in Africa: Culture, Controversy, and Change*, Boulder, CO: Lynne Rienner Publishers.

Sherwin, S. (1998) *The Politics of Women's Health: Exploring Agency and Autonomy*, Philadelphia, PA: Temple University Press.

Singh, S. and Darroch, J. E. (2000) 'Adolescent pregnancy and childbearing: levels and trends in developed countries', *Family Planning Perspectives*, 32 (1): 14–23.

Singer, L., Brodzinsky, D., Ramsay, D., Steir, M. and Waters, E. (1985) 'Mother–infant attachment in adoptive families', *Child Development*, 56: 1543–51.

Sjogren, B. (1992) 'Future use and development of prenatal diagnosis, consumers' attitudes', *Prenatal Diagnosis*, 12: 1–8.

Sleebos, J. E. (2003) 'Low fertility rates in OECD countries: facts and policy response', *Social, Employment and Migration Working Papers No.15*, Paris: OECD.

Slovic, P. (1992) 'Perceptions of risk: reflections on the psychometric paradigm', in D. Goldring and S. Krimsky (eds), *Social Theories of Risk*, New York: Praeger.

Smith, A. (1996) *The Contradictions of Change: The Relative Status of Women in the Workforce After the Fall of Communism in Eastern Europe*. Available at: http://titan.iwu.edu/~polysci/res_publica/smith.html [Accessed 11 May 2005].

Spallone, P. (1989) *Beyond Conception: The New Politics of Reproduction*, London: Routledge.

Stephenson, M-A. (2005) 'It will take all our energies to stand still', *The Guardian*, 8 March 2005. Available at: http://www.guardian.co.uk/comment/story/0,,1432589,00.html [Accessed 11 May 2005].

Stewart, M. (2004) 'Curbing reliance on abortion in Russia', *Human Rights Brief*, 11: 51–4.

Stoller, C. (1996) *Eine unvollkommene Schwangerschaft*, Zuerich: Theologisher Verlag Zuerich.

Strathern, M. (1993) *Reproducing the Future: Anthropology, Kinship and the New Reproductive Technologies*, Manchester: Manchester University Press.

Tang, Y-P., Shimizu, E., Dube, G. R., Rampon, C., Kerchner, G. A., Zhuo, M., Liu, G. and Tsien, J. Z. (1999) 'Genetic enhancement of learning and memory in mice', *Nature*, 401: 63–9.

Tempest, M. (2005) 'Blair courts evangelicals as Catholics back Howard', *The Guardian* 14 March 2005. Available at: http://politics.guardian.co.uk/ homeaffairs/story/0,,1437235,00.html [Accessed 11 May 2005].

Testart, J. (1984) *De l'éprouvette au bébé-spectacle*, Bruxelles: Éditions Complexe.

—— (1994) *Artificial Procreation*, Madrid: Debate Dominos.

te Veld, E. R., van Baar, A. L., and van Kooij, R. J. (1998) 'Concerns about assisted reproduction', *Lancet*, 351: 1524–5.

Thomson, J. J. (1971) 'A defense of abortion', *Philosophy and Public Affairs*, 1(1): 47–66.

Thompson, L. A. and Plomin, R. (1988) 'The sequenced inventory of communi-cation development: an adoption study of two- and three-year-olds', *International Journal of Behavioral Development*, 11: 219–31.

Thornton, J. G., McNamara, H. M. and Montague, I. A. (1994) 'Would you rather be a "birth" or a "genetic" mother? If so, how much?', *Journal of Medical Ethics*, 20: 87–92.

Tizzard, J. (2004) 'Sex selection, child welfare and risk: a critique of the HFEA's recommendations on sex selection', *Health Care Analysis*, 12: 61–8.

Tomasevski, K. (1995) 'European approaches to enhancing reproductive freedom', *American University Law Review*, 44: 1037–51.

Tong, R. (1997) *Feminist Approaches to Bioethics: Theoretical Reflections and Practical Applications*, Boulder, CO: Westview Press.

Toubia, N. and Izett, S. (1998) *Female Genital Mutilation: An Overview*, Geneva: World Health Organization.

Trehan, N. (2001) 'In the name of the Roma? The role of private foundations and NGOs' in W. Guy (ed.), *Between Past and Future: the Roma of Central and Eastern Europe*, Hertfordshire: University of Hertfordshire Press, pp. 134–49.

Triseliotis, J., Sellick, C. and Short, R. (1995) *Foster Care: Theory and Practice*, London: Batsford.

Triseliotis, J., Shireman, J. and Hundleby, M. (1997) *Adoption: Theory, Policy and Practice*, London: Redwood Books.

Tritt, R. and Human Rights Watch (1992) *Struggling For Ethnic Identity: Czechoslovakia's Endangered Gypsies*, New York: Human Rights Watch.

Trombley, S. (1988) *The Right to Reproduce: A History of Coercive Sterilisation*, London: Weidenfeld and Nicolson.

Tsien, J. (2000) 'Building a brainier mouse', *Scientific American*, 282: 62–8.

Tydén, M. (2002) *Från politik till praktik: de svenska steriliseringslagarna 1935–1975* [Sterilisation Laws in Sweden, 1935–1975: The Formation and Transformation of a Policy], Stockholm: Almqvist & Wiksell International.

United Nations Population Division, Department of Economic and Social Affairs (2002) *Abortion Policies: A Global Review*. Available at: http://www.un.org/esa/ population/publications/abortion/ [Accessed 11 May 2005].

United Nations Population Fund (2004a) *State of World Population 2004*, New York: UNFPA. Available at: http://www.unfpa.org/swp/2004/pdf/en_swp04.pdf [Accessed 11 May 2005].

United Nations Population Fund (2004b) *UNFPA Global Population Policy Update*. Available at: http://www.unfpa.org/parliamentarians/news/newsletters/ issue20.htm [Accessed 11 May 2005].

United Nations Population Fund (n.d.) *Country Profiles: Overview: Eastern Europe and Asia*. Available at: http://www.unfpa.org/profile/overview_eurasia.htm [Accessed 11 May 2005].

United States Holocaust Memorial Museum (c.2002) *Sinti and Roma: Victims of the Nazi Era*, Washington D.C.: USHMM. Available at: http://www.ushmm. org/education/resource/roma/roma.php?menu=/export/home/www/doc_root/ education/foreducators/include/menu.txt&bgcolor=CD9544 [Accessed 11 May 2005].

Van de Kaa, D. (1999) 'Europe and its population. The *long view*', in D. Van de Kaa (ed.), *European populations: Unity in Diversity*, Vol. 1, Dordrecht, Boston, MA, London: Kluwer Academic Publishers.

Vayena, E. and Rowe P. (2002) *Current Practices and Controversies in Assisted Reproduction*, Report of WHO meeting, Geneva: WHO.

Verhulst, F. (2000) 'The development of internationally adopted children' in P. Selman (ed.), *Intercountry Adoption. Development, Trends and Perspectives*, London: BAAF.

Verlinsky, Y., Rechitsky, S., Verlinsky, O., Masciangelo, C., Lederer, K. and Kuliev, A. (2002) 'Preimplantation diagnosis for early-onset Alzheimer disease caused by V717L mutation', *JAMA*, 287: 1018–21.

Villota, P. (2000) 'Reflexiones sobre una política fiscal y social más favorable para la conciliación de la vida familiar y profesional', *Compartir es sumar*, Barcelona: Institut Català de la Dona, Generalitat de Catalunya.

—— (2003) 'Políticas de cuidado de personas en la Unión Europea para facilitar la conciliación entre la vida laboral y familiar', *Aequalitas*, 12: 50–9.

—— (2005) 'Birth rate and women's rights in Europe' in H. Widdows, I. Alkorta and A. Emaldi (eds), *Women's Reproductive Rights*, Basingstoke: Palgrave Macmillan.

Villota, P. and Ferrari, I. (2001) *The Impact of the Tax/Benefit System on Women's Work (El impacto de los impuestos y transferencias sociales en el empleo remunerado de las mujeres)*, Brussels: Comisión Europea, DGV. Available at: http://europa.eu.int/comm/employment_social/equ_opp/women_work.pdf [Accessed 11 May 2005].

Waldron, J. (1988) *The Right to Private Property*, Oxford: Clarendon Press.

Warman, A. and Roberts, C. (2003) *Adoption and Looked after children – An International Comparison*, Oxford: Department of Social Policy and Social Work, University of Oxford.

Watt, H. (2004) 'Preimplantation genetic diagnosis: choosing the "good enough" child', *Health Care Analysis*, 12: 51–60.

Wei, F., Wang, G-D., Kerchner, G. A., Kim, S. J., Xu, H-M., Chen, Z-F. and Zhuo, M. (2001) 'Genetic enhancement of inflammatory pain by forebrain NR2B overexpression', *Nature Neuroscience*, 4: 164–69.

Weingart, P., Kroll, J. and Bayertz, K. (1986) *Rasse, Blut und Gene. Geschichte der Eugenik und Rassenhygiene in Deutschland*, Frankfurt: Suhrkamp.

Weiss, R. (2001) 'Study: rodents' higher IQ may come at painful price', *Washington Post*, 29 January editorial, p. A2.

Wertz, D. and Fletcher, J. C. (1989) 'Fatal knowledge? Prenatal diagnosis and sex selection', *Hastings Center Report*, 19: 21.

Widdows, H. (2002) 'The ethics of secrecy in donor insemination' in D. Dickenson (ed.), *Ethical Issues in Maternal-Fetal Medicine*, Cambridge: Cambridge University Press, pp. 167–80.

Widdows, H. and MacCallum, F. (2002) 'Disparities in parenting criteria: an exploration of the issues, focusing on adoption and embryo donation', *Journal of Medical Ethics*, 28: 139–42.

Wikler, D. (1995) 'Policy issues in donor insemination', *Stanford Law Political Review*, 6/2: 47–56.

Willems, W. (1997) *In Search of the True Gypsy: From Enlightenment to Final Solution*, Translation by D. Bloch, London: Frank Cass.

Winston, R. (1999) *The IVF Revolution: The Definitive Guide to Assisted Reproductive Techniques*, London: Vermillon.

Wolf, D. P. and Quigley, M. M. (1984) *Human In Vitro Fertilization and Embryo Transfer*, New York, Plenum Publishing.

Women on Waves (n.d) *Criminalisation of Abortion in Portugal*. Available at: http://www.womenonwaves.org/article-1020.52-en.html [Accessed 11 May 2005].

World Health Organisation (WHO) (1992) 'Recent advances in medically assisted conception, Report of the WHO Scientific Group', Geneva: *Tech Rep Ser*, 820: 1–111.

World Health Organisation (WHO) UNICEF *et al.* (1997) *Female Genital Mutilation*, Geneva: World Health Organisation.

Wrigley, E. A. and Schofield, R. S. (1981) *The Population History of England, 1541–1871: A Reconstruction*, London: Arnold.

Yarrow, L. J. and Goodwin, M. S. (1973) 'The immediate impact of separation: Reactions of infants to a change in mother figure', in L. Stone, H. Smith and L. Murphy (eds), *The Competent Infant: Research and Commentary*, New York: Basic Books, pp. 1032–40.

Yarrow, L. J., Goodwin, M. S., Manheimer, H. and Milowe, I. D. (1973) 'Infancy experiences, and cognitive and personality development at 10 years', in L. Stone, H. Smith and L. Murphy (eds), *The Competent Infant: Research and Commentary*, New York: Basic Books, 1274–81.

Zaremba, M. (1997) 'Racial purity in the welfare state: the hidden legacy of the Swedish folkhem', *Dagens Nyheter* 20 August.

Zhurzhenko, T. (2004) 'Families in the Ukraine: between postponed modernization, neo-familialism and economic survival' in M. Robila (ed.), *Families in Eastern Europe*, London: Elsevier, 187–209.

International Legal Instruments

United Nations

Convention on the Prevention and Punishment of the Crime of Genocide, adopted by Resolution 260 (III) A of the General Assembly on 9 December 1948.

Convention Relating to the Status of Refugees 28 July 1951, adopted by Resolution 429 (V) of the General Assembly on 14 December 1950.

Fourth World Conference on Women, Beijing Declaration and Platform for Action, Beijing, China, 17 October 1995, A/CONF.177/20.

International Conference on Population and Development (ICPD), *Programme of Action*, Cairo, Egypt, 18 October 1994, A/CONF.171/13.

World Conference on Human Rights, Vienna Declaration and Programme of Action, 14–25 June 1993, A/CONF.157/23.

UNESCO

Declaration on the Responsibilities of the Present Generations Towards Future Generations, Paris, 12 November 1997.

Universal Declaration of Future Generation, 1984.

European Council

Convention for the Protection of Human Rights and Fundamental Freedoms 1948.
Convention for the Protection of Human Rights and Dignity of the Human Being with regard to the Application of Biology and Medicine (Convention on Human Rights and Biomedicine). ETS No.: 164, Oviedo, 1997.
Additional Protocol to the Convention for the Protection of Human Rights and Dignity of the Human Being with regard to the Application of Biology and Medicine, on the Prohibition of Cloning Human Beings. ETS No.: 168, Paris, 1998. Available at: http://conventions.coe.int/treaty/en/treaties/html/168.htm
Additional Protocol to the Convention for the Protection of Human Rights and Biomedicine concerning Transplantation of Organs and Tissues of Human Origin. ETS No.: 186, Strasbourg, 2002.

European Union

COMMISSION OF THE EUROPEAN COMMUNITIES (2001) *Communication from the Commission on the Precautionary Principle*, Brussels, COM (2000) 1.

Domestic Legislation

Austria

Act no. 275/1992 on *Medically Assisted Reproduction.*

Denmark

Act no. 460/1997 on *Artificial Fertilisation.*

France

Act no. 653/1994 on *Human Body, Donation and Medically Assisted Procreation* (amendend by Act no. 800/2004).
Publique Health Code 2004.

Germany

Embryo Protection Act 1990.

Greece

Act no. 3089/2002 on *Medically Assisted Human Reproduction.*
Ireland
Constitution 1937.

Italy

Act no. 40/2004 on *Medically Assisted Procreation.*

Malta

Criminal Code.

Norway

Act no. 56/1994 on *Medical Use of Biotechnology.*

Poland

Abortion Act 1996.

Spain

Act no. 9/1985 *on Abortion, amending the Penal Code.*
Act no. 35/1988 on *Assisted Reproduction Technologies* (amended by Act no. 45/2003).
Act no. 42/1988 *on the Use of Embryos, Foetus and its Cells.*
Act no. 15/2003 *amending the Penal Code.*
Penal Code.

Sweden

Act no. 1140/1984 on *Artificial Insemination and Extracorporal Fertilisation.*

Switzerland

Medically Assisted Procreation Federal Act 1998.

Former Yugoslavia

Abortion Act 1978.

Russia

Family Code.

United Kingdom

Offences Against the Person Act 1961.
Abortion Act 1967.
Children Act 1975.
Prohibition of Female Circumcision Act 1985.
Children Act 1989.
Human Fertilisation and Embryology Act 1990.
Adoption and Children Act 2002.
Female Genital Mutilation Act 2003.

United States

Code of Federal Regulations (CFR).
Code of Virginia Annotated (Va. Code Ann).
Illinois Compiled Statutes (ILCS).
North Dakota Century Code (N.D. Cent. Code).
Revised Code of Washington Annotated (Wash. Rev. Code Ann.).

Table of Cases

International Court of Human Rights

Open Door Counselling and Dublin Well Woman v. Ireland, App. Nos. 14234/88, 14235/88, 15 Eur. H.R. Rep. 244 (1992).

Ireland

A. and B. v. *Eastern Health Board and C.* [1998] 1 I.R. 464.
Attorney General v. *X* [1992] 1 I.R.).
McGee v. *Attorney General* [1974] I.R. 284.

United Kingdom

R. v. Bourne [1938] 3 All E.R. 615

United States

Anna J. v. *Mark C.* 286 Cal. Rptr. 369. (Cal. App. Ct. 1991).
Curlender v. *Bioscience Laboratories*, 165 Cal. Rptr. 477 (Cal. App. Ct. 1980).
Harnicher v. *University of Utah Medical Center*, 962 P.2d 67 (Utah, 1998).
In re A.C., 573 A.2d 1235 (D.C. Cir. 1987).
In re Baby Boy Doe, 260 Ill. App. 3d 392, 399, 632 N.E.2d 326, 330 (Ill. App. Ct. 1994).
In the Matter of Baby M, Re 525 A 2d 1128 (NJ, 1987); on appeal 14 FLR 2007, 109 NJ 396, 537 A 2d 1227 (NJ Sup. Ct. 1988).
Jefferson v. *Griffin Spalding City Hospital*, 247 Ga. 86, 274 S.E.2d 457 (Ga. 1987).
Muller v. *Oregon*, 28 S. Ct. 324, 327 (1908).
Roe v. *Wade*, 410 U.S. 113 (1973).

Index

abnormal embryo transfer, 144
abortion, 3, 193–4
  abortion issue, access to, 167–9
  among teenagers, 77–81
  in Eastern Europe, access to, 20–4
  as a reproductive right, 17–32
  in Western Europe, access to, 24–31
Abortion Act 1967, 29, 30
Act on Assisted Reproduction Techniques,
  145, 146
*Act on the Use of Embryos, Foetus and its
  Cells*, 145
activity rate and vital cycle men and
  women, 57
adoption
  across Europe, 40–1
  challenges of, 41–5
  history and development of, 33–6
  and regulations, 33–49
  selection criteria for, 36–8
Adoption Act, 34
Adoption and Children Act, 36, 39
adoption outcomes, 45–8
Adsera, Alicia, 60
Africa, 100
Ahn, Namkee, 58
Albania, 18, 19, 78
Alkorta, Itziar, 9
Andrews, Lori, 9, 112
anti-Gypsyism, 94, 95
  in Europe, 89
apparent genetic relatedness, 157–8
Arab peninsula, 100
Artificial Reproductive Technologies
  (ART), 111–15, 118–21, 123n10,
  140, 167, 170, 173–4, 179, 182,
  186n8
Assisted Reproduction Act, Italy, 112
Assisted Reproduction Technologies,
  Spain, 112
assisted reproduction, for unintended
  childless couples, 169–70

asymmetrical relations, responsibility
  in, 178–82
Australia, 51, 101
Austria, 64, 80, 91

Barnett, Carol Beth, 127
Bavarian law, 90
Beijing Declaration, 18–19
Beijing Platform for Action, 19
Belgium, 64, 67, 122n9
Bioulac Report, 118
birth rate and women's rights in
  Europe, 50–70
births and abortions in women under
  20; proportion of, 79
Body and Soul report, 95
Bonino, Emma, 28, 102
Bowlby's theory, 35, 46
Britain, 33
Brown, Lesley, 125
Bucur, 106n9
Bukovská, Barbora, 97
Bulgaria, 81

Canada, 101
Children Act, 36
China, 171
Cholewinski, 23
cloning, 196–8
coerced sterilization
  in central and Eastern Europe, 94–6
  and female genital mutilation, in
    Europe, 88–108
comparative law, preimplantation
  diagnosis in, 147–9
contraceptives, 3
  access to, 167–9
contract motherhood, 194–6
*Convention on Human Rights and
  Biomedicine*, 113, 145
Croatia, 21
Crowhurst, Isabel, 7

current adoption practice, 36
Czech Republic, 75, 89, 95, 98

Danzig, 90
Darroch, J. E., 74, 75
data sources, on teenage pregnancies, 74
Davis, A., 107n20
Delgado, Margarita, 120
demographic background
   ethical considerations and proposals on, 86–7
   in European countries and in the United States, 80
   governmental concerns and policies on, 82–6
   multivariate analysis of, 81–2
   on teenage pregnancies 71–4
demographic changes, in developed countries, 57–62
'demographic crisis', 71
Denmark, 40, 64, 66, 89, 90, 92
designer babies
   and the commodification of children, 128–9
   dark side of, 137–8
developed countries, demographic changes in, 57–62
de Villota, Paloma, 6–7
Dickenson, Donna, 11, 12, 117
donor insemination (DI), 10, 151
   and embryo donation, 155–6
Dooley, Dolores, 162
Dorff, Rabbi Elliot N., 131
Dworkin, R., 185n3

Eastern Europe, 25
eggs, extra-commertium nature of, 117
Emaldi, Aitziber, 9
Embryo Protection Act, 112, 122n9, 144, 146, 148
'embryo' definition, 186–7n19
embryonic stem cell research, 172
embryo protection, 115–16
embryos legislative proposals, Selection of, 145–6
England, 35, 39
Estonia, 90, 91, 92

ethical analysis and future perspectives, of reproductive rights, 172–82
ethical considerations and proposals, on teenage pregnancy, 86–7
ethics
   and gender considerations, in female sterilization, 98–9
   and politics, change in, 201–2
ethnic minorities, experience of, 88–9
Eugenics, 136–7
Eugenics practices, 143–4
Europe, *see also individual entries*
   adoption practices across, 40–1
   anti-Gypsyism in, 89
   Central and Eastern Europe, coerced sterilization in, 94–6
   coerced sterilisation and female genital mutilation in, 88–108
   employment and family life in, 50–7
   female circumcision/female genital mutilation in, 99–101
   legislation within, 101–4
   Romanies in, 89–94
European Convention on Human Rights, 26
European fertility medicine regulation, women's rights in, 111–23
'European marriage type', 73
European Women's Lobby (EWL), 18
Even Broader License to Kill Children, 31
extra-commertium nature of eggs, 117

family/children benefits, 65
Family Code, 24
Feinberg, J. 210–12
female circumcision/female genital mutilation (FGM)
   and Coerced Sterilisation, in Europe, 88–108
   in the European context, 99–101
Female Genital Mutilation Act, 101, 108n30
Female Participation Rates (FPR), 59
'female self-determination', 141

female sterilization, problematising, 98–9
feminist reproductive ethics and reproduction rights, future of, 183–5
Finland, 64, 77, 81, 89, 90, 92
FORWARD (Foundation for Women's Health Research and Development), 104, 108n35
France, 40, 53, 64, 67, 89
French National Advisory Committee of Ethics, 147
Futris, T. G., 75

Gatens, Moira, 192
gene therapy, 142–3
genetic and reproductive technologies, merger of, 136–7
genetic relatedness
   importance of, 160–2
   and non-relatedness, new reproductive technologies impact on, 151–64
genetic services today, 129–31
genital mutilation, *see* female genital mutilation
German Embryo Protection Act, Italy, 116
German sterilisation law of 1933, 90
Germany, 40, 64, 89, 91–2, 197
germ-line gene therapy, 142, 143
gestational relatedness, 156–7
Gilligan, Carol, 170
global population policies, reproductive rights in, 199–213
global reproduction policies and original position, 207–8
Gordon, Jon, 137
governing women's bodies, 88–9
Governmental Action Plan against Female Genital Mutilation, Norway, 101
governmental concerns and policies, on teenage fertility rate, 82–6
Greece, 50–3, 64, 80
Green, Karen, 190
Guillod, Olivier, 112

Gypsy groups, 89–97, 105–6n2

Haarstad, Ragnhild, 93
Habermas, J., 187n20
Hajnal, John, 72
Haker, Hille, 10–12
Halliday, 21
Hare, R. M., 212
HARP (Health for Asylum-seekers and Refugees Portal), 108n36
Harris, John, 185n3
Hegel, G. W. F., 189, 190
Hellsten, Sirkku, 12
Hershey, Laura, 134
human embryos, research and experimentation with, 146–7
Human Fertilisation and Embryology Act, 38, 112, 123n11, 149
Humphrey, M., 45
Hungary, 22, 24, 78, 89, 95, 98

Iceland, 81, 89, 90
India, 100, 171
Indonesia, 100
infertility business, 119–20
inter-country adoption, 38–40
International Conference on Population and Development (ICPD), 17, 199
international regulation, on reproductive medicine, 113–14
in vitro fertilisation (IVF), 10, 140–51, 153–5, 171
involuntary sterilisation of minority women, eugenic history of, 89–94
Ireland, 18, 25–6, 56, 64
Italy, 31, 40, 53, 64, 66, 75

Jagger, Mick, 138
Jefferson v. *Griffin Spalding City Hospital*, 127
Jews, 91
Jonas, Hans, 178

Kant (philosopher), 189–90
Kenny, Catherine, 5–6
Kevles, D., 89
Keynes, John Maynard, 191
Kissling, Frances, 22

Klein, Mary Therese Meuldes,
  118
Koch, Lene, 123n12

laissez-faire model, 112
Latin America, 100
Law against Dangerous Habitual
  Criminals, 91
The Law for the Prevention of Offspring
  with Hereditary Defects, 90
Law on Abortion, 21
Law on Assisted Reproduction
  Techniques, 144, 146
'Law on Bioethics', 148
Law on Measures of Security and
  Reform, 91
Levinas, Emmanuel, 178
Levy-Shiff, R., 46
Lippman, Abby, 135
Lithuania, 91
Locke, John, 191, 192
Luxembourg, 51, 53, 64, 91

MacCallum, Fiona, 6
Mahowald, Mary, 154
making policy for making babies,
  138–9
Malaysia, 100
Malta, 18, 25–8, 31
Manuilă, Sabin, 94
Marriage Health Law, 91
Marx, 198
McGee v. *Attorney General*, 25
Medically Assisted Procreation Act, 112,
  115
Mertus, Julie, 21
Mill, John Stuart, 210, 211
minority groups, and reproductive
  rights, 88–108
minority women, reproductive rights
  for, 104–5
Mira, Pedro, 58
Moldova, 19, 75, 81
Montenegro, 19
motherhood, and changing
  technology, 124–39
Muller v. *Oregon*, 127
multivariate analysis, of teenage
  pregnancy, 81–2

National regulations in Europe,
  on reproductive medicine,
  111–13
'neo-institutionalism', 117–19
Netherlands, 40–1, 64, 75,
  80, 91
Network of European Women's Rights
  (NEWR), 1, 3
new reproductive technologies (NRTs),
  151–64
  impact on genetic relatedness and
    non-relatedness, 151–64
New Zealand, 51, 101
NGO activism, 96–8
'Non-European marriage type', 73
Norplant, 128
Norway, 67, 81, 89–92

Offences Against the Person Act
  (OASA), 25
Ombudsman, 23
O'Neill, Onora, 177, 180
Ordover, N., 90, 99
original position and global
  reproduction policies, 207–8
ova donation, 196–8
ownership, property and women's
  bodies, 188–98

paid work and unpaid work,
  reconciling, 62–9
parenthood, moral concept of,
  177–8
Pasley, K., 75
Paternalism on maternal choices,
  209–12
PGD (Preimplantation Genetic
  Diagnosis), 29
Poland, 18, 22, 23, 24, 91
Pope John Paul II, 28
population control, for and against,
  202
population wrongs, reproductive
  rights as, 202–4
Poradna report, 96, 97,
  107n16
Portugal, 18, 25, 32, 40, 64, 66
pregnancy, and prenatal screening,
  131–3

Preimplantion Genetic Diagnosis
(PGD), 9, 29, 171, 175–6
drawbacks of, 141–7
legitimising, 147–9
practice of, 140–1
and prenatal diagnosis, 170–2
problems and future perspectives,
140–50
technical problems, 141–7
prenatal diagnosis, and
preimplantation genetic
diagnosis, 170–2
prenatal screening, spread of, 133–6
Prohibition of Female Circumcision Act,
101
property in the body, concept of,
189–93
protected interests and rights, on
reproductive medicine, 114

Quinacrine drug, in sterlisation,
107n19

Ralws, John, 207
Ramsey, Paul, 133
Raymond, J., 117
regulatory abyss, 125–6
reproductive and genetic
technologies, merger of, 136–7
reproductive autonomy, notion of,
access to, 167–9
reproductive medicine, 113
international regulation on, 113–14
national regulations in Europe on,
111–13
protected interests and rights on,
114
reproductive rights
abortion as, 17–32
critical issues in, 17–108
ethical analysis and future
perspectives of, 172–82
and feminist reproductive ethics,
183–5
as human rights, 208–9
and minority groups, 88–108
for minority women, 104–5
as population wrongs, 202–4
projections for, 167–213

rhetoric of, 199–213
and scientific advances, 109–64
social–ethical approach to, 173–7
term of, 204, 208
in the twentieth century, 167–72
as women's rights, 3–5
Reproductive Technology Act, Spain, 115
reprogenetic medicine, women as
patients of, 114–15
Reprokult, German feminist
movement, 116
rhetoric, change in, 201–2
right to reproduce, 204–7
Riou, Catherine Labrousse, 118
Roe v. Wade, 19, 26
Romania, 18
Romanies in Europe, 89–94
Romeo, Carlos, 113
Rothman, Barbara Katz, 132
Russia, 21, 24, 39
R. v. Bourne, 30

Said, Edward, 89
Sauer, Mark, 125
'saviour siblings', 29
Saxton, 134
scientific advances and reproductive
rights, 109–64
Serbia, 19, 21
sex selection, 144–5
Siegfried, Alfred, 93
Singer, L., 46
Singer, P., 185n3
Singh, S., 74, 75
Sleebos, Joëlle E., 61, 62
Slovakia, 18, 89, 95–9
Slovenia, 75, 78, 80
social benefits for the family, 63
social–ethical approach, to
reproductive rights, 173–7
social expenditure, 62–9
social versus biological relatedness,
152–3
societal norms, change in, 131
Soros, George, 107n17
Southern Europe, 61
Soviet Union, 22
Spain, 6, 18, 25, 30–1, 50–1, 53, 56,
64, 66, 75, 121n1, 143, 145

Steinbacher, Roberta, 135
stem cell technologies, 196–8
Stern, William, 195
Strathern, Marilyn, 118
Surplus embryos, 146
'surrogate' motherhood, 195–6
'sweat equity', 196
Sweden, 40–1, 64, 67, 75, 89–91,
    122n9, 160
Switzerland, 75, 80, 89, 92–3

technical problems, of
    preimplantation diagnosis, 141–7
teenage births, 75–7
    in European countries and in the
        United States, 80
teenage pregnancy, 71–87
    data sources, on, 74
    demographic background on, 71–4
    'the tentative pregnancy', 132
Testart, Jacques, 122n7
third-party NRTs, 155–6
    and secrecy, 158–60
Thomson, Judith Jarvis, 193
Total Fertility Rates (TFR), 59
Toth, Olga, 6–7
traditional family structures,
    preserving, 117–19
'traditional' model of family life, 152
Trehan, Nidhi, 7

Ukraine, 73, 81
*UN Convention Relating to the Status of
    Refugees*, 102
unintended childless couples, assisted
    reproduction for, 169–70
United Kingdom, 20, 126, 147, 149,
    197
    abortion laws in, 29–30
    adoption in, 36–41
    assisted reproduction treatment, 37
    legalisation of abortion in, 26–7
    teenage birth rate in, 75, 80–1

United States, 6, 19–20, 40, 61, 71,
    74–85, 127–8
    artificial reproduction laws
        in, 112
    and regulatory abyss, 125–6
    sterilisation laws in, 90

Vatican, 22
Vaud canton, 90, 92–3

Wales, 35, 39
Walker-Lampley, Bree, 132
Weimar Constitution, 90
Wertz, Dorothy, 135
Western Europe abortion in, 24–31
Western women and motherhood,
    with changing technology,
    124–39
West Germany, 53
Whitehead, Mary Beth, 195
Widdows, Heather, 9, 10
Wikler, Daniel, 163n4
Wolf, Don, 126
Women
    activity rate and vital cycle, 55
    experimentation on, 124–5
    as patients of reprogenetic
        medicine, 114–15
    reproductive rights of, 5–12
    as vessels, 126–8
    women's reproductive rights, *see*
        reproductive rights
women's rights
    in European fertility medicine
        regulation, 111–23
    reproductive rights as, 3–5
Women's Sexual Rights in Europe, 18

Yarrow, L. J., 46
Yenish Gypsies, 93
Yugoslavia, 21

Zaremba, Maciej, 106n8